H.E. SHELLS BURSTING IN TRENCHES

EL

J. Hopham
June 24th 1914

TRENCHES SHEWING WHITE

VILLAGE OF BÉCORDEL-BÉCOURT

← edg
put in
which
had two

This sketch damaged through bein
sent to   in a friend's haver

d wide

INTO THE BLIZZARD

INTO THE BLIZZARD

WALKING THE FIELDS
OF THE NEWFOUNDLAND DEAD

MICHAEL WINTER

DOUBLEDAY CANADA

Doubleday Canada and colophon are registered trademarks of Random House of Canada Limited

Library and Archives Canada Cataloguing in Publication

Winter, Michael, 1965-, author
Into the blizzard : walking the fields of the Newfoundland dead / Michael Winter.

Includes bibliographical references.
Issued in print and electronic formats.
ISBN 978-0-385-67785-1

eBook ISBN 978-0-385-67786-8

1. Somme, 1st Battle of the, France, 1916. 2. Beaumont-Hamel, Battle of, Beaumont-Hamel, France, 1916. 3. Great Britain. Army. Royal Newfoundland Regiment. 4. World War, 1914-1918—Regimental histories—Canada. 5. World War, 1914-1918—Newfoundland and Labrador. I. Title.

D545.S7W45 2014   940.4'272   C2014-903151-3
                                            C2014-903152-1

Cover image © The Gallery Collection/Corbis
Printed and bound in the USA

Front endpaper photograph copyright © Canadian War Museum. Thurston Topham, Opening of the Somme Bombardment, CWM 19710261-0728, Beaverbrook Collection of War Art. Photo on pages iv-v copyright © The Rooms Provincial Archives Division, A 97-35 / E. Holloway. Photo on page 13 copyright © The Gallery Collection/Corbis. Photo on page 99 copyright © Imperial War Museums (Q 1530). Photo on page 195 copyright © The Rooms Provincial Archives Division, F 48-18 / E. Holloway. Back endpaper photograph copyright © Richard Baker/In Pictures/Corbis

Published in Canada by Doubleday Canada,
a division of Random House of Canada Limited
a Penguin Random House Company

www.randomhouse.ca

10 9 8 7 6 5 4 3 2 1

To the fallen

or to the children

or to families

or to the independent spirit

or to John Roberts, who was shot at dawn

or to Levi Bellows, who was stripped of a stripe

    for talking back at the colonel

or to Robins Stick, who was almost court-martialed for cowardice

    when in fact he was suffering shell shock

or to my grandparents

or to my grand uncles, who were never the same in the head,

    says my father.

To my son.

The only visible sign that the men knew they were under this terrific fire was that they all instinctively tucked their chins into an advanced shoulder as they had so often done when fighting their way home against a blizzard in some little outport in far off Newfoundland.

MAJOR ARTHUR RALEY, *The Veteran* magazine, 1921

It was a magnificent display of trained and disciplined valour, and its assault only failed of success because dead men can advance no further.

GENERAL HENRY DE BEAUVOIR DE LISLE,
Commander, 29th Division

They came out of the neat restored trench, and faced a memorial to the Newfoundland dead. Reading the inscription Rosemary burst into sudden tears.

F. SCOTT FITZGERALD, *Tender Is the Night*, 1934

Inverness

Edinburgh

Ayr

Hawick

UNITED KINGDOM
OCT 1914 – AUG 1915

Aldershot

Salisbury

Devonport

ST. JOHN'S
OCT 1914

UK to DARDANELLES
AUG 1915 – SEPT 1915

THE TRAIL OF THE CARIBOU

(SEE ALSO: P. 327)

ONE

In June a few years ago I set out to visit some of the World War One battlefields of Europe—the slope and valley and river and plain that the Newfoundland Regiment trained on, and fought over and through and under. I grew up in Newfoundland but, to be honest, had not thought much about our time as an independent dominion and our effort to contribute to wars fought in Europe. The tall green war memorial in our capital city of St John's is handy as a skateboard park. A Canadian writer, Norman Levine, who had dropped bombs on Leipzig during the Second World War, inspected the memorial with me one afternoon, and he approved of the skateboarders. Youth should make a game out of a memorial.

But a publisher approached me about a book and it was the sort of story and material that I had never attempted before. I felt an attraction. So much could go wrong with a book like this that I immediately signed on for the duration. There was money involved but there was also a chance to begin something new. I have a wife and child. *Yes, I'll write to you*, I said. I would mail to them the first postcards I'd ever sent to my own family. *Take care of each other.* And as I left for the airport to begin my solitary parade, I was cheered off at my own door on my way to fly over the roof of this encouraging family and head to England. I felt like I had volunteered for some public service for which I was not quite trained or well equipped.

My family and I were living in an apartment in Toronto. We had moved several times, just as many of the families of soldiers had moved throughout the war. Their letters, often dictated to a minister of faith, address the question of their sons' whereabouts. Some families—the widows of dead soldiers—had moved to Toronto and Boston and Halifax to be with other parts of the family and perhaps remove themselves from the place where they had loved another. Some parents had not heard from their sons. Or the son was missing and the letters said: *Have they found him? Is he a prisoner of war? My allotment has been cut off. The street address is changed now because I have moved.*

The men who were married with children were often

older, and sometimes officers. So I was more of an officer on this excursion—one of those officers who thought, naively, that the cavalry and the navy would solve a lot of things.

I hit the sidewalk in the evening twilight and turned north for a streetcar to the subway. From the Dundas West platform, I struck west towards Kipling station. Rudyard Kipling, I remembered, had a lot to say about the war. Perhaps no one more publicly had such a change of heart. His son was killed in the war. And it is a line Kipling chose from Ecclesiasticus that is chiselled into all of the allied war graves: *Their name liveth for evermore.* I thought this while waiting at Kipling station for the 192 airport bus which would take me to the international departures terminal. Commuters streamed up the stairs out of the subway much like I imagined men climbed out of trenches and crossed no man's land. I felt the compressed pummel of wind as a subway launched itself into the station and pushed air up the stairs like the concussion from an exploding shell.

I was standing amongst enlisted men now, the so-called other ranks. The pause here made me think of the photos I'd seen of soldiers in France waiting for their double-decker buses—sheathed in protective wood barriers, a coop for carrier pigeons mounted on top—to transport them to the front. You had to see those photos to believe them. They showed the type of scene I might have read about in a book and then described to my son. He likes old war photographs, and he was learning about the various weapons and when they were introduced during the war. Sometimes the weapons in the photos would appear more modern only because of the improvement in the photographic emulsion process; even a five-year-old can distinguish this technical improvement. My son, I knew, was now in bed watching a movie on my laptop. His movies involved a lot of Japanese figures firing at each other. He does this thing where he shortens his arms and jerks them around like the first Godzilla snatching warplanes from the air. I had tried explaining that the movie *Godzilla* was made as a result of war, the effects of nuclear weapons on Japan, but this puzzled him. Sometimes I thought of him and what the world would be like ten years from now, when he would be eligible fodder for the political powers that might push him into a war, but also eligible for his own gusto to ambush him and enlist, a hearty leap into combat. This thought filled my legs with lead.

I had a twenty-pound knapsack, and no checked bags; I had packed like a soldier. I crossed a road, allowed the automatic doors of the airport to accept me and made my way to the airline check-in. The comfort of interior air. The soldiers were always looking for a break from the elements, just as they had when they'd set out sealing in the spring. The Newfoundlanders would pack a lunch when they crossed the ice to hunt seals, for you never knew when you might get waylaid. In their little bag of provisions—"nunch" they called it—along with cartridges, they stowed hard-bread: "For who could tell what swift blizzard might cut off hunters miles from the ship?"

LEONARD STICK

I checked in and got in line for the walk-through metal detector. I love the tangerine and lime outlines of checked luggage on the computer screen; I think we should be allowed to purchase copies.

Near the departures gate, I saw that I was not the only one there taking an overnight flight. The queue made me interested to find out who had been the first Newfoundlander to line up and sign on when war was announced. It was not a hard thing to discover, as the Newfoundland Regiment gave out numbers to the men. Leonard Stick was the first man. Stick was from Bay Roberts, which is not far from where we have a summer house. I remembered how, a few years ago, the name of a major road in Bay Roberts was changed to L. T. Stick Drive; at the time I had no idea who Stick was.

Leonard Thretheway Stick was born in 1892 and was a member of the Church Lads' Brigade. He was nicknamed Eagle Eye. There's a little museum in Bay Roberts called

The Road to Yesterday where they have Stick's dress uniform in behind glass. It is odd to see the uniform presented on a headless mannequin inside a glass box. It reminded me of a reliquary I'd seen in central Turkey, a glass cabinet that housed the moustache of Mevlana, the whirling dervish, also known as Rumi. Small women dressed entirely in black leaned in to the glass corners of the Rumi cabinet and inhaled the air, trying to receive a whiff of vapour that had touched his moustache. This was in Konya when I was twenty-three.

The quest for souvenirs continues: People desire the caribou badge that was the Newfoundland Regiment's emblem. They find, in trunks in the attic, old tin helmets and boxes with medals. There were a lot of moustaches on the officers—you weren't allowed to shave off your moustache until 1916—and evidence of this survives in photographs. Men wore their hair short but kept a tuft in front. The men often visited European museums and wrote letters home describing the wonders of a Scottish castle or the view of the English Channel near a bust of Napoleon in Boulogne. Eight hundred and fifty years before, at the Bay de Somme, William the Conqueror had assembled his navy. Perhaps the only place where the Newfoundlanders did not visit a museum was in Turkey; they were too busy being shelled to death on the shores of the Dardanelles. So I place Mevlana in my book here now, for them.

I thought of Stick's great-grandson, Andrew Hillyard: there is a photo of him in the newspaper wearing a uniform, and in his youthful demeanour one can see a tremendous responsibility to carry out service. It is moving, and tragic, to see this yearning in the young to seek approval from their seniors. The Church Lads' Brigade's motto is "Fight the good fight." We all, in our bones, wonder if we have room to fight for a noble cause.

Leonard Stick had a long face, no moustache, much like my own face. Later, he was the first federal member of Parliament when Newfoundland joined Canada. His two brothers were also in the regiment. Robins Stick, a captain, was under scrutiny for abandoning the field during an attack. The youngest brother, Moyle Stick, was captured by the Germans. He was the only Newfoundland prisoner of war to escape.

FLORIZEL

I waited with the Canadians at the airport gate, much like the Newfoundland Regiment had waited aboard the *Florizel* a hundred years ago—its first shipment of Newfoundlanders, 537 of them, had to remain at anchor in St John's harbour for a day before joining up with the flotilla of Canadian ships rendezvousing off Cape Race to head across the

Atlantic. Cape Race was where word of the *Titanic*'s trouble, thirty months before, had first been received by telegraph. The *Titanic*'s overworked telegraph operator, Jack Phillips, had sent happy messages to Cape Race for several hours, messages that were postcards of people on board letting their families know that they were having a good time. Phillips did not listen to the ships who cautioned him of ice. Beleaguered, he told one telegraph operator to shut up.

The *Florizel* was out there the day the *Titanic* sank. The captain said they had passed sixteen icebergs, one that was eight miles long. Two months later it was the *Florizel* that docked in Halifax with the last victim of the *Titanic*, the body of steward James McGrady, recovered from the sea by the sealing vessel *Algerine*.

The White Star Line had chartered the *Algerine* from the Bowring family to help look for bodies. The *Algerine* was built by the same Belfast shipyard that laid down the *Titanic*, Harland and Wolff, in 1880 and its purpose was to fire on coastal targets. The *Algerine* was overhauled in 1910— she lay in drydock just as the *Titanic* and her sister ship, the *Olympic*, were being constructed in a twin gantry built just for these ocean liners. The *Olympic* survived the war, painted up in dazzle camouflage, ferrying Canadian soldiers to England for training.

The *Florizel* was held in port, mysteriously, until it was announced that she would be the ship conveying the men across the Atlantic. In the newspapers the day before the ship departed there was news from Belgium of barbaric warfare: "It is not by men but by devils that the people of Belgium have been confronted." A brother of a man working for the local merchants, Ayre & Sons, living in Manchester, had a cousin—a Red Cross nurse—whose hands had been cut off while attending another woman.

There was news, too, of the first Newfoundlander to go down in his service: Bernard Harvey, an officer on HMS *Cressy*, sunk by a German torpedo. It had taken ten days for the news to reach Newfoundland. That Saturday, the day before the *Florizel* departed, flags were flying on all the mercantile premises as a sign of respect for Harvey.

The *Cressy* was named after the Battle of Crécy in 1346 in northern France, a battle that had been part of the Hundred Years War. It took place after the French failed to force the English between the Seine and the Somme. The King of England ordered everyone to fight on foot. The French, while superior in numbers, were tired from travel, their crossbows wet. The English won. And over five hundred years later, they named a ship after that battle—a ship upon which a Newfoundlander drowned in the sea in late September of 1914. Bernard Harvey was thirty-two. He was last seen helping his men to keep afloat.

SHIPYARDS

I thought about Bernard Harvey while waiting in the air-port. I thought about marine traffic and how shipyards were coming back to life again. Warships were being built for this country. Lao-tzu wrote, "When the way does not prevail in the empire, war horses breed on the border." And I thought of my son and I wondered what way was not prevailing for us to resort to building a navy again. I am not opposed to the rebirth of shipyards. All one summer in St John's the sound of a piledriver reminded my mother, who was visit-ing, of the shipyards of England. I was born in Newcastle upon Tyne, a major shipyard city in the industrial north of that country. And when we immigrated to Canada we first lived in Marystown, Newfoundland—a shipyard. My father had a job there. Marystown, my father told me, was the place where the royal family were to be evacuated in the case of a German invasion of Britain during World War Two. The navy, if dispersed, was to use Marystown's natu-ral port of Mortier Bay as a place to reassemble.

I have a wrench my father used in the Hawthorn Leslie shipyards of Tyneside. It has his initials stamped in the forged steel—a wrench made in West Germany. You marked your tools or else they would drift into the hands of other apprentices. I am drawn to industrial cities and the lovely compounded names the shipyards receive. Once, I was walking through Hamilton, Ontario, with my sister and she thought Hamilton was a good place to live. She knew I was looking to buy a house. Hamilton, a port city, was a steeltown. Its airport was used, in the 1940s, as a wartime air force training station. I've seen my sister stop at overpasses to inspect railway lines below or look up to study a dockyard crane hoist a shipping container. It's the site of prior industry, she said, and that sort of history always has good bones to it.

St John's, 1914. The crowds paraded the soldiers down to the water and cheered them up the duckboards to the *Florizel*. People lined the streets from Pleasantville to the Furness Withy pier. The police and members of the HMS *Calypso* had to keep people from the pier so the sailors could cast off the mooring hawsers. Then the band aboard the tug *John Green* played "It's a Long, Long Way to Tipperary"—a song I had thought might have been written during the war, as it's a song longing for home, but was in fact composed two years before the war. In August 1914 an Irish regiment in France was heard singing it as they marched and it soon swept through the British army and across the Atlantic.

After this send-off, the people of St John's, puzzled, watched the *Florizel* come to anchor in the stream and then sit in the harbour all night. The men on board spent the evening "drinking to the health of everyone else." The next morning, the men aboard the *Florizel* waited for the thirty thousand Canadians and seven thousand horses aboard a thirty-ship convoy heading from Quebec. The Newfoundlanders stood on deck bare-headed (their Australian slouch hats had not arrived), many of them waking up at home for the very last time. They were used to saying farewell during the spring seal hunt when the large vessels congregated in St John's as part of the new method to prosecute the seal fishery. Some might have remembered the strike of 1902 when the sealers fought for and won an increase in their share of the sale of seal fat.

Eight hundred small ships had once been involved in sealing, but recently the large merchants had taken over with their big ships—the *Florizel* was built specifically to withstand the ice while sealing—and now those vessels had been converted into troopships. This first contingent of 537 men to join up were called the Blue Puttees because the material they wrapped around their lower legs was made of blue cloth instead of khaki. It is thought they wore blue puttees because they could not find khaki material for regular puttees. But here is a new idea: the Newfoundland Patriotic Association had a design in mind. They had ordered Australian slouch hats and Canadian army overcoats and, with the Church Lads' Brigade blue puttees, this "look" would make a distinctive regiment, intentionally setting the men off from the imperial forces of Britain and the convoy of Canadian troops they were to join on their voyage overseas.

JIM STACEY

I bought a *New Yorker* and found a seat in the departures lounge and waited. I was realizing now that I was embarking on a journey, that tonight I would not be sleeping in my own bed. A man nearby stood studying the flight monitor above him. He was wearing flipflops and shorts. His bare legs and feet were an offence to the serious endeavour which is international travel. A woman stared at my face and then came over and asked if I was someone she knew. She mistook me for someone else. Someone on television, she said.

As I opened my magazine I recalled that this misidentity had often happened on the battlefield. Men were injured, shipped to hospitals in France and England, patched up and returned to their regiment. I thought you were killed, Jim Stacey was told. And he realized he was being confused with another J. Stacey who had won a Military Medal at Marcoing for retrieving food and water and carrying it to the front line, saving the lives of many wounded soldiers. That other J. Stacey's parents read of their son's bravery and then quickly heard he'd been killed in action near the destroyed Belgian town of Poelcappelle. A tremendous correspondence traversed the Atlantic, packets of mail and wireless forms written out by hand and typed and then tapped across the ocean, reprinted and retyped and sent by mail or by hand to the families and read aloud by ministers of the cloth to those who could not read. Many formal and panicked letters, and telegrams in full capitals, inquiring and prodding and asking for clarification. "His final resting place" was a phrase that mattered, for many bodies were moved and trampled and run over in later battles by tanks, and then finally discovered and disinterred and buried for what everyone hoped was the last time. At the start of the war men had only one identification disc around their necks. Then people realized you needed two, so you could remove one as evidence of a death, but leave the other with the body in case the body was moved and confused with other bodies after the war. You left it so that, once the war was finally over, you could bury the body with dignity.

My plane was ready for boarding. I opened my passport and there was my black-and-white unsmiling face, much like the photos of the soldiers before they left for war. I got on board and the plane hauled our weight up over Lake Ontario. It surprises me how I'm now living surrounded by a continent of land, when I was born encircled by the ocean. Before leaving the city, I had visited the lake, looking for the Malibu condo tower in downtown Toronto. I bicycled there, forcing myself under the Gardiner Expressway. To live down there you have to subvert your natural instincts. Canoe Landing was nearby, a mound of earth made from redirected landfill, and the cluster of condo towers that is City Place. Toronto is trying to make this a neighbourhood. Civic leaders are gambling that the modern city will have little connection with the land except through monuments. There is a piece of public sculpture here that I was forcing myself to see. The sculpture is of two large toy soldiers from the War of 1812. They have those plastic-looking bases that toy soldiers have, but the sculptures are twelve feet tall. This, at the busy intersection of Bathurst and Lake Shore. There was the lake in front of me, but I couldn't hear it for the traffic. I looked at the statue. Standing over a fallen toy American was a toy member of the Newfoundland Regiment.

Now in the plane: the city, dark below me. They say that at the Battle of Waterloo, part of the reason Napoleon decided to fight was that the best British soldiers were here in Canada at war with the Americans.

I tried to sleep as we flew over eastern Canada in the dark. But I could not quiet my mind and so I opened and read my official history of the Newfoundland Regiment, written by Gerald Nicholson. While I read this battle narrative I saw below the necklace of lights that outlined the St Lawrence Seaway. At the outset of the Great War, the steamship *Morwenna*, on its way from Montreal to St John's, was shot at from the fort at Quebec. The captain had failed to note the war regulations which called for ships to have a special travel clearance from Quebec. He reversed his engine and brought the ship into the harbour where he obtained the required papers "and left on his way rejoicing."

The *Morwenna* would be sunk off Cardiff by a submarine torpedo in May 1915.

We flew over a dark East Coast until the little forlorn lights of the west coast of Newfoundland appeared. This is where I grew up. Where soldiers like Levi Bellows and Tommy Ricketts had been born. Where five German prisoners of war had built a wall in Curling. Those Germans, who were fishermen, were allowed to jig for cod in the bay. But they spent their days constructing a stone wall for the district inspector of the constabulary. The hundred-year-old wall, which I saw as a kid (we lived in Curling), is five feet high and five feet wide and a thousand feet long. One prisoner, Otto Rasch, wrote to the inspector after the war, when he was back in Germany, wishing in his rationed state that he could have a feed of rabbit and cabbage.

None of the soldiers knew what lay ahead. And I realized I too didn't know what emotions were in store for me. Germany had declared war on Russia on 1 August 1914. Then two days later it declared war on France. The following day it declared war on Belgium. Still, no one could have known what would come. Wars since 1850 (there had been about two dozen) had been brief and peripheral. Assaults involving the Turks and Greeks and the Balkans and the new state of Albania filled many columns of the local newspapers.

When Britain declared war on Germany on the fourth of August, 1914, it was assumed by her dominions that they too were at war. The governor of Newfoundland, Walter Davidson, sent a telegram to England saying that the colony would supply five hundred men to the war effort. Would this be accepted? The response was yes. But there was no standing army in Newfoundland, and no militia. There wasn't even a government office to arrange such a body of men. Small paramilitary groups, like the Church Lads' Brigade, the Catholic Cadet Corps and the Methodist Guards, had leaders who oversaw raising a regiment. They took it upon themselves to form the Newfoundland Patriotic Association, whose goal was to supply and support five hundred soldiers. Conventional thinking—to be loyal to Britain by contributing men to an army—had prevailed. There was little voice from those in power to stay out of the war, as was the case in America. The Americans had closed the New York Stock Exchange to prevent Europeans from selling shares and requesting gold from the US banks. The US markets were shut down for the last four months of 1914—that was America's response to war.

The British nurse Edith Cavell was visiting her mother in Norfolk when war broke out. She went to Brussels, helped two hundred British soldiers escape, was court-martialled and convicted of treason and shot by a German firing squad. It was this act that caused the surge in British and colonial volunteers signing up. In Newfoundland, a letter in a Twillingate newspaper implored the young to volunteer before more nurses had their hands and breasts cut off in Belgium.

What did Newfoundlander Frances Cluett think of that, volunteering as she did as a nurse? Her community must have believed the amputations and not known that it was propaganda, that their homes and women were not in jeopardy. But sailing above this land I realize none of us know the true hazards of work and travel. Those German prisoners found their way home. And so, too, Bertram Butler and Leonard Stick and the nurse Frances Cluett managed to get home.

A wing swept over my vista and I lost Newfoundland, the great carcass of it, until its bright little head reared up—the peninsula of Avalon, so like the head of a caribou, the perimeter of its antlers all aglow in the dark. This is where the majority of the men came from. The distinctive harbour of St John's, where most of this first contingent were born and bred. The men marched down past Ayre & Sons, which was draped in Union Jacks. Charles Robert Ayre had provided five grandsons and four were killed in the war—the only reason the fifth survived was that he was kept out of service after complaining of rheumatism.

Imagine being Charles Ayre and surviving the war because of pain in your joints. Ethel Dickinson, a first cousin to these Ayre soldiers, served as a nurse in England and then perished in the flu epidemic of 1918. Could the Ayre family have had any idea this toll would be the result of a European war? Of course not. There was no concept yet of a long, vast, deadly war.

The day after Britain declared war on Germany it was Regatta Day in St John's—a Wednesday. The banks were closed, and there were people who said they were closed because of the war. Germany was the chief market for lobster. Lobster, usually sold at twenty-three dollars per case, now couldn't fetch ten dollars; war risks were not covered for cargo, and no fish buyer would risk a cargo on the North Atlantic.

The English doctor Arthur Wakefield, who practised in Labrador, left Twillingate for Lewisporte on a small motorboat to entrain to St John's and join the regiment there. A naval reserve of a hundred men was shipped off to Nova Scotia to man the Canadian cruiser *Niobe*. Naval reservists were wished "good luck and a chance to small powder."

A couple in St John's reported being asked by a foreigner to describe the lay of the land. Two passengers with German names were kept in police custody. A man named Clarke in Trinity Bay claimed to be German and was put in an asylum.

A load of salt arrived from Cadiz. A local antimony mine opened up again because the war had driven up the price from eight cents to eighteen cents; antimony was used in batteries and was the best alloy in munitions for penetrating armour.

A Mr Roberts, while fishing, lost his knife overboard. The next day when splitting his catch, he found the knife in the belly of one of the fish. An electric storm struck the house of Isaac Young. The current came down the chimney then out the attic and continued through a bedroom partition. It split the partition in two and smashed some pictures. Isaac's wife was wallpapering and the current hurled her across the room.

I thought of all these things I had read in accounts of that time. The night sky out my plastic window was clear. No turbulence. I noticed the dearth of lights as we passed over Pleasantville. This had been the military encampment—where the regiment came together to train on the old cricket grounds on the north side of Quidi Vidi Pond. I've never seen cricket played in St John's, so this tells you of a British heritage that was outstripped by the introduction of American army bases, and baseball, in World War Two. Of course, I thought, staring down from thirty thousand feet, this is where you train: on the grounds where you play. War is an elevated sport. The commander of the Newfoundland troops, an Englishman named Henry de

Beauvoir de Lisle, wrote a memoir in 1939: *Reminiscences of Sport and War*. The frontispiece shows de Lisle sitting on his horse lifting a polo mallet to his shoulder.

But war is not sport. There should, by law, be a division between war and sport like the one between church and state. Soldiers should not appear with the flag at hockey games. Soldiers should not sing the national anthem in baseball parks. No salutes should be made to the flag when a game begins. No applause given to platoons watching in uniform from the gold seats. The military should be the first to support this separation of sport and war.

The first photographs of the Newfoundland soldiers were taken down there in Pleasantville. They showed the men in canvas tents, gathering together to form platoons, playful groups of men preparing for a lark as they would in a woods camp, kitted out in their British army-style pattern-1907 service dress uniforms and their blue puttees. These uniforms were made with wool grown a hundred miles away in Makinsons.

It is hard not to stare at the dozens of glass plates from the Holloway Studio, which was a house at the corner of Henry Street and Bates Hill in St John's. Beautiful men in groups suitable for playing football, photographed by Elsie Holloway and her brother Robert. You could have a print in a day, and a dozen postcards cost sixty-five cents. Robert Holloway joined up early on and the responsibility for photographing the regiment was left to his sister. There's a photo of Robert that his sister must have taken.

Now we were crossing the Atlantic. Those Pleasantville camps had been dismantled as soon as the *Florizel* left the harbour. Those engaged at the camp and firing range were paid off, and Governor Davidson wrote to his British counterpart that the men on their way over were "very hardy and accustomed to hard work and little food." There must have been a sense in the city that we Newfoundlanders had done our bit and now could return to normal life.

Inside the plane, the movie screens were broken and we were unable to use our phones. So many people, staring and alone with themselves. The dark of the plane as the pilots decided to let us sleep. How old-fashioned our presence of life was now, six miles above the middle of the ocean. A mile, I thought, is a thousand full paces of a marching army.

The *Florizel* had finally weighed anchor at ten o'clock that Sunday night, carrying a gift of forty barrels of apples from Ayre & Sons. It took the men on the ship ten days to reach dry land, over the very sea below me, as they received shelter within that Canadian convoy. Nine miles long and three abreast, that forest of ships, ditching dead horses as they ploughed through the sea. One day a man fell over from the *Royal George* and the entire fleet stopped to lower a boat and pick him up. A Canadian later said that often, in the carnage of battles to come, he thought of that care taken for an individual life, care that stopped that great fleet in order to save a man.

The convoy arrived at Devonport but had to wait six more days to unload because the troopships were backed up from all regions of the Commonwealth. Some of the officers were allowed onto dry land but the men stayed aboard. The British had made statistical sheets of populations and eligible fighting strength from all of the colonies and dominions. The Newfoundlanders, like soldiers from all over the world, did a lot of waiting.

DEVONPORT

England. The Newfoundlanders crossed the ocean in ten days and landed in Devonport after escort cruisers discovered German U-boat activity; the Germans thought the convoy was to land in Boulogne, France. In Devonport, the grandsons of Charles Ayre were just forty miles from where their grandfather had been born in Exeter.

The Newfoundlanders finally disembarked and gathered dry land under their feet. One hundred years later, my plane landed at eleven in the morning UK time and, because we were early, I had to wait to deplane. I had yet to experience, firsthand, any remnant of the war. I was not looking forward to the research or the wanderings or to the idea that I had to become an expert in an old war, but I was happy to shuck off my domestic life and get involved in a quest where meals would be cooked for me and shelter provided. I don't mean to make the life of raising a child and having a significant other sound arduous, but it is always good to complement that steady, secure life with a dash of abandon and singular adventure. The shuttle train arrived in a box like an elevator, the way subways should. An elevated track to South Gatwick. A lot of sky. This is how travel in the future will occur, within a depleted environment. I was the only one not looking at a screen or typing on a smartphone. I punched out my four train tickets from a machine, tickets I'd purchased with a credit card online from Toronto. But it was hard to figure out where and when to get to Salisbury. So I asked a turnstile guard. One train to Clapham Junction, he said, and then turned his hip as if indicating a stopover: a half-hour wait for a Salisbury train. The men a hundred years ago had to ask the same things in this very spot. They received, perhaps, the very same answer.

COMICS

The soldiers were on their way to train in Salisbury. Politicians and generals thought the broad clay plains were similar to the terrain the men would fight on in France. The weather had been mild and dull, with below-normal rainfall. The turnip crop was poor, and rod salmon fishing on the Don was a failure. But the weather was about to change.

I bought my first Cornish pasty from a legitimate kiosk that was all black with gold trim and lit with tremendous amounts of electricity. I had spent the night on the plane next to a huge man—we had both bought the extra-legroom seats. I was late boarding because I never line up, and he had already placed a tube of potato chips and a shirt on my seat. He never said a word, but I knew he was English. He was watching football highlights on the screen. He reminded me of Nick Fury, the British comic book character who was always losing his temper and bursting the buttons off his tunic before killing a lot of krauts.

When I was a kid my grandfather sent us comics from England, wrapped in a roll of butcher's paper. This was my first mail. I carefully tore off the postage stamps and soaked the scrap in a glass of water overnight. Then I slipped the stamps from the paper and dried them on a windowsill so that I could later insert them, with the lick of a glue hinge, into my stamp collector's book. And this is what I am doing here, collecting a gallery of individual scenes that matter to me, into a scrapbook of what I think has survived of an antique war.

My siblings and I devoured the comics. My grandfather, I knew, had served in the Coldstream Guards and fought in the Second World War. When I was twenty-two and backpacking through Europe and Africa and told my mother I was to see the pyramids, she said, You're not the first one in the family to go to Egypt. Your grandad was in a tank division. He fought Rommel.

My mother was sent to Workington as a six-year-old. She was an evacuee because she lived in a shipyard the Luftwaffe might bomb. Rommel, the Desert Fox, was in the comic books my grandfather sent. The British admired him.

While in Egypt I mailed my mother a letter with a postcard of the pyramids. I rented a camel and was led around the tomb of Chephren. I proceeded down the long hall inside the dark tomb and bent over to enter the room with the king's sarcophagus. The doorway is intentionally short so you have to bow to Chephren. A friend had given me a chunk of rough labradorite to toss into a corner of the king's chamber. He wanted to confuse the archaeologists. There was graffiti on the walls here, some of it from Napoleon's time: *Scoperta da G. Belzoni 2. mar. 1818*. I've seen photographs of the Newfoundland Regiment in Egypt, parading around in the same manner as I did. Even the regiment's doctor, Cluny Macpherson, who invented the gas mask, had his picture taken on board a camel. It was funny to see these photos, though I thought, too, how the comic strips the British created about the war did not have this type of humour. A confusing thing in the comics my grandfather sent was that they had both world wars in one edition. As a kid, the only way I could distinguish the wars was by the shape of the tanks and the structure of the soldiers' helmets. These black-and-white comic books were a contrast with those of my North American friends who read strips that were in full colour, including *Sgt Rock*. The American comics had Baxter paper covers that felt slick, like real magazines, not just the rough paper of newsprint. My first experience of English war was that it drained all the colour out of you.

SALISBURY

The Newfoundlanders had no idea they would end up, for a time, in Egypt. They were in Salisbury to train for the Western Front, a front which wasn't even formed yet. The two great armies were racing towards the sea—this is how it is often described. Trying to outflank one another, moving northwards into Belgium. That is where the men thought they were to go; they hadn't realized they would spend a year training in England before being sent to a theatre of war. They began to suspect that the English did not plan to use them at all.

A theatre of war. The Colosseum of Rome may have been the origin of such a phrase—an open place to stand in order to witness a spectacle. The writer Sven Hassel says war is like a cinema—all the best seats are in the back and the front is all flicker and noise. Carl von Clausewitz uses the term "theatre of war" in his 1830s book *On War*. He's the one with the following aphorism: "War is the continuation of politics by other means." He also was the first to describe the fog of war. "The solution to fog," Clausewitz wrote, "is a fine piercing mind, to feel out the truth with a measure of its judgment."

In Salisbury I asked for a bike hire and found the place that I'd seen online in Toronto: fifteen pounds for a bright yellow bicycle all day. This bicycle would not get stolen. It was not the type of bicycle Ernest Hemingway rode delivering mail to the Italian front. I had packed the first collection of Hemingway's correspondence—the gung-ho letters after he is wounded in a shrapnel blast, his exaggeration about being shot by machine gun. It's not true that war always changes you. It changes some people, but if you read Hemingway's letters, the joy over the intensity of warfare remains intact. Hemingway created a double life, for he was aware of the lack of romance in war, and used that in his fiction. But his letters are full of the exhilaration of being young, alive and lucky.

At Waterstones bookstore I spotted a poster with the face of Sebastian Faulks. He was to give a writing master class on the first of July here at the Chalk Festival. Faulks wrote *Birdsong*, a novel hailed as, I have it here, "an overpowering and beautiful novel" about the First World War. I bought an ordnance map at no ordinary price, the "130" of Salisbury. Then I asked about a grocery store. I was pointed towards a Tesco where I lined up, even though they sell live turtles in bags to China, to buy two apples and a banana. Then, suddenly, I was pedalling out of town, following a path along the river that merges onto a small road north to Amesbury. Thatched roofs passed me by, roofs which I had thought existed only on my mother's cork-back placemats. Then I saw that the roofs were covered in wire mesh, though the thatch was real. I passed a truck that advertised it was owned by Brian Chalk, who repairs thatch using combed wheat straw and water reed. The poppies were out, and wild pink roses, and bushes of rosemary.

I pumped the pedals up a hill and suddenly I was overlooking Stonehenge. It was five thirty. There were two bands of highway traffic splitting around the ruins, noisy with large trucks and commuters. I paid seven pounds eighty pence to walk the perimeter of these rocks with an audio guide pressed to my ear. I did this even though there is no record in any of the Newfoundland diaries of a soldier visiting Stonehenge. They lived and trained just a few miles down the road but it seems not one of them thought to visit this site, or at least to note it down. (Jim Stacey, I discovered, only visited Stonehenge during a visit he took later in life.) It was three in the morning when they reached their first camp, at Pond Farm. So they would have marched through rain and mud, with the Canadians, past Stonehenge in the dark.

The caretakers were changing the ropes and poles that herded you over the grass because the sod was turning yellow from all the feet. It was hard to tell, from this distance, how big or small Stonehenge was; human-scale figures should be placed near it. Postcards are deaf, and now I realized how noisy Stonehenge is. Above me, the vapour of a jet—perhaps one arriving from across the ocean. I had seen a World War One postcard of a biplane strafing the Stonehenge ruins and a rope cordoning off the site, much like the one that was here now. Over the course of a century only the planes have advanced.

SASSOON

I biked on to Shrewton, the closest town to Pond Farm Camp. Now and again I unfolded the ordnance map and marvelled at the detail. The scale was larger than the topographical maps I used when hunting caribou. I've never regretted spending money on maps.

My rear was sore from the heavy knapsack and the narrow saddle. I found the manor I'd booked, and I was sweating. It's a nice owner who isn't used to a patron arriving in a full lather aboard a bright rented bicycle. The barn, doors open, was full of the dozing bonnets of European cars.

You're in the Colonel Room, the owner said, and watch your head on the lintel.

I tore off my shirt, and washed it with a bar of soap, and hung it on the shower stall. The soldiers, upon reaching Pond Farm Camp, had done the same. After an inspection from the King they received regulation wear and their blue puttees were replaced with khaki ones. The training days in Pleasantville, the ten days on the sea, and their march to Salisbury Plains were the only time these soldiers would wear blue puttees. But the name stuck. It was the last image of the men seen by those from home. And it is home that makes the name. The men hadn't thought to call themselves the Blue Puttees but they read of the name in local newspapers shipped abroad. The other name given to them by people from home was even more poignant: Ours.

I threw on a new shirt and a blue cloth jacket—I was dressed like a colonel and felt proud of my exercise. I headed downstairs. I ordered the Stilton and broccoli soup followed by a sirloin steak with mushrooms, tomato and chips. I had to acclimatize and get ready for deprivation, and so I assuaged my guilt over this luxurious meal by reminding myself that Siegfried Sassoon, whose regiment fought very near the Newfoundlanders on the Western Front, would sometimes eat a meal like this, if not better. He had a hard time during the war, but when position and privilege allowed it, he indulged. Even the forty-three volunteer nurses from Newfoundland, such as Frances Cluett, who went across the water, were surprised at the meals aboard their converted luxury liner. I toasted the nurses with a big glass of wine. I too was a nurse of sorts, nursing history to tell me what had happened to individuals during war. But it was lonely eating by myself; I wished I had a little regiment with me. The officers at Salisbury had been serviced in a mess run by Harrods. They signed wine cards to their account, much like I was keeping my receipts to be reimbursed by my publisher. I was, in fact, an officer in an advanced position, with a hundred years of hindsight to draw from.

I finished my meal and retired to the Colonel Room. I remembered to duck under the lintel. I know short doorways from the house we own in Newfoundland. I have knelt on the floor there, whimpering with pain from having hit my forehead. I thought of the men on parade near here, and a story about a retired Lord of the Admiralty who thought he understood Newfoundland life. A soldier at attention wore a pair of woollen trigger mitts—mitts you could fire a rifle with—and Lord Brassey said, "I'll bet many's the drop of salt water you've wrung out of those." But the man was an accountant in St John's and hadn't spent a day on the water.

In Sassoon's *Memoirs of an Infantry Officer*, Sassoon has a meal with Lord Brassey. And Brassey tells him how proudly convinced he is of the uselessness of some of our colonies which, he said, "might just as well be handed over to the Germans."

I watched Spain beat Portugal on a penalty kick. The Queen shook the hand of an IRA leader.

CURSUS

The next morning I steered towards Bustard, where the Newfoundland Regiment had trained next to the Canadians. What I found was a trailer park. The artillery can shake the caravan, a local said to me, walking out to see who I was— he was the unofficial trailer-park mayor, carrying a cup of tea in a mug meant to be used indoors. At a sentry post the red flags were up, which meant live firing was occurring. The guard inside his box said he hadn't heard of Newfoundland Wood. I unfolded my gorgeous map, and we saw that it was better than his, which was thumbtacked to the bare wall. He read the words on my map and explained I wouldn't be allowed in the spot marked Newfoundland Wood.

The Newfoundland men, when they arrived on Salisbury Plain, had heard of a place called Newfoundland Wood and were surprised at the coincidence. Did they know, a hundred years ago, that the British army would still be practising here on this land a century later? The sound of exploding ordnance was coming out of the earth, sound that never fully disappears. It recedes into solid objects, and perhaps I felt that the percussion I was hearing was the echo of long-ago training. I got on my bike and followed horse trails through farmland to Larkhill and down to Woodhenge. The sound was verging on audible vibration. Woodhenge is older than Stonehenge—the same idea, but just a sketch made from wood. All that is left here is the remnants of wood pilings. The First World War, I thought, is the Woodhenge to the Stonehenge of the Second World War. The remnants reminded me of the fish weir built near Orillia by the Chippewa, a place of agreements and treaties. The land rising out of the water, the reflex action of retreating glacial ice. Sometimes the work of humanity is converted, over time, into geology.

I rode over to Cursus and the King's Barrow, the brilliant afternoon sun lighting up the small hills that were the graves of an ancient people. The invisible British artillery practising, as if they were a radio channel. Weapons may look new, but their sound remains old. And all I had here was sound. I used to operate a trap shoot at the local rod and gun club in Corner Brook, Newfoundland. It was my first job. I was paid with a free round on my father's Winchester over-and-under, and I could pick up all the brass casings from the rifle firing range behind us. It is a dangerous job, operating a trap. The machine is half-buried in a bunker and you feed fluorescent clay pigeons onto the arm of the machine. Someone else has control of the firing button. You hear a shooter shout "pull" and a man presses this button and the trap arm violently fires out an orange disc. You are protected from an errant shot by the earthen works. Then you lay another disc on the returning arm as it rotates with an electric growl.

After the war, people did a study of the live ordnance left in the ground at Salisbury and concluded it would take a thousand years to remove it all. And so Salisbury remains a military secured area. The red flags hoisted when live rounds are fired, as they were now.

I bicycled down the river Avon past Amesbury, then stopped to look at some swans through the trees. I must have walked through poison ivy because soon I had a rash. Stephen King describes shitting in the woods and wiping himself with leaves that turn out to be poison ivy. We don't have poison ivy in Newfoundland, and so I was innocent of its look and its effect, and reading Stephen King had done me no good.

The swans were beautiful and the River Avon made me think of Shakespeare. The troopship *Florizel* was named after a character in a Shakespeare play, *A Winter's Tale*. The story of an old war, I said aloud, and what it means to a new people—to civilians and swans who know nothing of war. We must all to the wars, muttered the Prince in *Henry IV*. And I realized those men who fought from my island were not soldiers but fishermen and lumbermen and commercial travellers and photographers; and the nurses who volunteered were schoolteachers. The soldiers were young, they had zeal. Perhaps war should be fought only by older people, when the thirst for adventure has dampened. If a war has to be fought, I—a man over forty—should fight it. We have laws about child soldiers. Well, how about an international law against anyone under forty fighting?

A ROSE TREE IN BELLEORAM

I took the horse trail around the Cursus. You could see the tracks left by the hooves, and the caution signposts. It would have been nice to hire a horse. Officers a hundred years ago rode horses. The graves I passed held ancient kings. They were called barrows and their hillocks rose out of the green fields straight through the territory where the Newfoundlanders trained. Soldiers, such as the photographer Robert Holloway, practised their shooting here. Holloway discovered he was an excellent shot so he was trained to be a sniper. The soldiers had marched deep inside an ancient burial site to learn the art of war, summoning the dead to aid in their fighting or, perhaps, innocently unaware that they were exercising in the cradle of their own graves.

I stopped at a nursery to get a packet of seeds for my mother. That's what I do when I travel the world: bring back seeds for my mother. The nurse Frances Cluett did the same thing. She wrote in a letter to her mother that she had included a slip from a rose tree growing in the hospital gardens of Rouen. She wondered if it might be planted in their garden in Belleoram. I have been to Belleoram and studied the garden of the Cluett house that still stands there. It was early summer and I had a flower book with me, but I could not find anything that seemed introduced. Rouen is near Giverny, where Monet had his garden, but there is nothing in Belleoram to compare to Monet. When my parents first moved, from Newcastle in England to Marystown in Newfoundland—which is close to Belleoram—my father wrote my mother back in England to not come. He had changed his mind. There had been forest fire down the entire stretch of the peninsula and it was like living on the face of the moon, my father said. But my mother ignored him and brought us over anyway.

Cluett sent her mother pressed flowers too, flowers like the purple aster. I was looking, I realized, for some transfer of the power of Edgar Quinet's comment that on all the battlefields of history the cities change, as do the leaders, but the hyacinth and the periwinkle still bloom. Quinet is buried in Montparnasse under a big block of cement. Someone has planted flowers behind his bust, but they are not hyacinths or periwinkles. Eventually, Frances Cluett made it home to Newfoundland. A German soldier had given her his Iron Cross—in 1919 she was caring for German prisoners of war. She describes the soldiers being given brandy to soothe their pain. She did not marry (she was thirty-three when she volunteered) but taught school and is buried where she was born.

At the nursery I found no seeds, just a tour bus full of seniors—men and women old enough to have been children during the Second World War, like my parents. I said hello in the tea shop, but no one replied. It was as if they were germinating some plan on a level that I could not reach. What are old people doing? I must find out, for soon I will be one.

I bicycled past four aluminum silos and saw a truck parked near them. The back of the truck barked and then a tall black and white dog appeared. There was a man ignoring the barks. The man did not say hello. The thatched roofs of the nearby houses had fat tall chimneys and I was surprised the roofs didn't catch fire. The Newfoundlanders had wondered no such thing, for it rained every day on the Salisbury Plain.

SANDBAGS OVER HIS PUTTEES

The ride back to Salisbury was pleasant and—I've rarely thought this about the environment—bucolic. I drank water and ate my apple and banana while still mounted and got back to the bike shop on the hour so I did not have to pay an extra fifteen pounds. I had to remind myself that the soldiers knew nothing yet of trench warfare or much of anything about the damage that can be done with shelling and machine guns. They had signed on for the duration of the war—or no longer than a year. That was the contract, and they expected to be home after a season of shooting rifles. They were bored with the training and exhausted by the bad weather and they smoked and learned to fire Lee-Enfield rifles. Some formed a regimental band and others took on cooking duties. The officers, and all the men, were careful with their expenses. They quibbled over accounts. They reduced the allotments given to family back home when they realized how much they had to spend on themselves. Men who had never bought things were suddenly stripped out of their usual environment of trade and self-sufficiency. Some men asked family for money to be deposited in their bank accounts. One man bought a Daimler and took "a tent-load of brother privates off to London." They bought new boots. The soldiers were tired from route-marches, and their feet chafed from bad footwear and from damp conditions on the plains of Salisbury. In their letters and diaries there was a lot of comparison of gear and clothing. The puttees were a menace when full of mud and the Canadian outfits had better boots, although if you read the Canadian accounts you discover that their boots were terrible too. Once, in France, Jim Stacey tied empty sandbags around his trouser leggings and puttees. The sandbags were there to keep his puttees neat, he told a baffled officer.

I was relieved to be done with the bike, although the trails had been fantastic. I sat near the cathedral in Salisbury to fill in some postcards for my family, just as the soldiers had done, although they had written from the gardens of hospitals using the same image of the cathedral. I looked but could not find a postcard with a reproduction of the Stonehenge biplane.

I ate a pasty and a coffee in the old section of town near the new market, which is closed to traffic. If we didn't have to eat, I wondered, would the world be a more peaceful place? Just sit us out in the sun and give us a drink and we'll all find harmony. It's the hunters and the gatherers who run out of animals and vegetation and meet each other to fight for territory, and that is what got in our blood and started all of the wars. I was near a Waterstones when I had this epiphany. The founder of Waterstones first worked for W. H. Smith, which is a bookshop from the 1700s. Everything you look at here has a long stem rooted in the past. Under the soil everything is holding hands and never dies.

Some nearby schoolkids were deciding what to do next—girls and boys, young teenagers. All the girls had phones, and some had two, and they wore narrow jeans or skirts with white low-cut sneakers. The boys were taller and wore caps and low-cut blue canvas sneakers with white laces. One girl, sitting, licked what appeared to be roll-on detergent—some liquid candy, I guessed. It made her infantile, although there was another suggestion in the way she carried the stick of candy and how near she was to the waists of the boys. I thought about how it was only when you looked in the medical records that you realized how much venereal disease there had been in the regiment. In David Macfarlane's book *The Danger Tree* a Newfoundland soldier training in Scotland has his feet praised for good dancing. You should see me on my elbows, he says.

A REMARKABLE KICK

The training was dull and repetitive and the Newfoundlanders only formed half a battalion. Join the Canadians, some people said; or hitch onto a British regiment. But the officers were worried they would lose their identity as a fighting unit. Thankfully, Lord Derby had a plan.

Edward Stanley—the 17th Earl of Derby—was in favour of compulsory military service. When war was declared the British cast around for ideas to bolster recruitment. Today we have this idea that there was a tremendous patriotic surge in enlistment, but in fact, during the first few weeks of the war men were not lined up around the block. Edward Stanley had been Lord Mayor of Liverpool. He said to a Liverpool audience, in August 1914, "This should be a battalion of pals, a battalion in which friends from the same office will fight shoulder to shoulder for the honour of Britain and the credit of Liverpool." He raised five battalions this way for Kitchener's new army.

Edward Stanley's idea took hold. Men were allowed to enlist, train and fight together. Stanley understood a man's loyalty to place. Men would sign up if they knew they'd train and fight with the men they worked with. Also, men would feel compelled to sign up if they appeared to be cowards in their own hometown. This idea was crucial to the war effort.

When younger, Edward Stanley had served as aide-de-camp to his father, who was the governor general of Canada. After his father died in 1908, Edward Stanley inherited sixty-eight thousand acres of land. The Liverpool soldiers trained in his park at Knowsley. Each original member of this Pals battalion received a silver badge for his cap that contained the Derby crest of eagle and child.

Prime Minister Asquith once remarked that in preparation for the battle of Agincourt in 1415, the Earl of Derby's forebear had undertaken much the same task to recruit men from Lancashire and Cheshire. This relation was John of Gaunt, the sixteenth-richest person in history—a man worth, in today's currency, $110 billion.

What Edward Stanley had done was pry open the ribcage and find the loyal heart and exploit it for the sake of recruitment. Instead of joining the British army and forming a unit with strangers, a soldier would stand on the battlefield with his friends. The notion that the Newfoundland contingent might be split up or diluted by attaching itself to another half regiment was supplanted by the vigorous campaign to have more men enlist. The little newspapers around the colony printed editorials that shamed men into joining up.

The basic tactical unit of the British army was the battalion. That's a thousand men with thirty officers. The Newfoundlanders were only five hundred in number— barely half of what was required to make the machine necessary for the British leaders to use you in battle. If they could not be encouraged to join with an unfinished regiment of Canadians, then a push had to be made to send over more Newfoundlanders to build a full regiment. And so this was done and drafts of men were shipped over through the early months of 1915. Once Newfoundlanders had seen battle at Gallipoli, wounded veterans were asked to tour the outports and give talks to encourage the men of the community to do the right thing and sign on.

But all this was a year away. The fall of 1914 marched into winter, and the men were cold and wet in their tents on the Salisbury Plain, and those who had experience with carpentry were asked to make platforms so that they could sleep off the ground. The Canadians saw how good the Newfoundlanders were with wood and asked if they might have platforms made too. But still the wet weather got to them. It poured all through November—twice the normal rainfall. In December a decision was made to move the regiment north, to Scotland. And so I, too, decided to move and follow them.

People see the war they want to see. They chase web links and footnotes across the planet, typing in names slightly misspelled in case someone wrote down a variant of the name on a World War One internet forum or census return, or misheard or guessed at the name. Revisionists are judged to be expecting something different out of the past, applying intentions that are impossible for the past to contain. Others are damned for selecting a history that can give us today's teachable moments. I have watched films of the men, footage now slowed to the correct speed and enhanced using the same software and techniques applied to the Zapruder footage. And I can tell you: World War One is slowly coming back, dear reader, all of it. People are ransacking attics and pawnshops, unloading old cameras that still contain undeveloped colour negatives taken during the war. The removal of black and white allows us to nestle into the arms of history. It is partly why we love stained glass in churches.

On the broad pavement behind Salisbury cathedral a woman walked her dog, and the dog—a black Labrador—sauntered over to smell my hand. The Newfoundland Regiment had a Newfoundland dog as its mascot: Sable Chief. The dog accompanied the regiment on parade in Scotland—there's a photograph of the dog trotting in step as the band marched. The dog was not from Newfoundland, but had been given to the regiment by a Canadian officer serving in England. Sir Edgar Bowring, the head of a merchant family in St John's, was the person who handled the transaction. Many regiments had animal mascots—the Third South African Infantry had a baboon named Jackie who dressed in his own uniform. The baboon ate with the men and marched with the men; he saluted officers, lit cigarettes, and accompanied the soldiers into battle. During artillery attacks, Jackie piled rubble around himself as the shells exploded. But a piece of shrapnel caught Jackie in the leg. He was operated on with chloroform, the leg was amputated, and he lived to return to South Africa after the war.

Sable Chief, at a hundred and fifty pounds, was heavier than most of the Newfoundland soldiers. His handler was the seventeen-year-old private Hazen Fraser. In one photograph, Sable stands up and lays his front paws on Hazen's shoulders as Hazen turns to the camera. The Newfoundlanders were short, and standing, the dog was as tall as Hazen. Sable was run over by a delivery truck on the base where the Newfoundlanders trained. The men were deeply upset by this. Sable's remains were given to a taxidermist. He is now in the museum in St John's called The Rooms.

Sable's handler, Hazen Fraser, survived the war. He married and had two sons. Fifteen years after the end of the war, his wife won a tennis championship in Newfoundland—she beat a LeDrew from Corner Brook. I went to school with a LeDrew, a triathlete. The Frasers lived on Winter Avenue in St John's. Once, in the middle of the night, while his dog waited in his truck, my brother and I stole the Winter Avenue streetsign.

The black Labrador sauntered off behind the cathedral and another woman strode by making a swishing sound. In each hand she was gripping a pink plastic ring filled with water. The rings had lids so they looked like two bottles of dish detergent.

I wished I could stay in Salisbury for the Sebastian Faulks workshop on writing about war. What did I think of *Birdsong*? There is a tail end to the novel that some people find distracting, about how the war affects a modern generation. But that is the part of the novel that interests me the most.

A half moon appeared while the sun was setting—very much like how I once saw it with my son out in the back alley behind our apartment in Toronto. We were sitting on plastic chairs and I had marvelled at how young a child can be and still appreciate the moon. I recalled a woman who had written a story about watching the moon landings. Her father had dragged the television out into their backyard and, under that very moon, watched the live broadcast.

I walked around Salisbury as though on leave. I passed the Poultry Cross, which dates from 1335. During the day, rowdies and the homeless gather here, sheltered by the crosses on each of the four sides of the gazebo, drinking canned beer. But no one was around now, at dusk.

On my way to the youth hostel where I was staying, I crossed a park and a football escaped from two boys so I kicked it back to them. Cheers, one said. Then the ball arrived again, intentionally, so I returned it once more with a nice arc. Cheers! And they sent it back a third time. I was quite a ways past them now, and had to concentrate and kick the ball hard. It was a return to admire. The Newfoundlanders had kicked a soccer ball around just like this while training in England—Frank Lind had been surprised with a ball landing at his feet, as I had. For a moment he'd thought that the Germans had arrived and it was a bomb.

A ludicrous fourth ball rolled in front of me—I was far across the park and could barely see the boys. I would not have known where it had come from without the previous experience. So I laid into it, into the wind, and it curved in the air, the wind got under it, and it dropped right at one boy's feet. I had registered my shellfire.

Cheers!

It was a remarkable kick and the boys knew it, and I pretended it was nothing, that I have that sort of kick stored in me. It made me think of the football played at Christmas during that first year of the war. Perhaps that game had begun because of an escaped ball. Perhaps, instead of being self-contained and orderly, we should spill over and be excessive and administer to the errors of others and shout out silliness. But there are cases, too, of soldiers attempting to be convivial with the other side, and being shot in the wide vulnerable open.

THE MODERN WORLD I'M WALKING THROUGH

On Milford Street I found, closed, a shop that sold Barbour clothing. Barbour is from South Shields, where my mother was born. During the First World War, Barbour supplied military clothing and coats for motorcycle riders. My father wore a Barbour coat when we were fishing or hunting in the woods. Both my parents had been children in the north of England during the Second World War. My mother was evacuated, but my father remembers the early evenings when the Luftwaffe came over to bomb the shipyards. The glint of their wings. But the British had camouflaged the shipyards and outlined decoy facilities further inland and south. And so the Luftwaffe bombed Sunderland.

The shop with the Barbour clothing opened at nine in the morning. Next door was a window display of little army figures and cowboys & Indians, just like the small figures I had as a child. We had driven across Canada, a family of five, from Newfoundland to British Columbia, towing a pop-up camper trailer, looking for a better place to live. We drew treasure maps and crumpled the papers and held them out the open window when it rained. In Victoria, British Columbia, our last stop before turning around, my parents had bought us figurines of cowboys, and of Indians with their plastic birchbark canoes and little spears you could remove from their clasped hands. It felt powerful installing and removing the weapons from their perpetual warring grip. And now, in front of this shop window, I wondered if I should get some for my son. But I had a long way to go, and surely, I thought, I'll see some like these again.

I remembered there was a pub I'd liked around this area, but where was it now? I was hungry. As I walked, I admired the residential doorways with bull's-eye glass for light. It was early glass, which meant these doors had been here a hundred years ago, experiencing the vibration of war. It was as if the street was providing me with the shops on my mind. Or perhaps, because the shops were closed and I could not find the pub that I wanted to eat in, they were somehow stymying my desire. The sun was now behind the trees.

I mention these things because it was a modern world I was walking through. This was what England had become one hundred years after the First World War. The American writer Nicholson Baker said that if there's only one thing a reader takes away from his work, he hopes it's that a person can think a lot of things. I agree: regular people think everything. And a hundred years ago they thought everything. I am naive, you'll say, and misunderstand the experience of war, or the necessity of it. I am not wise to how a society is coerced into war. Baker's approach? What I like about *Human Smoke*, his book on the Second World War, is the absence of narrative bias, a voice. And yet the selection of material becomes Baker's voice. The scenes he chooses to illuminate offer an opinion on the war. He ends the book with the one sentence he alone wrote: "By the end of 1942, the majority of the people who were killed in the war were still alive."

Inside one of the closed stores—it was "to let"—I spotted a poster of a sculpted sheep. The sheep used to hang from the second storey. The sheep had been there during the war, so I stood back and imagined it still hanging above me. I overlaid the image of the sheep upon the stone face of the shop. The head of the sheep had fallen and smashed on the ground right there at my feet. So they had built a new one. The sheep was from a company in the early 1900s that sold, on consignment, woollen goods from women in the area. I was reminded of the gas station near our summer house in Newfoundland that sold woollen trigger mitts. The cashier placed the money in an envelope under the cash drawer for the woman down the road who knitted the mitts. I imagined the money and the envelope, making its trip down the road to the woman, and a rifle, held by warm hands, in the woods trained upon an animal. It made me happy, being at the junction of this entire enterprise.

Two Americans were skipping rope outside the youth hostel. They followed this by doing pushups against two rings in the pavement. America had not entered the war until 1917, and their comic books reflected this. I watched the collapse and press as the two Americans pushed the earth away, then came so close to it again with their strong noses that they breathed upon the world. It was true that many, and especially the Americans themselves, felt they breathed the joy of life into both wars. The American writer James Salter says it's essential for a writer to travel. "It's not a question of meeting or seeing new faces particularly, or hearing new stories, but of looking at life in a different way. It's the curtain coming up on another act."

So says the ex-military man Salter, who flew fighter jets in Korea.

The hostel had a kitchen and I ordered the fish dinner, but I was late and twenty German tourists had just eaten all the fish. A part of me hated the Germans for this act and wished they had been forever banned from the soil of Britain. I ate potato-leek soup and sat with the Germans and ordered a pint, and twenty minutes on the internet for one pound. The waitress poured the flat Guinness from a tin into a pint glass and then placed the glass on a ledge and punched a button. Slowly a head formed—the result of a magnet of some kind on the ledge.

I used the code on the slip of paper my pound had bought me to access the internet on the public computer. A Toronto friend was in Paris. *You're probably in a war zone*, he wrote. I wasn't yet, and I explained that I could only visit him in Paris if the Germans had been there in 1915. *You are venturing*, he replied, *into the heart of war*. That's my friend's flat, laconic tone: sincere with praise, yet mixed with a spoonful of derision. The Newfoundland men, too, while training here in Salisbury, had been full of humour and light-heartedness alongside grievance at the hard training and resentment that their familiarity was being beaten out of them in order to instill the discipline required to turn men into military tools for tactical manoeuvres.

I received a flat stack of white sheets and a blue pillowcase. I was in Dorm 3, the attendant told me; there's a key. A man from Lancashire asked where I was from and what I was doing. He liked that I wasn't German. I explained my project and how I had chosen this dormitory so as to experience, a little, what it was like for the Newfoundlanders to sleep together in large tents in Salisbury. But there were Germans in the room. So I imagined myself in a hospital ward that treated both friend and foe alike. I reminded myself that Frances Cluett, the nurse, had ended up treating Germans.

ISLANDS

I like islands. Islands that are poor like Cuba and Newfoundland. Because I'm not rich. The islands that attract the rich I'm less interested in—the island of Britain, for instance, where I'm standing now, which is twice the size of the island of Newfoundland. Some islands lose their island quality—Manhattan, even though Manhattan is only a thousandth the size of Newfoundland. And yet most islands keep the essential parts that made them: a shoreline and density. What is called a littoral zone.

My father told me, when I was a child, of an island in Newfoundland called Glover Island. Glover Island is the same size as Manhattan. He'd pointed to it down the lake where our log cabin is. He had been to Glover Island once; it had rescued him, when an open boat he was in capsized. He had been moose hunting and the lake is a hundred miles long. The lake lies along the axis of the prevailing wind, as though the wind had made the lake. But the island and lake are built within a fault line that runs along the Appalachian mountains of Newfoundland. The fault disappears under the Atlantic Ocean and emerges again dividing the Hebrides in Scotland. There's a pond on Glover Island, my father said to me, and on that pond there's an island. Someday I'd like to spend a night on that island on a pond on an island in a lake on an island in the ocean.

I remembered lifting up over Toronto in the dark and noticing the other side of Lake Ontario. The lake does not look that big. In fact, I had wondered if what I was seeing were the islands that are very near the Toronto shoreline. I could understand the coastline down to Hamilton and then around to the American side of the lake. As the plane ascended, it was difficult to gauge how small things were becoming. This was similar to my experience of Stonehenge. How big is it? The roped-off area did not allow you to get close enough to tell.

I slept well in the bottom bunk, with my sleeping mask and earplugs. I sank deep into the mythical embroidery of an old war. The window was open about four inches. Three pairs of bunks, six men. Some Germans. Civil. And the bunk was long enough for me.

Very early the next morning, the Americans immediately jumped to the floor and began their pushups. Breakfast cost five pounds for buffet egg, sausage, bacon, beans, mushrooms, tomato, toast, cereal, and coffee. I made a toasted cheese and ham sandwich to take with me on the train. On the way to the station I bought a flat cap at the Barbour shop—made by Deerhunter in Denmark. It was a dark olive, and the only one that fitted me well. I tried on some of the larger Bond caps that men wore a hundred years ago but I looked too ridiculous—as if I was trying intentionally to enter the past. There were no English caps of the right colour or weight.

The Newfoundlanders, if they had money, bought new outfits that looked like officers' uniforms with big flat pockets. They did this in London, on their way north to train in Scotland.

A DISTURBANCE MADE OUT OF OMISSION

I took the train out of Salisbury and awaited a change at Southampton. This was the port where the *Titanic* had left England. It was where many soldiers had left to join the wars in Turkey and France. And where many troops returned to English hospitals, wounded.

But I was heading north. The flat lands and rises I saw through the train window were interrupted by little clusters of trees on hills—the disturbance the result of farmers cultivating the land and leaving the trees. So it was the smooth flatness that was deliberately created, and a disturbance made out of omission.

The Lancashire man back at the hostel had told me he had to work on Monday. I'll take a train with my bike to London and then back to Lancashire, he'd said. One of the Americans who had been doing pushups explained to the Germans that at his school a German student always won the scholarship in history, even speaking English as a second language. Imagine, he said, an American studying in Germany and pulling that off.

The Germans, someone else said, had lost the semifinal in the Euro Cup last night, 2–1 to Italy.

I opened my eyes and saw a sign with the word "alight": *Alight here for Mottisfont Abbey.*

The ticket collector woke me while he inspected a fallen

perforated gate over a fluorescent light tube near my seat. That's a fitter's job, actually, he said aloud but to himself.

Fitter's job. Such English words!

Each car on the train had two surveillance globes on the ceiling, one at each end. The signs that indicated the presence of recording devices had an outdated image of a camera; symbols have not kept up with the objects they represent.

I dozed while tall earthen banks with clusters of thick bushes zipped by the train window. Even on flats, trees blocked the view. Which meant people in their homes didn't have to see this train—but no one thinks of the needs of a train passenger. I required intimate views into kitchens and bedrooms for a fleeting second, so I could stitch these fractions of action together and form a country.

A trolley of coffee; this perked me up. The platforms at the stations where we stopped were sheltered by peaked corrugated roofs and it was difficult to see your connection because there were so many trains. Passengers who annoyed me: whistling and humming to music in their earphones, a man with a fluorescent orange bag who planted it in the aisle, people with cell phones that rang loudly with old-fashioned rings or mash-up reggae.

The public toilets cost thirty pence. You had to feed the coins into a turnstile. London Victoria was a lovely station, with the light coming through the arced ceiling. During the war, this had been the terminus for many trains arriving from France with the wounded. It was wonderful now to leave the train for awhile and walk along streets that had such permanence in their markings. You couldn't create this in a climate where snowploughs scoured the surface of roads. And I wondered, Did it make people here any closer to their history than we were in Canada?

See you later.

Yeah, take it easy.

This was the exchange between two young men on the train, their hair shorn like sheep. This was how men communicated at Ramsey East station. Departing, ready for service.

FORT GEORGE

It was a long day's travel climbing up the entire body of England and, finally, into Scotland. The Newfoundlanders had loved this landscape. The beauty of the little packages of farming and the thatched roofs, the mild weather. It all seemed so tame and without constant toil and hardscrabble effort. My train had passed, in the distance, my own birthplace of Newcastle. I have visited there, and considered the other life I could have lived if my parents hadn't moved to Newfoundland. My parents had some great-uncles who were in the First World War. They came back not quite right in the head, my father said, and they didn't talk about it. My father, as a boy, chopped splits for kindling and sold the bundles, on a cart, to the neighbours. He had trouble tying the bundles. An older man next door showed him how to do it. You take out a few sticks then tie up the rest and then shove the sticks back in. The man had been in the war. It was as if he was applying his own experience of what ties a bundle of men together. There is footage of the Tyneside Irish descending across no man's land on the first of July. Their movements are the same as the ones ascribed to the Newfoundlanders: marching with purpose over an open area. The soldiers of the Newfoundland Regiment thought, like those soldiers from Newcastle, that they were going to war in France. The Newfoundlanders had landed in Devonport, trained at Salisbury, found the conditions inhumane—there was twice the average rainfall that year—and finally were sent to Fort George near Inverness. The weather was better at least, and they were away from the Canadians.

Their train took them north past Birmingham to Ardersier, which is near Inverness. An old fishing village. They moved into barracks at Fort George and had, for the first time, real beds to sleep in. They had milk in their tea and butter on their bread, one Blue Puttee wrote. The commanding officer's horse stopped in front of a tea house every morning to receive his lump of sugar. Once, they went to a dance in Inverness, and near curfew, Frank Lind and a few other Blue Puttees jumped aboard a biplane and flew back to barracks in five minutes. *It is very exciting whizzing through the air at such an awful speed.*

The regiment's first death happened here at Fort George. It was Christmas. Parcels from home had arrived and continued to be delivered all through the season. The soldiers cut large biscuit tins down to make pans for cooking goose. The men had an excellent Christmas dinner: goose and roast beef, cabbage, potatoes, turnips and then plum pudding and tea. They opened presents and ten cases of cakes from the Daughters of the Empire. At New Year's, "sixty-seven barrels and thirty-eight cases of Christmas presents reached the Regiment from the Women's Patriotic Association." One Blue Puttee, fifty years later, said, of the bounty of cake: You couldn't escape it.

Jack Chaplin was the first to die. In his military records it notes "abdominal disease." He died at Fort George on the first day of 1915. He was buried there in the small town of Ardersier:

JUST IN THE MORNING OF HIS DAY
IN YOUTH AND LOVE HE DIED

He was eighteen.

The men trained at Fort George for another ten weeks. And then, in February, they heard that another contingent of men was on its way to join them from St John's: C Company. So they were on the move again, to be stationed in Edinburgh—the only non-Scottish troops to ever garrison Edinburgh Castle.

THE MONARCH OF THE GLEN

There was a painting I had to see in Edinburgh. *The Monarch of the Glen* portrays a glorious full-bodied elk, catching a whiff of the viewer, while in a misty background the purple crags of Scotland appear to be cooling after recent formation. It was painted in 1851 by Edwin Landseer. It's a famous painting and has been called the ultimate biscuit-tin image of Scotland. Artists like Peter Blake and Peter Saville have reworked the original image, saturating the colours and, eventually, collaborating with textile workers to create a tapestry of the same elk and landscape. The tapestry is stunning for the feeling you get: that you are looking at a digital work. But up close, you see the elk is a fabric composed of threads. The scene portrays what is often the subject matter in a traditional wall hanging: the hunting scene. Jonathan Cleaver, one of the weavers who collaborated with Blake and Saville, said that patience is not something he thinks of when he's weaving. If you're being patient you're waiting for something to happen. When you're weaving, you're making something happen with every movement of your hands.

Why was I struck with these reworkings of an old romantic image? Because I am dealing with the same trouble of sifting through an old war to find new meaning. It is not enough to reproduce the classic image of a nation and of the hunt. And this Scottish elk was the basis for a famous Newfoundland photo of a caribou called *Monarch of the Topsails* by Simeon Parsons. That Parsons image, from the 1890s, became the biscuit-tin image for Purity Biscuits, a Newfoundland company. And the caribou was adopted as the emblem for the Newfoundland Regiment. The five memorial caribou that stand in France and Belgium are based on this Parsons photograph. So I had to see this original painting, and then find the textile version at Dovecot Studios.

A note by one of the curators mentions Derrida's description of writing as weaving, that textile and text have the same etymology. We have all seen people, I thought, in the cemeteries, running their hands over words. Receiving the texture of that name—perhaps a family name—directly into their bodies.

The Landseer painting was on loan from Diageo, which is a drinks business that owns Bushmills and Johnnie Walker and Captain Morgan and Seagram's. Diageo had exited their food interests, selling off Burger King and

Pillsbury. Peter Blake's appropriation of the Landseer stag, called *After "The Monarch of the Glen" by Sir Edwin Landseer*, was painted in the mid-1960s for Paul McCartney's dining room. Blake then designed the *Sgt Pepper* album cover.

I studied my walking map and admired the castle above me. The weather was poor, but not as bad as what the men experienced: a foot of snow fell on them during one blizzard. I simply wished I had an umbrella.

My mother once gave me a ruby umbrella handle made of bakelite. She said it was the only ornament in her house when she was growing up. It had been her grandmother's umbrella, and so that handle had existed during the First World War; it had existed at the end of a functioning umbrella. The other thing my mother gave me was a glass paperweight with a photo-backing of the Scottish war memorial. We have some relatives in there, she said.

I thought she meant some of my Scottish kin—Hardys and Pippetts—had been killed in the war and buried in the memorial. Under the stone floor, like the poets of England at Westminster Abbey. All three Hardys in the Newfoundland Regiment had been killed in the war.

But now I saw that the Scottish war memorial here at Edinburgh Castle was created in 1927. The names of the dead who fought with Scottish regiments were listed on a scroll inside a box in this memorial. So I realized my kin had their names in a box here. The biscuit-tin interior of Scotland.

GRETNA GREEN

Let's tally up the days here: a month in St John's, ten days at sea, two months at Salisbury, another two at Inverness, three months in Edinburgh. Every day the men waited for word that they were being shipped to France. The route-marches and training were repetitive and boring. There was talk of an uprising in Ireland, of a politician—Roger Casement—who had been traitorous, and there was some suggestion of sending the Newfoundlanders to Belfast. Eventually, the men realized that the British weren't expecting the Newfoundlanders to go anywhere, were only expecting them to replace the British soldiers who were keeping the homeland safe.

But then an event happened at Gretna Green, which is near the English border with Scotland. I stopped outside a train station in Gretna Green—Hadrian's Wall is down the road, the wall that runs across the top of England to the city I was born in, Newcastle, where my parents met and were married. Gretna Green is famous for runaway weddings—centuries of young English couples eloping to the Scottish border and being married by blacksmiths. But it was too early in the day to happen upon anyone involved in a romantic marriage outside of England. Across the rolling hills here, you could see an elopement for miles.

In Gretna Green there was a monument to a train disaster

that had happened in May of 1915. It was an event that changed the fortunes of the Newfoundlanders and it was the reason I was here. Three trains, fully loaded with passengers and fuel, collided and a fire ripped through the wooden trains, ignited by the gas lamps used for lighting. Many passengers were burned alive. "The dead bodies lie in a white farm building near the railway and in a little hall in Gretna."

One of the trains carried two companies of the Royal Scots from the 52nd Lowland Division. Three officers and 207 men were killed. Five officers and 219 other ranks were injured. It remains the worst rail disaster in British history—the *Titanic* of train wrecks.

The Royal Scots were part of the 29th Division. They were on their way to Gallipoli.

For several months after, this gap in the 29th Division remained. And then, in August 1915, Lord Kitchener arrived to inspect the troops in Edinburgh. Over twenty thousand soldiers were present, but Kitchener addressed the Newfoundlanders. You, he said, are the men we need for Gallipoli.

HAWICK AND ALDERSHOT

The soldiers were vaccinated and met up with C Company and heard stories from home from the recruits. They felt

67

that C Company had received "the soft end of the plank." Then the regiment moved back into tents at Stob's Camp, near Hawick, and the men attended dances in this small town. James Paris Lee, the man who invented the Lee-Enfield rifle, was born here in Hawick. One man was found absent without leave, selling coal from a cart. He was wearing a bowler hat. The camp was low key after Edinburgh—a half-dozen sheep wandered around the tents. A detention camp next to Stob's Camp contained ten thousand German prisoners. The Newfoundlanders did route-marches and one of the men made a movie of their march, which they watched the next night at the picture palace in Hawick. There was a rumour that Turkey was about to withdraw from the war. That Germany was using poison gas. The men killed and ate twenty rabbits.

Hawick's war memorial in Wilton Park has been a winner of the best-kept memorial competition: a naked figure of youth by A. J. Leslie. In its day, it caused some controversy.

It was here the regiment was divided, the men split into two groups: those heading to Aldershot for a final "polish" before being sent overseas; while the remainder—mostly the recruits—were sent to their new depot at Ayr. At Aldershot the barracks were large, and there were great gymnasiums. There were dining rooms and rooms for playing billiards and rooms for borrowing books. There was a statue of the Duke of Wellington from Hyde Park, and Caesar's camp was nearby. The British built their airplanes here. The soldiers were told that Alfred the Great had fortified himself here eleven hundred years ago.

Dr Arthur Wakefield gave the men a lecture on how to use the gas helmet recently invented by Cluny Macpherson. The men turned in their thick-woven uniforms for lighter outfits and a St John's man with a camera made a movie of the men taking bayonet practice. Lord Kitchener spoke to the men about the Dardanelles and the King inspected the troops and then they took a train to Devonport and sailed, on a beautiful August day, aboard the *Megantic* straight to Mudros, on the island of Lemnos east of Greece and very near Turkey. They were guided by two torpedo destroyers. Then they backtracked to Egypt where they trained near Cairo and rode camels and learned to wear tin hats and took pictures of themselves with the pyramids. They slept on stone floors and then moved into tents.

And meanwhile, the remnants of the battalion moved to Ayr, Scotland.

AYR

When I got off the train in Ayr, I found that the land was similar to the land back home. The Great Glen Fault, a hundred miles north of Ayr, was the same strike-slip that cuts through the Long Range Mountains from White Bay, Newfoundland—the Cabot Fault. It is what makes the long lake with the island and the pond on that island and the island on that pond that my father told me about. The fault was broken up by the mid-Atlantic ridge formed two hundred million years ago.

George Ricketts was from White Bay. He signed up in the summer of 1915. He was eighteen. He marked an X for his signature. George was five foot ten, 144 pounds, a fisherman from Middle Arm. His aged father, John Ricketts, was imprisoned and his mother, Amelia Cassell, had moved to Canada and remarried. His sister, Rachel, was going to marry his friend Edward Gavin. All George Ricketts had left was a younger brother, Tommy. Tommy Ricketts was fourteen. George took the coastal steamer to St John's and signed up there and gave sixty cents of his daily pay to his sister, who was looking after Tommy. He was sent to the depot in Ayr.

"Simple service simply given to his own kind in their common need"—this Kipling quotation, from the poem "Sons of Martha," is used at the base of a Celtic cross that presides over the Newfoundland dead in Scotland—over two dozen who died here from accidents and illness. Kipling wrote the poem before the war; the poem is meant to honour those who work to serve others. Patrick Tobin, buried here, died of "syncope." Eric Ellis, who spent the war at the Ayr depot, wrote in his diary that this meant Tobin drank too much—Tobin was "found drowned" and he had lost his watch. He had served at Gallipoli and was wounded at Beaumont-Hamel, and it was Christmas of 1916, back at the depot, when he died suddenly of alcohol poisoning. He was twenty-one. Tobin's allotment of fifty cents a day to his mother was immediately stopped. Instead his mother received three hundred and fifty dollars and a photograph of the grave of her son—this grave here, where I was standing—which was sent to her in 1921.

Some of the dead, I noticed, were from the Forestry Corps, and their tombstones had a carved log motif.

The men in the regiment loved Scotland. They saw Charlie Chaplin movies and they saw Charlie Chaplin himself on stage. They stayed up at Halloween parties until three in the morning. They played field hockey against the ladies. They learned from a commander at the Gas School that it was considered a crime for men to drink water taken from shell holes of a contaminated area. The men watched plays at the Gaiety Theatre and ate boxes of chocolates sent over at Valentine's. *All of a Sudden Peggy* was a play about a spider that was found in a maid's food, and was taken to his lordship's room for inspection. "Real good," Eric Ellis wrote. Ayr was a town happy to host the Newfoundlanders.

The men found time to marry Scots ladies. And after the war the women returned with the men to Newfoundland.

The women thought Newfoundland must be an island like the Isle of Wight. They did not realize it was so far across the Atlantic. They were not prepared for outhouses and oil lamps. For skinning rabbits and turning salt fish over in the sun. The savagery of pioneer existence was too overwhelming for some of those who were used to simple service simply given. And so some of them returned to Scotland. For didn't Jesus scold Martha for working too hard? *Come, sit with Mary and listen to me.*

In June of 1917 Eric Ellis received leave and took a ship from Brighton back to Rimouski, Quebec. Then he traded a ferry for the railroad back to Newfoundland and spent a week in Kelligrews shooting birds—those would be the only things Eric Ellis shot through the entire war. He spent over three months away from the war. Then he returned to England: he sailed with a draft of men in October aboard the *Florizel* to Halifax, took the *Metagama* with a convoy of ten steamers and eight liaison ships back to Liverpool, and made his way north to the depot at Ayr.

EGYPT

The medical officer Cluny Macpherson, who had witnessed the men's physicals back in St John's, was one of the soldiers riding a camel in one of the photographs near the pyramids. He looks both distinguished and ridiculous on the camel. I knew of Cluny Macpherson because his name is on a plaque on a stone wall outside a house in St John's telling you that he was the inventor of the gas mask. That is not a statement you expect to read while walking down a street in Newfoundland.

Cluny Macpherson had been a doctor with the Grenfell Mission in Labrador when war broke out. He was the eldest son of a St John's businessman—Campbell Macpherson. Campbell and his brother owned, with William Job, the Royal Stores in St John's, which were built after the Great Fire of 1892. This was the world Cluny was born into—hearty conversation, the desire to study, an appetite for work. He had a brother, Harold, five years younger, who, among other things, saved the Newfoundland dog as a breed— Harold Macpherson's house is near the grounds of Memorial University, nestled in trees. I once bought a bicycle from an elderly man outside this house—a bicycle I still have. The Macphersons were fixtures at Methodist picnics; they were confident, with no room for doubt and laziness, just belting out talent and having the guts to create good in the world. That's what growing up proud with a strong moneyed family in a capital city of a great little nation can do for you.

The Royal Stores owned Riverside Woolen Mills, which operated in Makinsons out of Conception Bay—a community I've passed many a time. It was Riverside which made the Newfoundland Regiment's uniforms with wool from local sheep. When we bought our little summer house, we found a pink blanket on a bed that was made by Riverside. Its logo: the Newfoundland dog.

GAS MASK

Before the war, Cluny Macpherson worked with Labrador doctors like Wilfred Grenfell and Harry Paddon and Arthur Wakefield. After the war started, Macpherson was picked by George Nasmith, the Acting Medical Officer of Health for Toronto, to help in France with the development of the gas mask. A German prisoner had been found carrying a pad of cotton waste done up in some veiling, similar to the mask worn by surgeons and nurses in the operating room. The cotton was impregnated with a solution of sodium hyposulphite and washing soda. The Germans were trying to race for the Channel ports by using gas. The shell with gas would explode and the contents would enter the eye and make the eye wet. These were called lachrymatory shells. The word "lachrymatory" used to be associated with glass vessels that were filled with tears and bottled. The Greeks had these jars a thousand years before Christ. And then these canisters of chemicals were volleyed into the British trenches—gas that caused tears.

The scientists who were brought together to make the mask were called the gasoliers. Macpherson was sent to London for two large cylinders of chlorine. This trip allowed him to conceive of a superior pattern to the German model, where you survived the gas by not moving. You had to hold the contraption in place.

Macpherson bought a couple of yards of Viyella and some mica in London and took them back to Saint-Omer in France. Viyella is a blend of wool and cotton; the name comes from the road where the mill was built, Via Gellia (the road builder, Phillip Gell, claimed Roman descent). Macpherson knew a soldier could breathe through Viyella because he'd used it to cover the heads of patients being transported in winter from Labrador.

The team tried out the German masks in a French field, and two of the scientists had to be taken to hospital. Macpherson cut out his pattern in paper and asked the matron to sew it up for him using the Viyella and a mica window. The next day Colonel Harvey tried on the mask and stood in the chamber for five minutes. Colonel O'Grady tried it, too. The director general of medical services, Arthur Sloggett, declared it was so comfortable a soldier could fight in it.

Cluny Macpherson was shipped back to London and headed up a team to produce the helmet. Tanners complained that the gasoliers' use of hypo, which was also needed in the tanning process, meant no leather for the army. Mica cracked, so it was replaced with photographic film. The film was flammable, but less so if treated with an alkaline solution. Then Macpherson went to a lecture where a type of cellulose used as a dope, or lacquer, on the wings of airplanes was discussed. He got nine rolls of cellulose film donated from Pathé News. It was a thousand yards long and a yard wide. It came in wooden cases which he loaded aboard three cars and drove to Abbeville and on to London aboard a transport truck.

The rolls were mounted on trestles in the Great Hall of St James's Palace. For weeks the place reeked of acetone as women cut the film into sections for helmet windows. A trial lot of a thousand were used in France, and then the team was told to go full speed on the manufacturing. They took over three laundries in London to produce the helmets.

The mask was such a success that the Allies realized the Germans would have to change the chemicals they used from chlorine and sulphur dioxide to phosgene. So an alteration was made because exhaled breath would spoil one of the protective chemicals: an exhaling apparatus was added. The new German ingredient destroyed wool, so flannelette was substituted for the original Viyella. Hexamine was also added to protect against another gas, and the slightly changed helmet with glass eyepieces instead of film was called the PH helmet. This was the one British soldiers used in France.

The gas team went on to produce the box respirator, which used powdered carbon as a filter. Twenty-two million were made before Macpherson was put on other tasks: how to protect soldiers from flame-throwers; and figuring out a means to transport hot food to men at the front (a box inside a box separated with hay). Then Macpherson was sent to Gallipoli as a medical transport officer in Mudros. He got offers to join the engineers as he was a dab hand at manoeuvring hospital boats and wrecking tugs along the peninsula of Gallipoli. He had to board vessels and decide how many patients they could handle. He would roll out blueprints and do his estimation. Forty thousand wounded poured down the Turkish shores onto the ships for treatment. Siegfried Sassoon's brother, Hamo, was one of them—he died at Gallipoli. The *Aragon* was nicknamed the "Arrogant" and the "Featherbed" by troops coming down from Gallipoli. Macpherson wrote, "She was reputed to have grounded on a bank formed of empty champagne bottles which had been thrown overboard." A photograph from the time shows a cat wearing a lifejacket made of champagne corks. Eventually the *Aragon* was torpedoed and sunk off Alexandria. Later Macpherson would say he never worked so hard in his life, and the load was matched only by his time later in St John's, dealing with the influenza epidemic of 1918.

Cluny Macpherson also acted as an advisor on poisonous gas in Turkey. He was charged with building and equipping a redipping station for reconditioning gas helmets after they had been worn in the field. He had done this before in Abbeville and Calais. There was scarce fresh water where he was stationed in Mudros, but there was a condensing plant. Macpherson used a heavy boiler and a sheet iron smokestack and had Egyptian craftsmen working for him. When work got slow he learned a few Egyptian shanties and got the men singing, and the rate of work increased.

In Egypt, the men received letters from home, from family concerned they were so close now to the war. *But we are further away now,* they wrote back, *than we had been in England.*

Macpherson strikes me as an intelligent, warm, fast-thinking, generous person who posed as an innocent from the colonies naive on protocol. He loathed red tape and admired a job done effectively and quickly. He suffered migraines and temporary half blindness. He climbed to the roof of the Grace Hospital in St John's in the middle of winter and took a series of photos of the city to send to a woman whose uncle used to live nearby. He pricked holes with a pin through the photos and wrote on the reverse the names of all the new buildings.

He was injured in Egypt. His horse shied from a camel and fell, trapping his ankle and dislocating a joint. He noted there were four other officers in hospital with a similar injury. Fashionable, he said. He was shipped back to Newfoundland to oversee the medical operations there. But his eye travelled both near and far to subjects at hand. The *Calypso*, which by then was just a salt and coal hulk stationed in the city's harbour, was so successful at training naval reserves, Macpherson wrote, that Newfoundland outnumbered all other dominions combined in supplying men for the navy. He was that kind of guy.

He thought that the failure of combined operations at Gallipoli made it possible for the later success at Normandy during the Second World War. Forces had landed on the peninsula without the Turks knowing much about it, but because the soldiers could not find their equipment on board, they had to reroute to Mudros, sort out this material and land again. And by then the Turks and Germans were ready.

GALLIPOLI

The Newfoundlanders took their troopships to the Mudros peninsula on the island of Lemnos. They were thirty miles from the Dardanelles.

I love the Dardanelles because there is a short street in St John's called The Dardanelles and I used to walk it to get to the street my girlfriend lived on. I didn't know at the time that it was named after this strait that separates

Asia from Europe, that connects the Mediterranean to the Black Sea. I didn't know that the Dardanelles was also the Hellespont, and it was this stretch of water that Lord Byron swam to honour Leander, who crossed the Hellespont every night to meet his lover Hero. And every night I walked that lane in St John's to my girlfriend.

No Christmas parcels were delivered to the Newfoundlanders in the Dardanelles—and no house has a mailing address for The Dardanelles. The soldier Owen Steele described forty thousand bags of wet mail sitting untouched, with the canvas sacks slit open to allow the water to drain out: "They are sure to be in fine condition." The Christmas mail had been routed mistakenly to the Western Front.

The Dardanelles is a passageway to other things, a sea river you could say, and for the Newfoundlanders—the last regiment to enter the war in Turkey and the only troops from North America involved in this theatre of war—the Dardanelles was the way to Constantinople. They landed in the middle of the night at Suvla Bay in September, after the British and Australians and New Zealanders had been there already six months. This was a full year after the Newfoundlanders had signed on for the duration of the war or no more than a year. And so they had to sign a second contract with no time limit: until the war was declared over.

And here is where the troops were first shelled and introduced to trench warfare.

Private Hugh McWhirter was the first combat death, killed on the third day after landing. He was a brakeman from Humbermouth. Humbermouth is where the Humber River enters the sea at Bay of Islands. It is where I grew up.

Hugh McWhirter had survived the great sealing disaster of 1914 off the coast of Newfoundland. Then he had signed up in January 1915, at the age of twenty. His younger brother George signed up with him. George was nineteen. They embarked for England and spent five months in Scotland. In August of 1915, they joined the Mediterranean Expeditionary Force. They spent time at Alexandria, Egypt, and then, on the night of 19 September aboard the coastal steamer *Prince Abbas*, they landed at Suvla Bay.

What did McWhirter think of this strait, this peninsula, this shelling, this attempt by men to find a footing on land? He must have thought at first that the straits they were entering were a bit like the long estuary which is the Bay of Islands. He must have felt, in a strange way, that he was coming home. For Suvla Bay is a little like Humbermouth. This was a man who had witnessed firsthand a Newfoundland blizzard while on the ice sealing, and who now saw himself, on his third day in Turkey, blown apart. And what did the men who had to deal with this death think, knowing that Hugh McWhirter could not withstand the punishment of Turkish artillery? Seeing the shocking transformation of a man's experience from the bucolic to the savage, which is the brute result of modern war? Witnessing a friend turned into what the poet Ivor Gurney called "that red wet thing"?

Suvla was the regiment's practical contact with this conversion: a man tears apart in front of you, and what is left is inanimate, a trunk, the exposed interior. The fibrous meat and organs of Hugh McWhirter had remained hidden under the character and soul of the man, as they should be. But here, in an instant, the sack of his nature was obliterated by an overwhelming force. Men were no different now than seals, or caribou or rabbits or fish. Their vulnerability to extreme force had been exposed. Forty-seven Newfoundlanders were killed here. And hundreds more suffered from severe frostbite and trenchfoot and dysentery. More died later from wounds and were buried in Egypt and France. Some had injuries that stretched on for years and died back home, but they too were dead from the war. I once visited a house on Fogo Island where the photographs of a man who survived the war haunted the grandchildren because he was injured and insane with a wound that could not heal properly. Families learned to grow around these wounds. But who is to say when a war truly ends—when the effects of a war have quit smouldering?

Hugh McWhirter's mother had sent her son four pairs of socks in a cardboard box—two pairs of grey ones with pink stripes, one pair of plain grey, and one pair of white with blue stripes. She had also sent a tin box with two little cakes and four khaki handkerchiefs and cigarettes. After hearing of her son's death she wrote a letter to the regiment: If you find the socks and return them I will repack them and send them to our other son, George.

JAMES DONNELLY

They spent their days in a front-line position not fifty yards from the Turks. They picked their shirts clean of nits and bathed in Suvla Bay. It was hot and the flies were bad. They cut their pants down to shorts—a photo of Owen Steele at Suvla reminds me of his race-walking days in St John's. Dr. Wakefield led the Presbyterians in prayer, as there was no minister. The Turks used dogs to supply their snipers with food and ammunition. Richard Cramm, who wrote the first history of the regiment, says this of the New-foundlanders at Gallipoli: "The soldiers had come expect-ing to find in war a life of excitement. They found it, on the contrary, duller than the most dreary spells of lonely exis-tence in the back woods of their own island. The heat, the hard work, the flies, the thirst."

The regiment's first combat deaths occurred here at Gallipoli, but so did its first military success. Lieutenant

James Donnelly's party captured a rise in land they named Caribou Hill. Donnelly was awarded the Military Cross. Walter Greene, a police constable from Bell Island, received the Distinguished Conduct Medal for his act of gallantry and devotion. Greene drove off the Turks and brought in the wounded.

During the time of this raid, Donnelly was involved in correspondence with the Bank of Montreal, for they were complaining of an overdraft on his account. His apology to the bank was written while he was in the trenches.

Eroticism is the human desire to live. We are still missing these lives of men who are dead. We think of them because they did not get old. They had potential, and we are puzzled when potential is stymied.

To witness a corpse is a startling experience. A friend died when I was twenty-five. He had been ill for a year. I was the first to see him. I got a call from the hospital saying he had taken a turn and I put on my old army boots and called a taxi at four in the morning. It was extravagant, the taxi, but I had to get there fast. The sky over the harbour was just turning blue when I reached the palliative care unit of St Clare's Mercy Hospital. The nurse on duty said I was too late.

The permanence of my friend's death ran counter to the fleeting presence he had in palliative care. Already the nurses were unpinning his favourite artwork from the walls and, for lack of any place to store the posters, laying the artwork across his dead legs. The bed had wheels. He would be wheeled out of the room once his wife had arrived, and ferried on to the next stage of his death.

Rudyard Kipling's son, John, was killed at the Battle of Loos. The British advance at Loos happened at the same time as Newfoundland's involvement at Gallipoli. And everything that happened at Loos was to occur again to the Newfoundlanders at Beaumont-Hamel.

THE DARDANELLES

One winter some years ago, several planeloads of Bulgarians on their way to Cuba stopped in Gander, Newfoundland, to refuel. The Bulgarians fought security to get off the planes and then they asked for refugee status. They piled into St John's. If you saw someone on the street reading a book you knew they were Bulgarian. I met several of them and they told me that they could not return to Bulgaria, and that they missed their families. One night I woke up and thought, But I can go there. I bought a plane ticket and put my belongings in boxes and sublet the room I was living in. I flew to London and then Athens and worked my way through the islands and took a ferry to Marmaris. The fabulous Mercedes-Benz buses delivered me through Turkey. I hitchhiked from Ankara in the snow and was picked up by two serious military men in a private car. We drove silently until a truck passed us and kicked a rock up into our windshield. The glass caved in. We stopped and cleaned out the glass remnants and then tried to continue but it was too cold. We had to leave the windows down to prevent wind drag inside the car. The driver pulled over again and we all got out and one of them popped the trunk. They were speaking Turkish and ignoring me, which made me nervous. But then they withdrew out of the trunk these brand-new pillows encased in clear plastic. Six pillows and they handed two to me. We sat in the car again and drove, all three of us hugging the fat crinkling pillows and the freezing wind blew through the car and the military men with their wide moustaches could not stop laughing.

Turkey. I thought about what a tremendously difficult position the Turks were put in by the war, and how Mustafa Kemal Atatürk led them to a place that Britain and France were not happy with. But Atatürk said this, after the war, about the foreign dead on Turkish soil: They were all Turks now, and would be looked after. His words were conciliatory.

The weather turned in November and the Newfoundlanders were issued an extra blanket. Half the regiment was sick with dysentery. Then the men had to endure a tremendous flood that washed out their trenches and sleeping caves and while they survived this they read, in the St John's newspapers, that enormous packages of food and clothing were being sent to them. But no socks or shirts reached them and, instead, they had to put up with seeing their Australian and New Zealand comrades celebrate with their gifts from home.

The flood swept away parapets and filled the trenches with three feet of water. There followed two nights of frost, the men soaking wet. "It reminded one of the *Greenland* disaster"—a sealing disaster from the late 1800s. "One was expecting to find them [the men] lying dead from exposure."

What was I doing in Turkey all those years ago? I had been happy in Newfoundland, and yet the same impulse that compels a young man to join the infantry is what made me apply for a passport and purchase an international youth hostel membership and select a knapsack and a sleeping bag and sew a flannel sheet to fit the sleeping bag. I brought with me a Bible my mother had given me when I was twenty-two, and I did not shave for six months. I ended up sleeping in a cave in the Sinai peninsula and thrashing olives in Crete and touring through Turkey during Ramadan and achieving the Newfoundland Regiment's dream of entering Constantinople. I had to slow down my evening eating habits when I hit Bulgaria, for there was no fasting in Bulgaria.

When it looked like Bulgaria was to join the fighting on the side of the Turks and the Germans, that's when the

British decided to evacuate Turkey. When I returned to Newfoundland from Bulgaria, I met the woman who made me walk through The Dardanelles and I tried to learn how to live with someone else. There's a line from a Heather O'Neill novel: The smallest a family can be is two members. But always the smaller number of one tries to destroy the two. The army, in its way, defeats this impulse of the individual. The army tries to be the biggest family you can have.

I drove, with the woman from Newfoundland, to Toronto in a brown Chevrolet with green flames painted on the rocker panels. We took turns driving and crying because we did not want to leave St John's, but I loved Toronto if only for the ease with which you could get around on a bicycle. Those were my twenties and thirties in a nutshell, trying to live with a woman and search for a place to live and be happy. I was allowed to do this because there was no war during my youth, no war that demanded a military draft.

Owen Steele describes the war at Suvla and how, when the order came to evacuate, it was the Newfoundlanders along with the Australians who set up, in the dark, rifles with twine and dripping water weights to pull a trigger and fire a bullet thirty minutes after they had all left the beaches, to make the Turks think they were still in the trenches. It was a model for a successful amphibious withdrawal. Steele was the last British soldier to climb aboard the side of a ship and leave the Helles peninsula, shouting out to the commander of the 29th Division, who had returned in the dark to retrieve his valise. During the war, the British suffered two hundred thousand casualties here. It was a good thing that the British decided to change their minds. Caribou Hill was the closest anyone got to Constantinople.

Gallipoli is near the site of Troy. Ephesus, where the Gospel of John was written, is across the Dardanelles and over a shoulder of hills. Ephesus is three thousand years old and used to be a port city, one of the largest cities in the world. And now, from the high ground of its amphitheatre, you can see the ocean almost three miles away.

GEORGE MCWHIRTER

Three years after her son's death, Hugh McWhirter's mother wrote the military to ask why her monthly allowance was being stopped. Reply: The pension ends after three years. In March of 1917, she asked after her other son, George, and his allowance of seventy cents a day, which she had not received. All I have at home, she wrote, is a ten-year-old boy. She wondered if George had intentionally cut her off or if it was a mistake. She mentions, privately, that her son had been accused of drinking but that at home in the Bay of Islands he neither smoked nor drank. And she didn't want George to know that she had been asking.

The paymaster, James Howley, informed her that George had cut off her allowance in November of 1916. There was no record of another allotment being made, Howley said, and George McWhirter was now in France. In December of 1917, McWhirter had been captured at Cambrai; he had a gunshot wound in the left arm. In his papers, from a German POW camp in Lazarette, his place of birth was called "Bayoffillans." This word on the German forms startled me when I read it: a German had been listening to this young man tell him where he was born. Bayoffillans.

George McWhirter was in Camp Dülmen, James Howley wrote. His mother, hearing this, wanted to know how to send him a parcel. Once a season, Howley said, a parcel weighing no more than eleven pounds can be sent.

George McWhirter was repatriated on 18 August 1918. Cluny Macpherson, the medical doctor in charge of the regiment, told James Howley that he authorized McWhirter to be furnished with a railway warrant to get home. McWhirter had three large scars over his left upper arm, including one weak scar that might break down, and considerable limitation of movement at the shoulder joint.

Here is McWhirter's statement as a prisoner of war:

> I had my arm shattered by a piece of trench mortar and
> then taken prisoner and taken to hospital at Cambrai

and stayed four days and sent to prison war camps. Put in hospital there and was there nine months tended by British Prisoners and no German Doctor, no nurses, food bad, cabbage and potatoes mixed and no meat, sour crout and potato peelings all the time and not much of that, no underclothes only one shirt I had on at capture, wash it myself. Bed, one brown blanket on the floor and a sort of pillow never washed for the nine months. An English Prisoner conducted Divine Service once on Sundays. Treated well in Holland on way to England via Rotterdam now getting five dollars no pension, my arm still weak and only able to do very light work.

PS: arm still only dressed once a week and only paper bandages which used to fall off before the Doctor would come.

LEVI BELLOWS

The Newfoundland soldiers evacuated the peninsula in the middle of the night. They took transport, wherever they could find it, back to Egypt. They did not travel as a regiment. They were dispersed into companies and platoons and even groups smaller than that, not fighting units at all—much like information travels today, separated into tiny packets that are then regrouped at their destination.

In this case, the destination was Alexandria. Where the soldiers took camels for rides around the pyramids. Where time alone after Gallipoli renewed their independence. The men trained, but some of them rebelled at the harsh conditions and marching in the heat. A sergeant, Levi Bellows of Curling, was stripped of his rank for muttering at Colonel Arthur Hadow, the commanding officer, who had joined the regiment during Gallipoli. Three months of harsh training had made the men hostile. The nurse Frances Cluett had heard from other wounded British officers that the Newfoundlanders were hard to discipline.

When Levi Bellows muttered at him, Arthur Hadow paused before climbing into his car. And then he returned from leave early. I have to stop this, he said. It is a sign of the soldiers' lack of training. Hadow made the men march in the afternoon. He broke them. He broke their individuality in Egypt. He did it for their sake, or at least for the sake of the army. And Owen Steele was embarrassed. Owen Steele rode horses and had a batman. He'd had a rubber sheet over his dugout in Gallipoli. Once you have privilege you forfeit the rights of the individual man.

But Levi Bellows was stripped of rank in Egypt. Levi Bellows was in trouble. And then, in France, he was captured by the Germans and made a prisoner of war in Limburg. He survived the war and married Agnes Taylor.

He died at the age of eighty-three in 1977. He is buried in Curling, where he was born.

Levi's brother Stewart Bellows had enlisted, too, and was reported as wounded; he died of his wounds in France in August 1917. He was buried at Canada Farm Cemetery, Belgium, aged nineteen. Levi and Agnes had a son and they named him after his uncle. Stewart William Bellows died at eighty-two, in Curling, in 2008. My father knew him. He was a "pillar of the community of Curling."

There's a photograph of Levi Bellows taken back in Pleasantville, outside his tent sitting in a chair, and he has the look of someone with an independent spirit. The men had yet to develop the unfamiliar method of address used in the military. They came from small communities—coves like Curling where you knew everyone intimately except for the minister and the schoolteacher. But these men had been thrown together into a regiment of a thousand souls and were forming their own cove. Colonel Hadow was the teacher, Father Nangle the minister. "If there's one thing in the world that I loathe," writes P. G. Wodehouse, "it is unremitting ceaseless toil." That, perhaps, sums up Levi Bellows's feelings, too.

The spirit of the individual does no good in war. It is not one army against another; there is a third element involved in the machinery of war: the turning of men into the machine, and the functioning of that machinery. Owen Steele was a convert to this way of thinking, which at times makes him look as if he wanted to satisfy staff and move up the ranks.

Morale is the sinew that ties together a regiment. Without morale a regiment will not perform the duties assigned by a superior. Morale is what kills the independent, free-thinking individual and renders that energy into loyalty towards the group. Looked upon from the other side, though, to champion the morale of each individual soul against the machinery of the group whose aims are often ambiguous, or are directed towards a goal not necessarily good for any of the other ranks, can be seen as the most courageous act of all.

OWEN STEELE

We know of Owen Steele through his own words, which have been published, with a great introduction by David Facey-Crowther. Steele was a merchant's son, full of patriotism and a fervour to improve himself, and when he joined up—one of the first five hundred—he quickly was promoted. His entire two years in the army he was hellbent on further promotion and driven by a sense of duty, and even when things were bad in Turkey he was game. While knowing they were in a terrible place, he hoped that somehow they were making a difference in the war.

He was a racewalker. His brother, James, was a racewalker, too. Racewalking was a big sport back then. Their father, Samuel Owen Steele, was a merchant in downtown St John's. He did not run a big enterprise like that of the Ayres—instead, Steele was involved in dry goods and then moved into glass and crockery. He had come from England and married a woman who was living with her aunt and uncle—they were originally from Devon, England. Her uncle, James Martin, brought the architect James Southcott from Devon to build a row of townhouses in St John's. Devon Row survived the Great Fire of 1892. The beauty of these buildings is in the roofline, in the detail around the windows. It's all still there, as if James Southcott was waiting for an elevated era, when you could see things from above.

And so we move from a man to a book to a building, and closer towards another man important to this journey. This is Leonard Stick—the first man to sign up for the regiment. Stick grew up, with his brothers, in one of these Devon Row houses. I have stood by the door of the house he lived in.

Owen Steele and his family, meanwhile, lived above their store on Water Street. When war broke out, Steele and Leonard Stick and George Tuff were all part of the first contingent—the Blue Puttees. Owen Steele was twenty-seven. When I was that age I worked across the street from his father's store in the old King George V Seamen's Institute on Water Street. One day after lunch I crossed the street and bought, from an old man who served me, a Royal Doulton saucer that was on sale. This man, I knew, was related to Owen Steele; you can tell from the photographs. The man asked where I worked and I pointed out the building that faced the war memorial. Oh yes, he said. That was the building they put the dead sealers in. And that was all he said. I didn't know then that the King George V building was where the corpses of the sealers from the 1914 disaster had been placed in the basement for identification—their bodies thawed in bathtubs. And then, during this war that I am now retracing, the building became a place for seamen and military personnel to congregate—it was known as Caribou Hut. During the last year of the war, it became the resting place for the bodies of the dead from the influenza epidemic. That was the building in which I worked.

WALTZING MATILDA

I travelled to Turkey and the Newfoundland Regiment fought in Turkey and were the last to leave Turkey and you'd think I could leave Turkey behind. But I was walking by a bar called Hugh's Room in Toronto one night and saw Eric Bogle's name on the marquee. How did I know that name? I opened the door and heard a song I knew. I had thought the composer of that song, who turned out to be Eric Bogle, was a dead musician from the 1950s. This song I heard is one of the saddest songs on earth. Bogle was halfway through the song when I climbed the stairs to the bar, and I did not stay to hear the end of it. It was enough just to have a verse and the chorus. That song is earnest and particular—you can only really hear it once a year.

"And the band played Waltzing Matilda."

I once went to hear the Pogues play, expecting that exact song, but the singer Shane MacGowan never got off the tour bus. He was hammered and unconscious, sleeping it off on the bus parked at the curb. Music critic Robert Christgau wrote of the Pogues' version of Eric Bogle's song that MacGowan "never lets go of it for a second: he tests the flavour of each word before spitting it out." I stared at the tour bus, where Shane MacGowan's body was asleep behind sixteen-gauge sheet metal.

I don't mean to be disrespectful to the men who died a hundred years ago in the Great War. In fact, I mean the opposite: to celebrate what they aimed to restore. If you look at footage of the Newfoundland Regiment, you see they are at rest and giddy and being silly with one another. Silliness is the antidote to trench warfare. If you ask a woman who is grieving the death of her son or husband how she feels, she will, through the tears, laugh at you. It's absurd—the question and the situation. Of course we would all prefer a different kind of absurd, the kind that did not depend upon pain. And so I want these men who died or were injured in the war, and who are all dead now one way or another—as every last person involved directly with that war is now dead—I want to let them know that I am the king of cornball, and I love life and I've made life, and I think we should all encourage people to go on, even in the face of doom. Surely that's what those men would have wanted.

At his Toronto show, Eric Bogle had announced that he was ending his touring, that this was his last chance to meet old friends across Canada. He probably wouldn't see them ever again. Near the end of the tour, he was invited to play in Newfoundland. If it was anywhere else, he said, I would have declined. But he had always wanted to come to Newfoundland. He said he knew the importance to Newfoundland of the Turkish war that had killed so many Australians and New Zealanders. He played in Corner Brook, my hometown, and in St John's, the city where I first realized I wanted to be a writer. I went to see him, and this time I listened to "Waltzing Matilda" all the way through.

TWO

The Newfoundland soldiers were shipped, through the Suez Canal, to southern France. From Marseilles, where "the peach trees were in bloom," they took trains through territory where now a factory is being built that will harvest energy from a star. Their troop train drove through a snowstorm, passed along the Rhone Valley and the vineyards of Burgundy. They were given tea and cakes along the way and the only men they met were cripples. They arrived at Pont Remy and marched towards Amiens. They slept in stables and billets and, over the course of several weeks found themselves, at last, on the Western Front. A torrent of mail and parcels from home had finally hunted them down. The soldiers sang a song James Murphy, a St John's composer, had written about parcels stolen from the mail. They watched Charlie Chaplin films and visited the ashes of Joan of Arc. They returned from illness and the effects of frostbite and trenchfoot from Gallipoli and were near the Somme to take part in the Big Push that was meant to relieve the French defending Verdun. Germany had decided, at Verdun, to bleed the French white. So the French needed help.

I found my way, like the drafts of soldiers from the Ayr depot, through Dover into France at Calais. I got into Dover Priory in the late afternoon and bought a two-pound ticket for a bus to the terminal. I was the only passenger. At the terminal, I paid a five-pound fee for being late for my ferry booking. I listened to a class of Dutch schoolgirls and their male teacher, who was younger than me. Their chatter was in English. Not full sentences but fragments of song, made-up lyrics, guttural noises. I thought: A weekend of this would kill me if I was that teacher. It had been drizzly all day, but a bit of sun peeked out now. I was wearing my Dutch hat and I thought it helped me understand their conversation. We had lost an hour because of the shift in time zones. It would be late when we reached Calais. I was hoping to get to Amiens that night.

We boarded the *Spirit of France*, and the boat left its mooring at six o'clock.

Ten minutes out, the horizon held the French shore. To

appreciate it, you must see it on a clear day. How far across is it? I wondered. And how wide, in comparison, is Lake Ontario near where I live? The land on the French shore looked high. I saw white buildings and the hills above; a large container ship, the name HATSU along its bow. These ships operated out of Zeebrugge and Thamesport. It's a life I miss, living on an interior great lake, the marine traffic of ocean ports. We say "landlocked" but never "sealocked"—being surrounded by land is the problem. In St John's, the big shipping line is Maersk. Their slogan: your promise delivered.

I had often taken the ferry from North Sydney, Nova Scotia, to Port aux Basques, Newfoundland. The new ferry along that route is called the *Blue Puttees* and it boasts five hundred reclining chairs. I don't know whose idea it was to have the same number of reclining seats as men in the first contingent of the Newfoundland Regiment. I have sat in one of those chairs, which you have to reserve, and reclined my body and stared at the ceiling above and the sea out the windows, and for a moment thought of myself as one of the dead men in a field in France.

CALAIS

We eventually landed in Calais, but I had missed the last bus out of the port. I realized I would not make it to the little towns in northern France that billeted the New-foundlanders. A man with no English suggested I accompany him to the train station. He presented the invitation through some movement of his shoulder and a warm eye, but I explained I wanted to take a taxi. His stare was that of someone who could not ever consider a taxi and did not know how to share one. You have to call one, was his pantomime. But I had no phone.

I found a woman at P&O Ferries who could call me a cab. My taxi arrived and I shared it with another man, a Dutch businessman who was staying at the nearby Metropol Hotel in Calais. I showed him my hat but he looked at it as if not even his grandfather would wear such a thing. The cabdriver told us: There are no trains at this time of night. He checked his phone for connections. Lille, Flanders—nothing. I could drive you to Amiens.

I asked how much. He did a calculation: 270 euros.

The Dutch man and I split the cab, and I checked the train station on the way past—it was indeed dark inside the glass walls. To the Metropol! I exclaimed. I followed the Dutch businessman into the hotel and got a room for 76 euros. I had lost my hotel room in Amiens that cost a hundred dollars, so really a taxi there might have been a good bet. Still, there were trains departing for that town at 6:30 the next morning. If I decide to go, I thought. At worst, I would miss the morning of July first, the anniversary of the morning when so many Newfoundlanders died, in Beaumont-Hamel.

Well, that worst would be terrible.

A draft of men on their way to the Somme, like me, had missed the July first attack. George Ricketts had been one of these men. They had learned of Kitchener drowning and the results of the Battle of Jutland and needed some good news. The men heard of the push and the attack's success, but then they were met with hospitals full of the wounded that showed something different from a victory. They learned how to put together the evidence of a disaster.

I asked the concierge at the Metropol Hotel for a restaurant tip and found myself crossing the canal and sitting in a little place with checked tablecloths. Café le Tour, at the end of the main strip. That was me in Calais: passing by shops and restaurants and resigning myself to the last place of record. I sat there without a French/English dictionary or a map. The red wine was chilled. Corked or normal? Corked is fine, I said.

SHOT AT DAWN

I wandered along the groomed river at Calais and looked westward towards Boulogne. I would travel that way in the morning. A Newfoundlander named John Roberts is buried in Boulogne Eastern Cemetery, between a football pitch and a hospital, twenty miles from Calais. He was buried at this time of year. Born in Newfoundland, Roberts spent four years in the Royal Navy Reserve before he enlisted in May 1915 with the Canadian Mounted Rifles. Many Newfoundlanders fought with the Canadians. The soil at Boulogne is unstable, so the grave markers are placed flat. This is true for those buried on the hill in Thiepval near the Somme, too, but at Thiepval the ground is unstable from all the tunnelling that the British and Germans did in the war.

In those English comics I read as a kid there were stories of tunnelling. There was also a story of a soldier who grew scared in the firing line and managed to escape the trenches and rush off into a small French village. He looked worried about what to do and, as a kid, I was concerned for him. I wondered how, once found, the authorities would help him. He was in a war and he was afraid—how terrible or wrong could that be? He was rounded up by the military police and they returned him, roughly I felt, to a locked room. A few days later he was removed from the cell and faced a tribunal and then a solemn parade of his old army buddies. They took him outside and blindfolded him against a wall and shot him to death.

I was horrified. Why would they do that? It would never have occurred to me to do that to someone who felt afraid.

It was what they did to John Roberts. He was a sailor, but he learned to ride a horse. He went absent without leave while still in Canada and served twenty-eight days in prison. Then he was deployed here in France. He had to leave his horse—his regiment had trained as cavalry but were reclassified as infantry. In January 1916 he was sent to a medical camp in Boulogne; he was released a month later. Then he disappeared from the Marlborough Details Camp, near Boulogne. He was gone for four months. His regiment was fighting at the Battle of Mount Sorrel, in the Ypres salient. On 13 June, behind a smokescreen, the Canadians advanced and managed to take two hundred German prisoners. Today, every June, there is a Sorrel Day parade at the Fork York Armoury in my home city of Toronto—a marching band and many coloured flags and a formal routine conducted within a congested site of condo development. They celebrate the battle. A member of the royal family is sometimes present.

John Roberts was arrested by military police on 26 June 1916. He was wearing civilian clothes. It must have been galling for his compatriots in the army to realize that, while his regiment was fighting in Ypres, Roberts had been absent without leave. He was court-martialled and found guilty of desertion. On 30 July 1916 he was executed by firing squad—it was less than a week before his twenty-first birthday.

From near Roberts's grave in Boulogne you can look over the Channel and see England. Boulogne is six miles from Étaples, which was the bullring of fierce training for the Western Front. The Newfoundland officers were posted here for a refresher course to "inculcate the offensive spirit." The poet Wilfred Owen spoke of the soldiers in Étaples, after recuperating from wounds in the hospitals of Boulogne, preferring to return straight to the front rather than face the training drills of Étaples. How severe were those sergeants, many of whom had not been to the front. "The men here," Owen said, "had faces unlike any I'd seen in the trenches or in England: faces with the eyes of dead rabbits." And Siegfried Sassoon wrote a poem about the mutiny that occurred in Étaples only a year after the execution of John Roberts. The mutiny was against the same military police who had arrested Roberts. A soldier had been imprisoned, unfairly, for desertion and a thousand men rebelled.

One hundred years later, in a cemetery near Birmingham, England, there is a Shot at Dawn Memorial for the more than three hundred British and Commonwealth soldiers who were executed for desertion. These men, once considered cowards, had been suffering from post-traumatic shock. It took guts or craziness to amble away from your regiment, or the front line, on your own.

I thought about John Roberts and his twenty-one

years. His brain knocked clear of the rules of behaviour. That animal instinct of preserving oneself which annihilates the military's attempt to indoctrinate an *esprit de corps*. A bird will preen when it realizes defense is futile and it cannot escape. These soldiers who have wandered away are preening themselves, devoid of morale. I salute you, John Roberts, Newfoundlander, wrongly executed.

It confirmed something in me. Yes, I decided, I have to see the land around the Somme, the land at Beaumont-Hamel, and I have to see it before the Big Push occurs. This book is partly about the land. The men were either buried in this land or blowing the land up. Of all that ordnance buried in Salisbury, not a round of it had been fired in warfare. So much of war is training. So much destruction happens in the preparation.

I WALK TOWARDS AUCHONVILLERS

The next morning, I was up so early that the hotel lights in Calais were still on, giving off that fatigued glow that dawn presents. How tired the night is—and still you have to swing yourself away from the party of the night and join the bristling morning or you are lost. I hate paying for a room and then leaving it halfway through the morning. But I did so in order to arrive in Beaumont-Hamel on July first.

This is what the men did: a lot of route-marches. And much waiting for buses and trains, and walking through the dark. A young man asleep on a bench at the train platform had been on the Calais ferry with me—I could tell by his deflation that he'd slept on the bench all night. Two pairs of white socks with coloured bands. I thought of the mother of Hugh McWhirter and the socks she'd knit and mailed to him, that she wanted to transfer over to her other son, George. That would be me, I thought, if I was not writing a book. If I didn't have a modest travel budget. If I was, like him and John Roberts, only twenty-one.

I took the train and it was practically dawn as I zipped past the death of John Roberts and then the bullring of Étaples and managed to lift my head to see the town of Flixecourt, where Sassoon went to training school. Sassoon had a bath at Flixecourt and thought it important enough to write this: "Remembering that I had a bath may not be of much interest to anyone, but it was a good bath, and it is my own story that I am trying to tell, and as such it must be received; those who expect a universalization of the Great War must look for it elsewhere. Here they will only find an attempt to show its effect on a somewhat solitary-minded young man."

I arrived half-dead in Amiens and cast a bitter look upon the hotel I should have slept at. Instead, I had slept with my head against the vibrating train window, but I opened my eyes to see the Carlton at Amiens slide past and stop and I had a sense that objects in the distance could affect the vibration in your forehead. The Carlton was where Siegfried Sassoon had stayed. I went in and sat at the dark plush bar and ordered a beer. It was early and no one else was drinking. There was no music, but there were the sounds of staff resuscitating kitchen life. I thought of the officers who tried to remain civilized, who had the luxury of periodic picnics of lavish eating and comfort behind the lines.

I walked through the town of Amiens. Men were working on the modern road and the plastic flatboards over holes had on them "trench limit" and, on a computer store sign, the word "reparations." Words that had other meanings in 1918, happily being used again. My parents used to call the radio in our kitchen the wireless. Then I walked past the old Godbert's restaurant where Sassoon ate; it is something else now but I darted in to the tall bright foyer that hosts a theatrical venture. He ordered lobster and roast duck, two bottles of champagne. Strolling out in the sunshine, his friend Edward Greaves suggested looking for a young lady to make his wife jealous. There was always the cathedral to look at, Sassoon said, "and discovered that I'd unintentionally made a very good joke." The Notre Dame cathedral used to house the head of John the Baptist.

It was overcast. Officers kept sending in receipts for taxis and meals they took, and there were tussles over bills unpaid. The discrepancies were beneath the officers, but they still spent time and energy making these quarrels over bills go away. I've seen adults with mortgages and bank loans and lines of credit use the persuasion of their economic clout to have a banking fee waived. The poor have not this option.

I found a taxi and asked for the fare to Mailly-Maillet. It was a grey afternoon in this small farming village near the Somme. I passed high stone walls and a large galvanized barn where you can hear the echo of cattle inside and your nostrils are full of the funk of animals bunched together in soiled hay. This was where I was spending the night, at the Delcour's cow farm. In April of 1916 the Newfoundlanders first went into the line near here. Arthur Wakefield, who had joined the regiment but then left to attach himself to the Royal Army Medical Corps, was delighted to see the regiment arrive with the 29th Division. Back home, the seal fishery was happening, and there were reports of men who could not return to their vessel because of a trench of water. The *Florizel* was pinched off Newfoundland in a crack in the ice and men were marching over ice pans for thirty miles with a piece of hard-bread and nothing else. Wakefield knew of these dangers as he had, during a winter in Labrador, got his party lost for two nights while following the trail of a caribou through the snow.

I climbed the stairs to my billet and slung off my pack and fell on the thin bed, spent from having travelled over the surface of the earth—sea and land—between England and France over the past few days. The modern ceiling was hard to admire. I stared at everything around me, looking for significance. The unobstructed view out the window looked over a thousand green acres of French farmland. I had asked the very short pension owner about a bicycle and she'd told me the nearest hire was some distance away, in Auchonvillers. Now I unfolded my map and measured with the top joint of my thumb. It was only four miles to Beaumont-Hamel. I could walk there.

So instead of falling asleep without brushing my teeth, I exerted myself. I switched on the button within me that willed myself into life and decided to march to Beaumont-Hamel on this, the anniversary of the very last night of so many Newfoundlanders' lives.

I unpacked my extra shirt and socks and took a slug of water and stashed in my bag a picnic that I'd bought in Amiens. I hoisted the bag to my shoulder, felt the heavy heel of a bottle of wine clunk me in the back, locked the solid door of my room, and made my way downstairs. Au revoir, I said to my host who knows no English. And then I was on the street, and along the road out of Mailly-Maillet in the gathering dusk. I walked towards Auchonvillers, happy to be on this road now and to have come to this decision that was not passive. It is hard when you have no commander to tell you to get off the bed and out the door.

The Newfoundlanders had stayed in Louvencourt, just down the road from here. Arthur Wakefield, on his bicycle, visited the men. As the historian Wade Davis puts it, Wakefield "had no idea that he would never see any of them again." On the night before July first—this very night— they marched towards Beaumont-Hamel. A draft of sixty-six men had arrived that day from England and most of them marched too. It was nine o'clock at night when they started out. They marched seven miles and got to their third line of defence, about four hundred yards from the Germans, at two in the morning.

I followed the road signs and entered Auchonvillers and collected scraps of noise from behind a hedged tavern called Ocean Villas. I was trying to put together a conversation. Several British men were talking animatedly, dressed in the olive drab uniforms of the First World War. One man ran dramatically down to his modern car and opened a door and dug out a German pickelhaube helmet and forced it unconvincingly onto his fat head. He shouted out to his friends, asking what did they think?

Brilliant, mate!

But I thought: This travesty of re-enactment, on the evening before the Big Push.

RAID BY BERTRAM BUTLER

I ignored the spectacle and kept marching. Up ahead, a long line of trees on the horizon. There was a beginning and an end to the trees—they stretched perhaps half a mile. I did not know at this moment that I was approaching the memorial to the Newfoundland dead, though I wondered if I might be. I walked to the park entrance within this line of trees and found quiet signs pointing me in under the canopy of great coniferous branches. These trees had been brought here from Newfoundland.

The path bent to the left and I thought of how, a few nights before this one, Bertram Butler had led a raid and Arthur Wight of Bonne Bay was one of the men killed. In the record of Wight's list of offences while in the regiment there is: missing the military tattoo, being late for church parade, refusing to obey an order, using profane language in the tent. The last offence listed is: killed in action. I had learned about Arthur Wight one night in Woody Point, Newfoundland, a village in Bonne Bay. I was there at a writers' festival, and there was a dance at the Legion Hall and, as we wildly partied and drank, I noticed behind the live musicians on the bandstand ten sober photographs of soldiers from Bonne Bay and Trout River who had served in the war. Every one of them, I have discovered since, had been killed. Arthur Wight was the first.

Bertram Butler, who led the raid that killed Arthur Wight, was an intelligence officer for the regiment. It was his duty to report on activity in the German lines. That meant a lot of night patrols. He and two others would crawl into no man's land and listen to the German pump push water out of trenches, and a creaking windlass remove chalk from the dugouts. The British were preparing for the Big Push and needed to know if their artillery shells were damaging the lines.

Butler was selected to lead some men on an intense raid a few nights before the July drive, to capture Germans and get a sense about how prepared they were for an attack.

I've seen the photographs of the men Butler led that night. These were published in *The Veteran* magazine. The men are Charlie Strong (the smile of the battalion), Walter Greene (who had distinguished himself at Caribou Hill in Gallipoli), Harold Barrett (who won, later, the Military Medal at Gueudecourt) and George Phillips (the only member of the regiment to have won the Russian Medal of St George). They were all killed during the war. The men had spent weeks training by stabbing a dummy named Hindenburg.

Bert Butler was in charge of more than fifty men, divided into three lines. There were bayonet men, wire cutters, bombers and Bangalore torpedo carriers, with more bayonet men to protect the rear. The centre line had a telephone and operator, and a man who laid white tape as the soldiers advanced to guide them back to their lines when their work was over. There were two flankers on each side. They had an hour for their mission, synchronized by shelling from their own guns that would afford them cover while they crept over the ground. With their faces blackened and carrying guns and revolvers, they walked two miles to the trenches and then waited two hours for the artillery to open fire at fifteen minutes to midnight.

A Bangalore torpedo is a twenty-foot iron pipe filled with high explosives. Both ends are sealed and a fuse is attached to one, an igniter that is set off by giving the end a slight twist. This torpedo was meant to be placed under the barbed wire of the enemy, making a gap from four to six feet wide and a yard longer than the torpedo. The raiding party had two of these.

But that night, the enemy wire remained intact. Butler's men kept losing contact with the sound of their own shelling as it moved off and then returned to where they were in the wire. The shelling was supposed to disrupt the German front line and then interfere with the German reinforcements. Butler and his men tried to breach the line two nights in a row, but on neither night did they enter a German trench or even get through the wire. Instead, they were illuminated by flares that lit up the night as if it were day. One torpedo had only made a gap through half the wire and the second Bangalore did not ignite. So the wire cutters had to be sent up. The wire was fifteen yards deep, and on the second night several men were killed and many others wounded as they tried to cut through. Two were taken prisoner. Butler reported the failure of the raid and said that the Germans were more prepared than expected, well fortified and strongly held. He was not believed.

Five months later, when the position was finally captured by General Bernard Freyberg, military experts reported that the position had been impregnable to a frontal assault.

TREAD SOFTLY HERE

I accepted the path through the gateless shaded entry and the trees opened up for me like curtains on a stage. Standing in the distance, in profile, was the tall bronze caribou: the memorial to the regiment. The sun was still above the trees, but sinking fast and already distant. The sun was on its way to Newfoundland. Only the surfaces of things were warm; underneath there was dampness. There was no one there; just blue sheep grazing in this rich grass. Clusters of sheep moseyed along a funnelled dip that I understood to be an old trench. A strange thought occurred to me that the wool uniforms the soldiers had once worn had been returned back to the sheep.

I recalibrated my thinking and positioned myself in a trench in the dark, listening to a foreign country talk. I recalled Frank Lind remarking that when the Newfoundlanders first got in the line, the Germans called out to them, "Hello, Red Men," and it startled him. How did they know this was a regiment of Newfoundlanders? And how did the Germans know that Newfoundlanders had taken over the territory of the Beothuk? Perhaps, I thought, Germans have always been interested in Indians—the original Red Indians were the Beothuk, called so because they smeared red ochre on their skin. They had lived along rivers much like the Somme and hunted caribou. They had erected great long fences that directed the caribou to small gaps where the Beothuk lay in wait, much like the Germans were now waiting for the Newfoundlanders. The Beothuk and the Newfoundlanders had fought each other because the Newfoundlanders took over valuable fishing grounds and denied them access to the sea. But before that war, there had been an earlier altercation: the first meeting of Europeans and Native Americans had happened in Newfoundland. A thousand years ago, Vikings, approaching the land, had recorded seeing a uniped; and this uniped had fired an arrow at the Vikings and killed a man. They pursued but could not stop this hopping figure. Newfoundland's involvement with war and Europeans stretches back a thousand years.

In 1914 it disturbed Lind, this satiric heckling, for he had no idea what type of Germans he and his fellow soldiers were facing, but they knew him.

The wide battlefield was now before me, spreading out and drifting down to a copse and, to the far right, a small graveyard of white stones like tablets laid out carefully in the grass.

On this path is the inscription that made Rosemary, in F. Scott Fitzgerald's *Tender Is the Night*, burst into tears. It begins:

> Tread softly here! Go reverently and slow!
> Yea, let your soul go down upon its knees,
> And with bowed head and heart abased strive hard
> To grasp the future gain in this sore loss!
> For not one foot of this dank sod but drank
> Its surfeit of the blood of gallant men.

This was written by John Oxenham. Just before the war, Oxenham published *Bees in Amber: A Little Book of Thoughtful Verse*. In that book he offered an apology—that his poems derived from bees in his bonnet that he strove to set in amber. The verses were expressions of ideas, and Oxenham said he doubted the trouble it took to write them down would ever make him any money.

John Oxenham was the penname of William Dunkerley,

who got his alias from Charles Kingsley's novel *Westward Ho!* Kingsley had published that novel when Dunkerley was three years old. I set down to read it myself last summer. It's a novel that fed a myth of English superiority over the Spanish, a myth that, like all good myths, never dies. Novels like *Don Quixote*, on the other hand, were supposed to make certain kinds of literature no longer possible to write because no one would read the content with earnestness. The great romantic quest novel; heroism—that's what Cervantes was out to demolish. And yet here we are today, surrounded by such books. The Germans were reading the westerns written by Karl May—that's how they knew of the Red Indians. We read these romances and love them and we want life to be that way.

This caribou before me stood on a knoll of rock— "from this vast altar pile the souls of men"—probably the Oxenham line that made Rosemary weep. This caribou was something else. He did not see me but was aware of danger. He is smelling the air, and he is haughty and dignified. Looking at him, I was reminded of the general in the Russian film *Burnt by the Sun*, the dignity he maintains until the last few minutes of the movie when mid-level Soviet officials invite him inside a car to be taken to Moscow for questioning. And then, when the general arrogantly corrects their insolence, they beat him up with short punches, and we cannot see the action but we hear the great man whimper. The whimpering is unsettling. The caribou before me stood on this side of arrogance, maintaining his caution. He would never get into that car. The caribou understands the mounting opposition. His expression is not what the guidebooks tell you—one of defiance. The caribou is saying to danger: I disagree with you, but also, I will return to the safety of the woods. You can kill me but I am the guardian here. And then he turns his great shaggy neck and melts into the forest as all great animals do when they recognize a superior, though brutish, force.

I walked down the roped-off path and passed, here and there over the undulating green mounds, the screw picket that used to carry barbed wire. I felt a great unease. Sometimes, when I run, I can feel the dull ache of the pockets between my teeth and jawbone; it feels like mortality. It was this sense of mortality I was walking healthily through now. I walked in the same manner as the Newfoundlanders were instructed to walk. Witnesses saw them march as if on parade. Even though the entire morning had gone wrong for the British, the Newfoundlanders were commanded to attack in lines of platoons and they did. They faced the blizzard of machine-gun fire with their chins tucked into an advanced shoulder, just like they did back home in a snowstorm. And that is what Major Arthur Raley later reported seeing. The Newfoundlanders had trained for weeks to step over barbed wire and keep themselves spread apart and not to run. The generals understood that they were fighting a war with hardly any professional soldiers now. The professionals were all dead. And so they were developing simpler tactics, such as forty-five thousand tons of artillery shelling to destroy the German defences, and they hoped that, with this third wave of men which the Newfoundlanders represented that morning, they might walk across this field and occupy the empty space left by a dead German army—dead from the ten days of artillery bombardment and the two prior advances of British men. The Newfoundlanders waited in their trenches and understood that the attack was not progressing as planned. They were weighed down with ammunition and rations and water bottles, a waterproof sheet and shovel or pick and flares and wooden pickets and Mills grenades and smoke helmets. They had sixty pounds of equipment to carry but it did not matter because they were expected to meet little resistance. They lay now before me with all of their equipment, their helmets with the initial N upon them, and on their haversacks a triangular piece of metal cut from a biscuit tin, seven inches to a side, attached so that reconnaissance airplanes could observe their advance. This biscuit-tin image of war.

Before this first morning of July, the sum of what the Newfoundlanders had experienced of war was the fighting in Turkey. And Turkey represented the worst of the acceptable wars that all of Newfoundland had read about in local newspapers, such as the *Twillingate Sun*. There had been several Balkan wars and wars between Greece and Turkey, and within a calendar year these events had taken place and been resolved and the soldiers who fought in them had returned home to civilian life. And so, naturally, Owen Steele's last diary entry looks upon this attack by the Newfoundlanders at Beaumont-Hamel as the beginning of the end of the war. He was proud to sense they were a part of this end, this July drive.

But Steele had nothing of the outsider in him. He had no flâneur instinct. When his regiment was destroyed in an hour, he could not write about it later in his journal. Yes, he was busy, but also he had not the words. He did not know what to say. He had been loyal and dedicated to the manner in which war worked, and this result was incomprehensible. The tally left him mute. All he could do was write down the names of the dead and wounded. And then, far from the front lines, a few days after this failed assault, he was killed by a compound fracture to his thigh caused by an exploding shell. It would have been very interesting to know whether, if Owen Steele had lived, he would have learned the new language.

Hugh Anderson was a soldier in the regiment who wrote a long letter to the prime minister of Newfoundland nine days after the attack, to describe what had happened.

Anderson knew the prime minister, Edward Morris, because his own father, John, was a politician. John Anderson had arrived in Newfoundland from Scotland in 1875 as a draper's assistant to the James Baird Company. Soon Anderson opened his own dry goods store and, in the early 1900s, he ran for the Liberals and won a seat in a district of St John's controlled by Morris—Morris was by then the prime minister. Later, in 1917, John Anderson would persuade the government to adopt daylight savings time. He meant to give citizens an extra hour of daylight for recreation, but it also helped to save an hour of coal and electric use during the war years. Newfoundland became the first jurisdiction in North America to adopt daylight savings.

Hugh Anderson wrote that the men had marched smartly over the ground for ten minutes until they had passed through their own defences and belts of barbed wire and began to encounter the shot from machine guns. The guns, Anderson wrote, seemed to be brought up on platforms out of the bowels of the earth. The week of British shelling, and that morning's intense bombardment including the detonation of a mine that made a crater sixty feet deep, had done little to interfere with the preparedness of the German defences. In fact, the explosion signalled the infantry attack, and the Germans prepared for the bombardment by standing on the lower steps of their dugouts:

In a few minutes the shelling ceased, and we rushed up the steps and out into the crater positions. Ahead of us wave after wave of British troops were crawling out of their trenches and coming towards us at a walk, their bayonets glistening in the sun.

A. A. Milne, who served briefly in France along a similar stretch as the Newfoundlanders, believed that war is poison and not, as others have said, an over-strong extremely unpleasant medicine. "War is something of man's own fostering," Milne wrote, "and if all mankind renounces it, then it is no longer there."

I came to the shattered husk of the Danger Tree. This is a spot in the downward slope of land where the men had hoped to congregate before heading further into the German lines. It was as far as any of the men got that morning. The tree before me looked real but I was told it was a replica. The Germans the Newfoundlanders faced here were the 119th Infantry Reserve Regiment of Stuttgart. They are described as stiff veterans who had been in the line for months. But photographs show these Germans at the front wearing various collars, and some sporting Brandenburg cuffs rather than Swedish cuffs, and a Queen Olga monogram. The noun "uniform" was something these German soldiers could hardly pull together, but they fought in a uniform manner.

The British had shelled the German line for a week. The push was scheduled for June 29, but the weather was so bad they postponed the attack and kept up the shelling. The German soldier Ernst Jünger wrote in his diary during the bombardment:

> In the morning I went to the village church where the dead were kept. Today there were thirty-nine simple wooden boxes and large pools of blood had seeped from almost every one of them. It was a horrifying sight in the emptied church.

WORLD WAR ONE IS COMING

I found myself now in the cemetery of the fallen. I sat my pack down and walked along the quiet rows of the dead.

I strolled there for an hour. Alone. I heard bagpipes and birdsong. I saw rabbits with their ears rotated towards me. A hawk on the wire in the middle ground, his neck tensely twisted in my direction. I had been in tears since arriving here, I realized, and tears felt like a normal state of being. The tears were the suit one wears for a special occasion, and I did not feel particularly overwhelmed by them. I unwrapped my picnic. A cucumber, tomato, salami, cheese, a bent baguette and a bottle of wine. I unfolded the blade of my pocketknife. I was happy to think of my picnic but worried about committing a sacrilegious act. I am in the place, I thought, I have travelled so far to see and, unlike when I visited the pyramids and Ephesus, I have no idea what this moment will be like.

It was powerfully moving. The cambered hill that sloped to the east.

On the last night of their lives.

I remembered, then, visiting my friend on my last night in Newfoundland before returning to Toronto and coming here. My friend is a curator at the Newfoundland museum. We had stood in his kitchen in St John's drying the dishes after a dinner with his family, and he talked to me with great openness about the war and its artifacts and what was on display at the museum and, as he spoke, the expression on his face grew more concentrated, and beyond his face, in the long window that looks over the harbour, I could see a corner of the old Newfoundland Museum. There was a calendar on the wall of his kitchen. He pushed a hand through his short hair and turned to me with a panicked look; he had noticed the year on the calendar. World War One is coming, isn't it? he said.

The museum's attention would have to be focused on marking this centennial, and the thought energized him but also filled him with a certain fatigue over the responsibility of it all. World War One is coming. It had jumped out of the trenches of history and marched towards him, slipped through the razor wire and was proceeding with bayonets fixed. He would have to mow it down. Send withering machine-gun fire at its hundred-year-old chest.

I realized now, standing in the small cemetery to the Newfoundland dead, that my friend had been ambushed by the thought of memorializing the dead. Something would be expected from him and the museum. But as of yet he had been ambushed only by the planning, just as the Germans had realized, weeks ahead of time, that a big event was arriving. The Germans had monitored the swelling ranks, the moving up of materiel, the increase in British shelling.

I had blurted out to my friend that I'd agreed to write a book about Newfoundland's involvement in the First World War. I had signed up, enlisted, volunteered to do this. Write about one tiny regiment, the lives of six thousand men, in an army of six million. A thousandth of the British army. I told him: That battle narrative has already been written; many books have explained aspects of the war and Newfoundland's role in it. But I wanted to talk about something else. How war and the past creep into everyday life. How does the past ambush us? How can we be accurate about what happened, how can we be true to it? And can war ever be declared over? And can we ever evolve from the notion of war, of nations, of us versus them?

We spoke in my friend's kitchen with its tall window that overlooks Duckworth Street, the green roof of the old Newfoundland Museum, as I said, over to the right, a building I still associate with my first interaction with artifacts preserved behind glass—I would bring my niece down here and she asked me what the word "museum" meant. She confused it with "moose." There was, in fact, a taxidermied caribou in the museum, so we took to calling the place the cariboueum.

The caribou herd in Newfoundland is the most southerly in all the world, trapped here because of the island nature of our province, even as the climate warms. The caribou are native whereas the moose were introduced. And as we have seen, the caribou is the emblem of the Newfoundland Regiment—a battalion that fought in the War of 1812 and continues, in some ceremonial manner, right up to this day. It is known as the Royal Newfoundland Regiment today, having received the "Royal" title during the Third Battle of Ypres in 1917, a battle we will get to. It is the only regiment in the British army in two hundred years to receive that honour during wartime.

Do you see that sentence, those facts, I just wrote? That's the type of sentence you can Google and perhaps retrieve word for word from a dozen sources. There is a touring circus of freak trivia like this. For Newfoundlanders, the sideshow tent includes being the only North American troops to fight at Gallipoli. The only Commonwealth troops to be used at the Somme. The only regiment—on either side of the war—to be composed purely of volunteers for the entirety of the war. These are the type of facts that mean little to me and should mean less to you. These facts accrue to every colonial army, and serve only to make us proud and distinct and loyal to war. They are the beads that bought Manhattan. But let's be honest here, I am not a historian. I don't want to brush up on my history and facts and recreate them as if they sit in my mind as bright articulate jewels—there are many important books that have done this very well. What I am interested in is this: What do we recall, and how does it move us, or not?

This is, I guess, the opposite of jingoism.

I was staring at the empty field above me, barren except for the understanding of an event. I was lying in wait like a German. And the empty feeling, the pause in action, reminded me of a car accident I'd had at eighteen. It was New Year's Eve. I was accelerating past traffic on the highway outside Corner Brook in a snowstorm, four of my friends in the vehicle with me, and the car lost control and slipped off the road and slammed into a retaining wall and flipped three times in the air. As the body of the car revolved over the face of the earth I had this experience, this empty moment as if death were awaiting me, and I was not in control of that death. The headlights shone into a slow-motion spiral of snow and out over the river at Humbermouth. We landed, softly, upside down and we unclicked our seatbelts and hit the roof. This, from the accounts I've read, was as close to the battlefield experience as a civilian can get. I was not exerting myself to come to this feeling; the museum of the park was laid out in a way that encouraged the feeling.

NORMAN COLLINS

I got up, half-drunk, and walked around the field, and discovered the Scots Regiment Memorial for the 51st Highland Division. The Scot stands upon a fifteen-foot cairn, the butt of his rifle at rest. The Scots were the ones who captured Beaumont-Hamel in November 1916. The Germans called the kilted Highlanders "the ladies from hell." Unlike with much of the front, the two armies had stayed put in their positions here. So when the Highlanders took this field they found the area still covered with the dead from the first of July—fabric and bones. A soldier named Norman Collins was one of the men instructed to bury the Welsh dead and then the dead Newfoundlanders. He and the others were upset to move the bodies of their Welsh friends, but they did. They buried them, each wrapped in an army blanket with their arms folded, in a long trench behind Mailly Wood. But then, the Newfoundlanders. Collins said in the cage of each body—that is, the ribcage of the chest—there was a rat's nest. And when they moved the Newfoundland bodies the rats ran out. They buried the bodies in the craters left from shells. They removed from each soldier's breast pocket his paybook, which held his will and his letters from home and photographs of his family. They placed these in a new sandbag and brought them down to Brigade Headquarters. The identity discs they left on the soldiers, so they could be reburied after the war.

I saw grave markers with inscriptions that verged on solemn exasperation: Here lie six dead until the Germans pushed through and then the British retook the land and the graves were lost and found again and then three years later, after the Germans retreated to the Hindenburg Line and then advanced before the Americans entered the war, they were lost a final time. Or: Somewhere here lie the bodies of three soldiers, perhaps disinterred and moved again during the Second World War. Everything moved during this British advance, everything except the brothels—the British ended up using the brothels that had once served the Germans.

When my wife and I bought our house in Newfoundland, a clever man told us that if we wanted an accurate survey, to measure the land in relation to the cemetery nearby. Cemeteries don't move, he said to us. Well now I've found a pile of cemeteries that do move.

The Scots Memorial is a thick-set soldier in his kilt. I thought of him as being Norman Collins. I thank you, Norman, for what you've done. Like the biscuit tin, the kilt is a piece of invented tradition. Thomas Rawlinson, an English Quaker, moved to Scotland and found that the full kilt interfered with the men working in his iron foundry. He devised the half kilt with a belt and did away with the top half. There was a ban, during the Jacobite revolution, on wearing the kilt and then, in the mid-1700s, that ban was lifted. As Hugh Trevor-Roper reports, various groups of men took to wearing the modern kilt: highland noblemen, anglicized Scottish peers, improving gentry, well-educated Edinburgh lawyers and prudent merchants of Aberdeen. "Men," he writes, "who would never have to skip over rocks and bogs or lie all night in the hills."

GALLOPING OVER THE FIELDS

I returned to the caribou with the sun sinking, a red sky. And it struck me that this caribou I had seen before, in Newfoundland. There is a lake I paddle at my father's cabin in western Newfoundland. And there's a brook that runs into the lake—it's that big lake with the island that has a pond and an island on it. I have taken my wife to this brook to fish. And as the sun set we hooked into some big trout. We were about to leave, at dusk, this very time of night, for the flies were bad, when there was a sound, a hollowness in the ground, a sound that almost came from one's own chest, and my wife pointed to an embankment. There, charging out of the woods and lifting his face above the water, was this enormous stag. His terrific fluffy chest and the tension in his shoulders. He was getting wind of danger and he paused in his movement. That moment is what this monument before me captures. The animal is not stable: you can see in his stance that he is about to turn, that he has the instinct of a survivor faced with overwhelming odds. The Newfoundlanders had this instinct beaten out of them, and loyalty and obedience trained into them. If Levi Bellows had had his way, they would have run, run and been shot in the back by their own people.

I walked up the winding path to the rear of this caribou, perched ten feet above me, and knew this animal would not retreat. I was tremendously moved to be so close. I thought of Jim Stacey who, a few days after this first day of battle, had noticed a beehive that hadn't been destroyed. He knew because it was alive with bees. And so he donned his gas mask and retrieved the honey. The bees did not bother him but they did attack the troops—he saw them running and waving their arms.

I climbed a little up the rock that had been transported here from Newfoundland. All these trees, I thought—

Newfoundland trees, just like the trees back home at the brook. The back heel of the caribou, just there. I reached up to feel his hoof.

Please do not touch the caribou.

It was a woman's voice, funnelled through a speaker or a megaphone. Then again it came, the command in French.

Yes, I replied and backed down. The voice was amplified and I felt deeply embarrassed. What was I doing? I was, of course, drunk from my bottle of wine. If the woman's voice hadn't called out I might have got aboard that caribou—who knows when or where I would have stopped? Galloping over the fields of the Newfoundland dead.

The men on this field were very tired. They had marched here the evening before and would not have slept for being so nervous and excited for the beginning of the end of the war. Later that year, before the November charge of the Highlanders, Norman Collins wrote that his batman had asked if he could purchase some whisky. Still the soldiers would not have been drunk like me. They would have walked soberly into the fire.

I walked the long lonely road back towards Ocean Villas. Along the way, I heard voices inside a barn. A group was showing a film there. Hobbyists were sitting in rows of portable chairs. High up on the barn wall was the projection. The men in the film held up souvenirs to the audience.

And I realized that's what I was doing by touching the hoof of the caribou. The perversity of a souvenir.

The man who was doing the live narration of the film stood a few yards from the barn wall and lifted a stick to point. He stared up at the projection and said, explaining the silent footage, "The cavalry help escort the German prisoners—they had to use the cavalry for something."

The audience laughed.

The horses, I realized, were walking along the road I was walking now. This barn wall—they were marching past it, a hundred years ago. I was watching historical footage of the very fields and town I was walking over. Those horses were pulling up the past and projecting it into the same space in the sky.

DRINK LIKE AN ANIMAL

As I walked back to my pension I thought of the men who had suggested sending Newfoundlanders to war. Walter Davidson had been the governor of the dominion. He was the son of an Irishman, and was born in Malta in 1859. He'd studied at Oxford, graduated from Cambridge, entered the civil service in Ceylon, got involved in postwar reconstruction in South Africa, was appointed governor of the Seychelles in 1904, and then married the daughter of Sir Percy Feilding.

Sir Percy Feilding was the son of a general. This general was the son of an earl. That earl was the son of a major-general who was in turn the son of an earl—and this earl and general business extended back another ten generations until we meet a man, Sir Geffery Feilding, who served King Henry III in various wars in the 1200s.

Walter Davidson had married a woman from this lineage of men.

In 1913 he was appointed governor of Newfoundland for four years. When war was declared, Prime Minister Morris asked Davidson to become commander-in-chief of the Newfoundland forces, to become involved in recruitment and to chair the Patriotic Association. Davidson rounded up twenty-five men, of all denominations but mainly from the merchant class, to oversee the building of a battalion. In 1917 he left Newfoundland to become the governor of New South Wales. A world war was not about to alter the strict term requirements for these colonial governors.

I packed my bag at the Delcour cow farm, then walked, on the morning of July first, into Auchonvillers and found the chalet of a woman named Julie Renshaw. Les Galets. I was to stay at Les Galets for the next few days. I asked Julie if she had a bicycle I could borrow, for I had to attend several memorial services at Thiepval and Beaumont-Hamel. She said her sister, Avril Williams, might have one. Avril ran the Ocean Villas—that was the gaudy place with the pickelhaube helmet. I changed my shirt and packed a lunch and walked to Ocean Villas, feeling less caustic about how my fellow humans participate in commemorating a past war. How judgmental I am about respect when I am leery of earnest and sombre reflection.

I found Avril to be very warm—she had a bike I could rent and so I pedalled to Thiepval. I got lost on a side trail and grew anxious that I might miss the official ceremony. So I doubled back, taking the main road, standing on the bicycle to make it briskly up the road. Then the road turned and there were crowds and cars parked and, in the woods, a few acres of gravel which you could not ride or walk on without making noise. It was very quiet as I gasped for breath, a voice on a speaker system.

I leaned the bike against a stone wall and turned towards the backsides of several thousand people. They were staring ahead, so I followed their gaze and there it was: the solid monument of Thiepval. It is stout and made of brick and has three tall arches. You could fit the delicate Newfoundland caribou underneath one of the arches. The crowd was British and French and they were listening to an amplified and dull minister of defence.

I saw a line of ceremonial blue-and-yellow flags. In the audience were four French soldiers and one British dressed in period costume: the drab military garb of World War One. I was drawn to them and stood behind them and inspected their meticulous uniforms while the monologue continued on, antiseptic and lifeless. I knew a man in Newfoundland who hunted with beagles and he once told me that, at the end of the day, he'd often be missing a couple of dogs. He'd leave his coat on the ground and take the beagles home and then return for his coat. The lost beagles would be sitting on his coat. I felt that in some way all of us gathered here were a tribe of lost dogs returning to the scent of home.

We listened to the politicians and senior military officials drone on. The civilians, I thought, should honour the military rather than the military honouring their own.

It was a dreadful service, and when it was over I found my bike. Twenty thousand British soldiers were killed on this day in 1916. Forty thousand more were wounded. They captured just over three square miles of territory. General Haig, in his diary, found this number of casualties reasonable.

Halfway down the hill, I stopped to watch a man and his daughter fishing through a ploughed field. The man saw my interest and came over. They were picking up loose bits of shrapnel and shell casings. They had a bag of old ruined brass. Here, the man said, and gave me a lead weight the size of a marble. That came from a shell, he said. That's shrapnel.

Most old battlefields in France have now been converted back to farmland but there is still an iron harvest. And I understood then, holding this ball of lead, that

Ernest Hemingway could be forgiven for saying doctors had removed a bullet from his leg. He hadn't been shot at directly, true, but a shrapnel shell has a cavity full of these large round pellets. And so Hemingway, at nineteen, was given a souvenir of a ball of lead extracted from his knee.

We all, if we have to be killed in action, want an eye on the other end of our specific death, the enemy intentionally choosing us to die. Death from an anonymous exploding shell is not humane.

SERRE

I nosed my bike down to the Ancre River and stopped on the bridge and looked down into the slowly moving water. I looked to find my face. My father, when I was a kid, would pause at brooks like this and drink from the brook. He'd lie down over the river, using rocks to plant his hands and feet, and press his chest to within an inch of the water and dip his mouth in the brook and drink like an animal.

I was well on my way to Serre now. As I travelled, I visited cemeteries in the trees along the Ancre. I filled my water bottle at a sink, and wondered how water that's been transported in old petrol tins must have tasted. I remembered siphoning gas from my father's car to fill the lawn mower and getting a mouthful of bitter gasoline that I spat out. A soldier's tea was never hot. It tasted of vegetables because everything, including the tea, was made in two big cookers. I studied the road and the revolution of my feet for ten miles. I was bicycling through sun and showers along the northeast corner of Beaumont-Hamel and out of the slopes and valleys grew a little hilltop graveyard. I made my way to it. Quiet. And displayed at the entrance was a laminated column from the magazine *Stand To!*, published by the Western Front Association. The note was written by Royal Marine officer Ian Gardiner, who had been a captain during the Falklands War of 1982. He'd served with the dismounted unarmoured infantry and had visited this little cemetery. He wrote:

> I feel like a company commander who has a platoon missing and has been looking for them. I find myself saying "Ah boys, there you are! How did you get here?" And then I sit down and have a cigarette with them and hear them tell their tale with pride, self-deprecation, and irreverent good humour. Nowhere else that I know evokes so strongly in me the sense of brotherhood shared over the centuries by the soldiers of the final hundred yards of the battlefield.

I remembered the Falklands crisis. I was seventeen, the age of many of the soldiers buried here in Ten Tree Alley. My brother was twenty, and he saw an opportunity to fight.

But you're Canadian, I said. No, I'm not, he replied. And he reminded me that he was the only one in the family who had not applied for Canadian citizenship. We had emigrated from England in 1968. So my brother had British citizenship and could indeed be called up, if things got bad. I saw the zeal he had for battle. He'd been in the air cadets, and all our young lives we'd been shooting guns—pellet guns and shotguns and rifles. We'd collected the plastic shotgun cartridges and refilled them on a manual machine our father had in the basement. You expelled and replaced the shot-priming pin, then filled the shell with gunpowder, a plastic wadding, the gauge of shot. And finally you recrimped the end of the plastic casing.

We listened to the progress of the war on the radio. It took ages for Margaret Thatcher's navy to reach the Falklands. This was a conventional war, and it seemed as if ships had not increased their speed in sixty years. There was an arrangement to have hospital ships, Argentinian and British, nearby in a neutral sea. They exchanged patients— Geneva Convention stuff.

Reading Gardiner's words in the graveyard, I was reminded that the intense pleasure of being alone comes after the pleasure of intense company.

I bicycled on in the heat, passing a strange Jesus on the Cross by Segui Fernand, an "artisan cimentier." Then I ate my picnic in the Serre cemetery and considered the dead. Jeanette Winterson grew up in Accrington, in Lancashire. She mentions the war in her memoir. The men of Accrington formed a Pals battalion much like the Newfoundland Regiment and they were sent here, to Serre. Five hundred and eighty-four of them were killed, wounded or went missing on the first day of the Battle of the Somme. Newfoundlanders like to mythologize their losses, but everyone suffers. There is no massive difference.

I reminded myself that all I mean to do is illuminate for a moment the experience of the men who made up a thousandth of the British army. To say, what happens to these men, and to the families and economies back home, happens to all of us.

If you read about the 11th East Lancashires—the Accrington pals—you will see the same language used to describe the fate of the Newfoundland Regiment—the valour and the waste, and their utter destruction.

Thiepval, I suddenly remembered from some history book, had been refaced with brick from Accrington. But I had not noticed the brick. I had, I realized, not noticed anything about the memorial for the dour ceremony that suffocated it.

I drank my water bottle dry. If I hadn't refilled it I wouldn't have made it here. I would have fallen, dehydrated and thin, on a road south of Thiepval. A victim to withering sunfire.

WOMEN AT BEAUMONT-HAMEL

I rested in the shade and then flipped the frame of my bicycle around to head for the official ceremonies that were to take place in the afternoon at Beaumont-Hamel. It was a clear warm day, and the earth offered no interference for this event we were marking. The parking lot was full of vehicles. Several hundred people stood now at a roped path while a Newfoundland politician, near the caribou monument, slipped out a bright sheet of a speech from her canvas portfolio. The site hardly seemed the same one I'd visited the night before. At least, unlike Thiepval, women were speaking here. It should just be women speaking, I thought, or civilians. A representative from the women's group that had bought this land, through Thomas Nangle, from a hundred and fifty French farmers and erected this monument to the dead.

The woman who spoke that day was the minister of health for Newfoundland. She spoke in bright sunshine. There were no shadows; the shadows were buried under our feet. We were here for the shadows, yet the shadows were denied. They were not acknowledged. Tandem loads of sunshine were poured over the battlefield as if to clarify its truth, when in fact it obliterated the truth of what stood here. We should all have been lying in shallow graves telling filthy jokes.

A student read out a poem about remembrance. There were many flags waved that day, and a Scotsman played his pipe. It was the Scots who managed to take Beaumont-Hamel from the Germans. I thought again of Norman Collins and the dead. I thought of Father Nangle, and Henry Snow who'd had to unbury the dead and then lay them to rest where they lie today. It was Nangle who chose Basil Gotto's caribou design and Nangle who arranged the landscape architect, Rudolph Cochius, to design this park. Nangle had advised Basil Gotto of the importance of the animal to the regiment. Gotto had never seen a caribou. The antlers are all wrong. The image of the caribou astride a rock comes from that photograph Simeon Parsons took in the 1890s, *Monarch of the Topsails*. The Topsails are the highest mountain ridge in Newfoundland. I used to visit the Topsails with my father and brother to hunt birds and pick berries. The train passed transmission poles; every second pole had been sawed down to use as firewood. And the train would not stop, merely slow down and the door slide open, you'd throw your gear off and then bend your knees and jump from the moving train and roll down the embankment. You'd spend three days on top of this mountain ridge, nothing to halt the wind, living in a little hut sheathed in plastic realty signs, eating canned food like a soldier and then waiting for the erratic train service to return you home.

It was Thomas Nangle's idea that this *Monarch of the Topsails* become the model for the Beaumont-Hamel memorial. There had been a lot of submissions. He chose wisely.

The words, the tone, the sunshine all seemed barely permissible. I thought: There should be no distinguished guests who sit in chairs while we stand. Only the old should sit. A man with a moving camera bumped a family aside to train his lens on the podium where the minister spoke. I thought of the British camera that took moving pictures of the men that July day. A small choir under a canopy began singing the "Ode to Newfoundland," and I was cheered until they stopped after two verses. Well, I conceded, at least they had sung a piece of it. But really, that song is just gathering steam. The earnestness of the song is undercut by its last verses. It was written over a hundred years ago by Cavendish Boyle. He sent the lyrics to his friend Hubert Parry. Parry went on to compose the music for the Blake poem "Jerusalem," which is all about Jesus travelling to Glastonbury.

The song begins, "When sun rays crown thy pine clad hills and summer spreads her hand." And it goes on like that but makes gradual inroads into something ominous, with the land frozen in winter and the snow driving deeper until . . . well, even I can't sing this line without laughing, nor should you be able to: "when blinding storm gusts fret thy shore." The song is saying, Why on earth are we living here?

The "Ode to Newfoundland" is meant to be both sincere *and* sarcastic. It should be sung with hammy effects, as if the singer is embracing the punishment: By God it's terrible here, and we love it. It is a ridiculous and most genuine anthem because it acknowledges that the line between existence and death is unclear. The history of settlement in Newfoundland is one of barest survival. The ode is a march through those raw elements, just like the march towards Beaumont-Hamel was. The line between the two is not fine at all. The Newfoundland soldiers were placed, without their knowing it, in harm's way. They were used to fifty-fifty odds. They were told the weather would be fine.

And then we get to the prophetic, moving line that Boyle wrote in 1902:

> As loved our fathers, so we love,
> Where once they stood, we stand.

We will stick it out through the blizzards and the bad times, for where we stand they stood. And here I was, my brief visit to Beaumont-Hamel an attempt to transform my understanding of how history works in a soul, to turn this battle into an experience of the mind. I was standing now on Newfoundland soil with Newfoundland trees around me, trees that had grown huge. They had grown old and to their natural height in this green and pleasant land while the men below died young and far before their time. Even Cavendish Boyle, who had written the anthem, outlived these men. He married, at sixty-five, a relative of Siegfried Sassoon's, then died in September 1916. He would have read of their massacre here at Beaumont-Hamel.

The minister of health spoke of the battle that day, and she said the phrase I knew she would have to say. I had promised myself to be good and not wince. Her eyes lit upon the glorious line on the sheet of paper in front of her. There was a pause in her voice and I understood she knew her tongue was to say those words. There is a cold-bloodedness in the words that I have grown to hate. I was hoping she would not say the sentence, that I might get out of that afternoon without hearing the line all Newfoundlanders have heard since grade school, but her speechwriter would have had to be brilliant to withhold from the minister's comments a line such as this, a line writers have been repeating for almost a century:

Of the 778 men who went into battle that morning, only 68 answered the roll call the next day.

This visual of sixty-eight men climbing out of bed and pushing buttons through a tunic to stand dutifully in line after such a ludicrous failure instills in the listener a knee-buckling awe. You are forced to conjure up the vast missing without mentioning their absence. This allusion to an ineffable predicament hits a moral nerve that is raw and unexpected. But once you hear that phrase enough times, when you hear it from a politician who you know has heard and read it on numerous other occasions, who is about to move on and say other things from a speech prepared for her by others, it becomes a cliché that insinuates some kind of pleasure at the utter travesty the words represent. Sometimes I have heard commentators use the word "decimate" to approximate the slaughter which the Newfoundlanders suffered that morning. The regiment "decimated"—how we wish it had been! How I would love to read that sixty-eight men refused roll call and turned and walked away, not as a group, but individually, throwing down their rifles, each taking a route personal and unfathomable by all in command, their disdain clear for the betrayal of a group who were volunteers, who were only meant to be consolidating a position, who were not meant to invade. Not a shot was fired by a Newfoundlander that morning.

But the general who would have fought this war differently had not yet been born.

At this point in the ceremony, all of us onlookers were handed a pamphlet that had the words to the Canadian, French and British national anthems. If I had been running things, the entire "Ode to Newfoundland" would have been sung and nothing else. I would have had buckets of salt water at the ready to "lash thy strand." The ode gradually reduces the singer to fits of desperation as the elements get worse and worse. And that is when I realized that this valley in which I stood was the only place where I'd seen the hills clad with pine. It was a genuine museum of Newfoundland—how Newfoundland used to be before confederation with Canada, before the largest pulp and paper mills on earth reduced our forests to spruce and fir, easily manageable farms of softwood.

The minister reiterated what the premier had said the year before: that we must give more money to the veterans. And we must remember them. Such solemnity! I remembered listening to a John Cleese speech on creativity—he described how laughter does not make the thing we are discussing less sombre. Solemnity, he said, serves arrogance. The pompous know their inflated egos are going to be ruptured by humour and so dishonestly pretend that their deficiency in humour makes their views more substantive. Their sober demeanour makes them feel bigger.

John Cleese's father, Reginald, was the one who changed his surname to Cleese; before that, it had been Cheese. He was embarrassed by the name and changed it when he enlisted in the army during the First World War.

Would it be too much to have a picnic here, to have a thousand children with streamers and music, to perhaps hear a poem read aloud? Would that lack dignity and decorum? Well, the issue is not "lest we forget" the vets. It's lest we forget the stress of military service, the pressure of combat, the grief over losing friends and brothers. It's the need to remember how politicians get us into shitty places, and to remember how the military must sometimes be used.

Newfoundlanders would wear forget-me-nots on the first of July—little sprigs of blue to remind people of the Blue Puttees. Listening to the ceremony now, I recalled a German tale where a knight walked with his lady near a river and bent down to pick a posy of flowers. But the weight of his armour caused him to fall into the river. He threw the flowers to his love and shouted, Forget me not!

I bicycled away, disheartened by the structured, public event I had just witnessed. I hunted down a cemetery to help dissipate my chagrin. I felt like an arrow that chases the deer, and I did not want my animal to be taxidermied and filled with slogans and propaganda that would continue the ways in which we conduct ourselves. I wanted to find the true wild beast and sink myself into its heart.

In Auchonvillers there were many Newfoundland graves, for men who died on the first of July. The wounded had been transported here from the front, and medics and nurses in a mobile hospital had tried to save them, but they had died and been buried close by. The same thing had happened at Mesnil Ridge Cemetery, and at Knightsbridge

Cemetery. All these little parcels of cemeteries existed alongside the green pastures of agriculture. There were able seamen buried here as well, a hundred miles from Calais or any ocean. These sailors who'd died must have thought they'd drown, not fall deep inland, near a river.

I knew that back in Newfoundland, on this very date, there had been much discussion about the Battle of Jutland. The Newfoundlanders had wanted to stop calling the stretch of water east of Britain the German Sea and refer to it as the English Sea, "so that forevermore the Germans will be reminded that they have no future on the water except as a trader." A new mayor in St John's had been elected. And it was announced that Captain Bert Butler had been wounded in that scouting party prior to the Big Push and was to be awarded the Military Cross. For the next few days the advance made that Saturday morning of July first was mentioned in abstract terms, as differing from the German assault on Verdun. Sir Edgar Bowring (presented a knighthood by the King the previous New Year's Day), after twelve months in England, had returned to Newfoundland aboard the *Stephano*. Great praise was heaped upon him for the amount of money he had spent looking after the regiment's sick and injured. Bowring acknowledged the beginning of the offensive drive and said he hoped that hostilities would soon cease with a victory for the allies. Bowring was chairman of the patriotic finance committee and, it was reported, he was motoring to his summer residence in Topsail.

Much was written in the local papers about the tremendous power of the British artillery, the Germans' lack of food, and the caution that still must be taken to emphasize that the advance was not a walkover. Results from the Great Offensive assumed that the French would take over Péronne and then the Germans would be cut off from Saint-Quentin. Germany was meant to feel the brutal arithmetic of the manpower available to General Haig.

They did not read the German side of things. Prince Rupprecht, a commander of the German 6th Army, reported that "our losses of territory may be seen on the map with a microscope. Their losses in that far more precious thing— human life—are simply prodigious. Amply and in full coin have they paid for every foot of ground we've sold them. They can have all they want at the same price."

Siegfried Sassoon, who was there at the Somme on that first day, received a Military Cross during this campaign. He wrote, later, that he felt for the rest of his life that the left side of his chest was more often in his mind than his right. "Much could be written," Sassoon wrote, "about medals and their stimulating effect on those who really risked their lives for them." The distribution of medals "became more and more fortuitous and debased as the war went on."

News travelled by ship, and the *Stephano* and *Florizel* were at that time making regular trips between St John's and New York. It took over a week before the city and the dominion began to realize the truth of what had happened at Beaumont-Hamel. The death of a son of the newspaper owner, William Herder, took a week to discover and print. Three Herder brothers went over the top together. Hubert killed, Ralph wounded in the face, and Arthur badly wounded in both shoulders.

At the public ceremony I attended at Beaumont-Hamel there may have been eight hundred people. This is how many Newfoundlanders walked over the field that first morning of July a hundred years ago. But of the eight hundred people I stood with, only thirty or so were Newfoundlanders. It would have been good if someone had said, "Will all the Newfoundlanders please step forward. We encourage you, walk across this field of the dead. You have the earth's permission."

BEREAVEMENT

I bicycled back to Auchonvillers and made my way to Les Galets. It was just getting dark. In some war memoirs I've read, a Yeats poem is quoted, and there is a line in that poem about pebbles rattling under the receding surf. These are "les galets." Julie Renshaw's husband, Michael Renshaw was there. Michael, I knew, had written some guide books for the area. He usually lives in London, he said, but his childhood friend Brian was visiting and staying at the inn.

Julie asked if I was hungry. I was emotionally exhausted and ready for bed, but yes, I said, I could eat. I went to my room for a while, and read Michael's *Mametz Wood* on my bed and thought I'd pass out. But after an hour, he called for me and we ate—chips and eggs and bacon and sausage, just like my mother might make. English rashers. Bread and butter. Brian was from Sunderland, as was Michael. I told them I was from Newcastle and related the story about my father as a child watching the Luftwaffe bomb Sunderland.

Are you a footballer? Michael asked.

I said I followed the Magpies.

I'm not biased against Newcastle, Brian said. I don't care who beats them.

This was a line from his favourite player, Len Shackleton. Shackleton was known as the Clown Prince of Soccer, a maverick. He did this trick, Brian said, where he kicked the ball a short distance at the keeper, and as the keeper came out to stop it, the ball spun back to Shackleton and he flicked it in over the keeper's head. He would bounce the ball off the corner flag to elude a defender. Another time he dribbled through a defence and past the keeper and stopped the ball on the goal line, turned around and sat on the ball, then kicked it in with his heel just as a defender reached him. In Shackleton's autobiography, he writes that during the Second World War he chose to work in the mines. And, he said, he didn't overwork himself.

Brian's grandfather had been in the Great War—and this was the reason Brian was here now, to mark that occasion. When he was a kid, the adults had called his grandad "the sergeant major." He'd stood five foot three inches, and been a joiner and then a heating engineer. He'd worn coveralls every day to work, but underneath he'd had on a shirt and tie all buttoned up. His word of advice to his grandson: when you go to work, dress so you can work anywhere, from a mansion to a sewer.

We talked about my travels. How I had seen Ten Tree Alley Cemetery. The look Michael gave me. Not many people have seen that, he said. What made you look there?

I had a bicycle, I said, and saw a shortcut to Serre, and Ten Tree Alley was on the way.

When I described the event at Beaumont-Hamel, Michael Renshaw told us of the orange sodium lights that used to light up the caribou. In those days, he enjoyed spotting the caribou through the trees when he was driving home. And you could see the incandescence from this window in Les Galets.

There was something consoling, he said, in the daily presence of the caribou. But the lights were extinguished and that made him think of a friend of his who was unable to get over a daughter's death. He used the word "bereavement." Even after ten years, Michael said. Her ashes visible in the parlour. They were Catholic but she expressed the desire to be cremated. She died of an asthma attack. The father slept in his daughter's empty bed. They couldn't move on.

In bed that night I thought of the caribou lit in the distance and that father, of sleeping in my own son's bed. If such a thing came to pass. How do you get over bereavement.

AT THE BOTTOM OF HAWTHORN CRATER

In the morning I wore my peaked cap and blue linen jacket, for I knew I was to be out all day and needed protection from the elements. I bicycled to Hawthorn Crater. The crater is the depression left from the massive underground bomb that was detonated just before the advance on 1 July 1916. You can't see the crater until you're upon it, for it's now full of trees. It's like discovering the ravines in Toronto or the rivers in Saskatchewan. I found thyme growing in the cemetery beside Hawthorn Crater, and I wondered how this place got its name. The hawthorn has thorns when the stems are young. The fruit of a hawthorn helps birds and wildlife get through the winter. I know this because of a place in Brigus, Newfoundland, where a family called the Bartletts lived; I've written about Bob Bartlett, the man who helped Robert Peary reach the North Pole. Hawthorne Cottage is the name of the place where they heard the news that Bob's brother, Rupert Bartlett, was killed on the Western Front. I also know that the oldest tree in France is a hawthorn. It is said that this tree might be more than a thousand years old.

I climbed down into the crater, and it felt like walking into woods. The place was dense with trees. Someone had made a cooking fire down here, and there was evidence of a rushed bivouac. I stood at the bottom, at the very centre of the explosion. Under my feet the Royal Engineer tunnellers had dug and planted the mine, the largest detonated in the war. It felt seedy here. There were strips of toilet paper.

I pushed on my knees to help get me out of the crater and found my bicycle tangled in the bushes. I toured, casually, the seven miles to Albert cemetery. It was a lovely route along the shaded Ancre valley. At Bapaume, outside Albert, there were lots of headstones with the Canadian maple leaf. Rows upon rows of them with the sun banking off their soft white stone. As I studied them, standing over my bicycle, I noticed a car had stopped to my left. I looked, and a large camera was pointed at me. The camera wavered.

Do you mind? the driver asked in a French accent. You are so typically English.

I glanced down instinctively at my torso straddling the bicycle, my damp and hot blue jacket and the little peaked cap. I felt the English sweat in my armpits and on my forehead and the pale English flesh of my hands. A cream-faced loon, a friend once called me. I admitted the truth of his statement and stared at his camera with as much typical English drama as my face could muster while his camera shutter made soft expensive clicks.

I had lunch in Albert and bought pretty stamps and dropped off postcards to my family. Then I rode east towards Fricourt and appreciated the rolling hills here that William Topham had painted during the first days of the barrage before the Big Push began. In Fricourt I was startled by a congested German cemetery with its dour grey iron crosses, two names on each side so that there were four men under each cross. This was a burial under stress, or perhaps graves marked after the war with fewer funds than the British and French shovelled onto their dead. This war was fought on and over and under French and Belgian land. Manfred von Richthofen, the Red Baron, had been shot down here and buried in this slope until his brother Bolsey took him back to Germany in 1925. Now another German is buried in the Baron's cavity. They still name this place in the travel brochures, marking where the Baron lay temporarily for five years. I stood for a while before his grave. I thought: a dogfight with a Canadian, and killed from below by an Australian machine gun. Yes, Lord Brassey, you're better off without the colonies.

The sun shone but there were clouds arriving. I detoured off the road and biked deep into the woods and found the red-and-black Welsh dragon memorial to Mametz Wood. The directions had been in Michael Renshaw's guide book. What a stunning piece of fantasy the dragon is. I had wanted to find it because I had discovered that the first Newfoundland casualty was Noel Gilbert, but he had died while fighting with the Welsh. He had joined the Newfoundland Regiment in England and shared a tent with fellow Newfoundlander Frank Lind in Scotland, but then received a commission and shifted to these very Royal Welsh Fusiliers and was killed in the Dardanelles. Captain Moody of the Fusiliers, wounded, recalls being carried down while slung on his puttees between two rifles. "It was an exceedingly painful journey," he said. But I was happy to hear that the puttees had come in handy. Sassoon was with these Fusiliers as was Robert Graves. The story of the Welsh here is the same as that of the Newfoundlanders at Beaumont-Hamel—artillery hadn't knocked out the Germans and so the Welsh were mowed down with machine-gun fire. The Newfoundlanders and the Welsh were killed before the notion of leaning on the barrage was invented.

The trouble, I thought, was in the training: the intense and precise drills the men learned, as though this could save them while traversing open land covered by a Maxim gun and its twenty bullets a second.

The other, ongoing trouble is in the writing about this battle. How often have I read that the men faced "withering gunfire." That word, withering. I associate it with flowers thirsting for water. Nothing withered here. Flesh and blood faced a crossfire of water-cooled MG 08s, each churning out seven rounds a second.

I carried on and came across Donald Bell's lovely memorial. It was sitting there beside the road. Bell was a Victoria Cross winner and football player. He played for Newcastle. The first professional footballer to enlist. Dead.

It began to rain so I took shelter under some trees in the Dantzig cemetery. There was an old man here, also on a bicycle. I explained who I was, and why I had come. He seemed to appreciate my interest in the dead. We both leaned hard against our handlebars to talk over our front wheels. And when the rain looked like it wasn't about to stop, I pushed out into it and tried my best to enjoy the saturation.

DELVILLE WOOD

At the South African monument at Delville Wood I realized I needed to find a bathroom. I was deep in the woods when this need struck me. Perhaps it had been all the riding but I wasn't going to find a facility and I remembered the toilet paper deep in the undergrowth of Hawthorn Ridge. I did my business as discreetly as I could, remembering that the latrines the soldiers used were often a little bend in the trench close to the German lines. The latrines stank of lime. I rubbed my hands in some leaves and found the famous tree in Delville Wood, a hornbeam, which is the last original tree surviving the battles of 1916. I bumped into Michael Renshaw and his childhood friend Brian. Brian had just been in a trench where his grandfather had fought. He showed me the image on his camera. It was an earnest still of Brian, a photo Michael must have taken: a man, in his sixties, going over the top. His ruddy face was full of the weight of responsibility of becoming his grandfather, and the viewer could sense that weight in the photographer too. Much depended on getting a good shot; it was important to visit these sites with respect.

I felt terrible because of my shit in the woods. And something in the mix-up of emotions I was feeling made me realize that I should go to Thiepval again. That when I'd gone the first time, it was like watching a monument take its annual public shit. Thiepval wasn't ready for my advance and the least I could do was meet the monument to the missing one-on-one.

I was making great time on the bicycle—a bicycle is a bit like a hobby horse. What I mean is, a bicycle is a convivial companion. And my bicycle, or perhaps the bottom half of me—which is what controls a bicycle— agreed with me that I should give Thiepval another chance. When you are alone too long you start having conversations with your bicycle, as though it were a horse. The mythological creature in me, part man, part bicycle, sensed I should go to Thiepval when no one else was there, just as I had with Beaumont-Hamel. And so I had encouraged my bicycle to take me up the hill. I enjoyed the hard incline, which reminded me of all the hills of Newfoundland I'd ever climbed. The big joy of climbing a hill is knowing that soon you will be whizzing down it. The brief thrill I had in Toronto was of riding the flats—they give you the peculiar feeling that all directions in the city are slightly on a downgrade. This feeling, I understand, is shallow and after one summer in Toronto the thrill had boiled away; all I knew then of landscape was that I missed hills. There is one hill in all of downtown Toronto and it's on Churchill Street. I don't know if it's named after Winston but it is a hill I have never climbed but only accepted the crest and plummeted down, much as we often avoid Churchill's constant war mongering and bullying vengeance and concentrate on his tenacity and vigour. There must be some slight progression of inclines that takes you to the top, but then going down, the street itself is all St John's.

POZIÈRES

On my way to Thiepval I bicycled past the first tank battle, and then the windmill battle in Pozières. Tanks had once been called landships, and the British had disguised what they were building by calling the vehicles "water carriers for Russia." So from "water carrier" the name "tank" was derived. The British, when training armoured crews, used canvas models that men carried over themselves like hobby horses. And when the Germans first heard and then saw the real tanks, they thought the devil was coming.

Pozières. The official war historian Charles Bean said this ridge is more densely sown with Australian sacrifice than any other place on earth. They talk of high points of ground, but to my untrained eye there is not a contour line anywhere except for Thiepval. A few feet in elevation must have mattered a lot. Certainly, it mattered for the artillery. If I were asked to take this ridge, I might have had to say, What ridge? It is possible, too, that the British generals Haig and Rawlinson reduced the ridge to rubble and wiped out the contour line. I wouldn't put it past Douglas Haig and his methodical approach. Step by step. The butcher Haig, they called him. Germany had a butcher too, Crown Prince Wilhelm. The French had Charles Mangin. All armies call at least one commander "the butcher." But this excuses the system. The system encourages reasonable men to become butchers.

I once drove out to Brantford, in southwest Ontario, to investigate the Earl Haig Family Fun Park. There's a spray-pad and waterslide and what is called a lazy river. I wondered what Haig would have called that river. Today you can hit a baseball and play a round of mini-golf at the Fun Park. I write this with a straight face. The park hosts birthday parties and summer fun-day camps. There is also a school in Toronto named after Haig. There must be a lobby group trying to rehabilitate the Haig name.

The Somme. Many pages have been written about the cost of this success. What a terrifically dismal way to bury the truth: that the Somme was a colossal failure. Wreckage upon wreckage, as Walter Benjamin writes. I wish I could awaken the dead from this catastrophe.

I salute you, Australia; you were here at Pozières three weeks after Beaumont-Hamel. You attacked in the dark, and then at dusk. The generals had begun to adjust their storm of progress because of what had happened to the Newfoundlanders. This was true, too, of the Germans: the Red Baron had begun the war on a horse.

If you rode a horse and you did not fly, then you were put in the infantry. This logic occurred to me while drinking a Leffe draft—a sweet beer—in the Knightsbridge Cemetery. I studied the Canadian infantrymen buried in Sunken Road—there were so many dead that two cemeteries had been built to house them.

I stepped off my seat when I hit the crunchy gravel at the gate to Thiepval. I petted the saddle and chose to walk on the quiet grass. As I had expected, not a soul was around now. Kipling called these vast graveyards silent cities. I pushed my bicycle like the white pony I found in a painting of the general Beauvoir de Lisle. Snowy was the white pony's name. Amazing to think that Beauvoir de Lisle was unaffected by this war, that war was an interruption to his instruction in polo. In his autobiography, de Lisle describes shellshock as something that rarely happened in his division, a division that included the Newfoundlanders. The way to treat shell shock, he said, was to present something even more terrible. He recommended lying down on a mattress full of electricity. He turned a blind eye when the men who were shellshocked were strung up in the wire overnight. That seemed to cure them.

And yet Beauvoir de Lisle gives a statement about the Newfoundland Regiment that we read today with poetic understatement: "Dead men can advance no further." I think de Lisle was unaware that there was more than a literal meaning to his words. In contrast, Douglas Haig's comments after July first were uninspired. The acting colonel of the division, Sir Aylmer Hunter-Weston, said to the Newfoundlanders, "I salute you, individually. You have done better than the best." This "better than the best" was said six days into the Battle of the Somme, at Englebelmer. John Robinson, a local journalist, said this praise "savours of extravagance."

Finally, the New Zealand general, Bernard Freyberg, rode up to the Newfoundlanders and asked who they were. When told, he said, with relief: Good. I don't have to worry about my left flank, now what about my right?

You cannot look at a website to the Newfoundland Regiment without finding these fleeting platitudes from great men. "The best small-boat seamen in the Royal Navy," the Admiral of the Fleet, Lord Beatty, said—or was it Winston Churchill. Perhaps it is apocryphal, but nonetheless we believe it and swoon, because we Newfoundlanders love to hear praise from the powerful heaped upon our dead.

Beauvoir de Lisle loved polo and wrote books on polo. His sporting critics say that even when the offside rule in polo was dropped—which changed the game considerably—de Lisle's advice remained the same. That tells me something of the man. He was a man who could not change his attitude to cavalry, or to horses who were heard to die on the battlefield, which was one of the worst sounds one could hear, as though the earth itself were dying, some men said. Eight million horses perished during the Great War.

The vast arches of the Thiepval monument were in front of me now. The bricks looked heavy, Jeanette Winterson's brick, but as I came closer the three arches diminished and the sky inside the arches expanded. It was an odd experience of broadening, as though the ribs of the brick arches were inhaling. I realized the monument was framing the sky—that the sky *was* the monument. Climbing the stairs, I moved into the monument. In two registry boxes were six thick books containing the names of all the men who had been killed on the Somme. There were—I counted them—thirty-five Winters. On the wall, there were towers of names belonging to the soldiers who were without burial. This effect of the names alongside the monument that had disappeared into sky broke me down. I was on the threshold of life and death here, standing in a pool of sky. Again, I thought: How quiet and how magnificent. What appeared from afar to be a heavy, dull English monument without imagination suddenly vanished as I approached it and become part of it, and I was left with a frame around me, and the names of all the dead hanging upon my perimeter to heaven.

I understood then what I hoped for this book: to escape the ponderous heavy weight of research so that the whole artifice lifts, like the arch, the closer the reader comes to its pages. I hope that somehow the soldiers and sailors and woodsmen and nurses and civilians will animate themselves and a world of death will feel, if only for a moment, alive.

I still do not know if that is possible to achieve. Instead, I will tell you that the Newfoundlanders played football near here, against other regiments. They put ribbons on a mule and rode him to the match.

BEES IN CELLOPHANE

I bicycled back to Beaumont-Hamel. The trees appeared on the horizon and I coasted down the quiet paved road towards them. I turned in at the now familiar entrance and dismounted. I left the bicycle in the trees and walked towards the caribou. There was something different: at the foot of the monument was a heap of wreaths and bouquets. And I heard an interior motor: a buzzing. A tremendous buzzing in the plastic wrap on the bouquets. Bees. The work of bees that I could not see. I looked at the cellophane wrappers: India had sent a bouquet. And so had small towns from around here, towns like Authuille. The flowers from the Royal Canadian Legion did not move me, for they were mandatory. But flowers from a small French village and India—yes, that was touching. I imagined that every year at a town council meeting, someone must approve the expenditure of a wreath for the war dead of Newfoundland—and they continue to do so.

While the bees worked, I read the list of names below the caribou. There were two brothers, Stanley and George Abbott. Stanley joined up at the start of the war. He was an upholsterer. His brother signed on six months later—George was a cooper. They had a sister who was close to their age, and then two younger siblings, aged ten and thirteen. George listed William, the ten-year-old, as his heir. The parents were in their early fifties. The Abbott brothers fought at Gallipoli. George received frostbite and rejoined the regiment in April of 1916. Stanley, the older, was sick with a venereal disease for six weeks; I had read that the soldiers were seven times more likely to be in hospital with a venereal disease than with either trenchfoot or frostbite. Stanley finally rejoined the battalion just ten days before the opening of the Battle of the Somme. Both brothers were killed here.

Their mother, after the war, applied for a separation allowance but was refused in June 1919 because her husband, Harry, was considered able enough to care for the family.

I walked back down to Y Ravine to get drunk again. It seemed the only thing to do—and I thought it was what these men would have done if they'd survived the absurdity of their tactical formation. They knew, from sealing on the ice, that in order to survive you had to stick together.

There was a letter displayed in the visitors' box at Y Ravine—a quote from the Newfoundlander Ernest Chafe three days before the start of the Battle of the Somme:

I am far from thinking, mother dear, that I will be
killed for I am not built that way, but then, as we
cannot see the future, fortunately, it teaches us not to be
too sure.

I continued in past the rows of cemetery stones, inspect-
ing the troops as it were, then stared up at the tops of the
intensely tall Newfoundland trees and wondered at their
marvellous virility. I kicked off my sneakers without unty-
ing the laces and I removed my socks and threw them into
the clipped grass. On someone's gravestone I read this:

LORD ALL PITYING, JESU BLEST
GRANT HIM THINE ETERNAL REST

I felt unruly. I was drinking another bottle of the Côtes
du Rhône, a wine from the valley the Newfoundlanders
had passed through before they died. A valley of grapes
ripening while the men were shot down.

I found the headstone for Ernest Chafe. He was twenty-
five. Dark brown hair and grey eyes. He had attested for
general service in September of 1914, trained in Scotland,
suffered frostbite at Suvla, and was invalided to England.
He went missing on the first day of the Somme offensive
here in France and the thought was that most of the missing were prisoners of war. "I am not built that way." It took

them nine months to declare him dead. A year after his death, his parents received fifty-three dollars, the balance of their son's estate—roughly a thousand dollars today. His mother was Jane Chafe, of 140 Casey Street, St John's. Three photographs of Ernest Chafe's grave were sent to his parents in 1921. Father Nangle and Henry Snow would have overseen this photography. And here was the grave before me, Chafe's name inscribed in upper case, the lettering designed by the Englishman MacDonald Gill.

The sun was going down. The trees, full of birds. Lots of pheasant-type birds. And doves. Owls, perhaps. A hawk. Up by the base of the caribou I'd seen a handful of rabbits hop about. Unipeds. It was quiet here and I thought of my son; he would be watching the *Lord of the Rings* movie now. And I recalled how Tolkien had served here during the war. In his letters, Tolkien describes how he'd converted his war experience into the passage over the dead marshes.

I lay down and looked up at the convergence of tree-tops. It was dark now under these immensely tall spruce. A full moon was coming up over the hill—over Thiepval. I wished I had a second bottle of wine. The trees, as I looked up, leaned their crowns together as if peering back down at me. *Who is this lying at our feet?* I was at the bottom, I knew, of a deep well of living things. This well reminded me of an accident I had lived through—an accident where I fell into an incinerator. I recalled the ambush of that accident. It was a falling—I could not control how I fell. Falling is the earth and the sun controlling you. It is succumbing to that grand subtle force of gravity and feeling that you are inside a cathedral of fire. Falling, grave as it is, is the source of much humour. That sensation I felt, the paralyzing terror of what must occur—it may have been similar to being shouted at and goaded into going over the top and realizing what awaits you. The Newfoundlanders understood the advance was a failure. The forward trenches were full of the dead and wounded of other regiments. But the men did their duty, and the lucky ones, the wounded, all asked the same thing. They lifted their heads from their gurneys and asked, Is the Colonel pleased?

Those men fell into death. They were not brave—courage requires a choice. The choice to flee was courageous, especially when the penalty for fleeing was a firing squad. And the shame of it all—a shame that falls on future generations. Shame is always unfair; it serves no good purpose. It is employed by those in power to force followers to toe the line. If, even today, shame exists for those who are absent without leave, then that force still exists. I do not want to be part of that machine. When we admire those who refuse, we know another force has taken the place of the first, and trauma can heal. And here, beyond this line in the sand, I defy the stately historical manner of honouring war. I defend my son against a missed encounter with the real, which is what trauma is. Let the real poke through in these words I have written, and not through the process of repeating words that become detached from experience.

This is what is real: The Newfoundlanders fell and died and lay here for a hundred and thirty-five days. Until the Scotsman Norman Collins buried them. And there they lay for another two years. Until Father Nangle and Henry Snow exhumed the corpses from their filled-in shell craters and laid them out properly.

I walked back to find my bicycle and it was quiet now. The bees were asleep in their sleeves of cellophane. F. Scott Fitzgerald wrote in his diary that the world will one day be made of cellophane.

The First World War now contains only a faint wisp of trauma in our memories. We have nipped off the trauma and it no longer carries any threat to us. It is becoming, like the War of 1812 and those toy soldiers near Lake Ontario, an event without direct effect on us. The bottomless fear is an experience that we can connect with only through some ironic re-transmission. We have to walk up to the war and inspect its corpse to realize some thoughtful verse is still buzzing in the cellophane-wrapped flowers. There is something alive here, but it requires our sensual interest. The Second World War still clings to fragments of threat and horror, but it too is turning over and Hitler will soon hold hands with Napoleon. One thing leads to another.

Recently, I watched the comedian Louis C.K. describe his experience of tuning in to the movie *Schindler's List* on television. There is a scene where a seven-year-old Polish girl stands on a mailbox and shouts, "Goodbye, Jews!" This line, he says, is probably based on a true story. Spielberg got wind of it and thought, That's going in my movie. I know how movies are made, Louis C.K. says, and somewhere there's a tape with fifty little girls shouting out "Goodbye, Jews!" And that knowledge disturbs him. This is the modern experience of the Second World War.

I have, once again, fallen into thinking about a future war. But it bears remembering that Hitler did serve here on this western front, ten miles from where the Newfoundlanders fell. Corporal Hitler suffered a shrapnel wound in his leg near Bapaume. He had a dog he kept during the war named Fuchsl, which means Little Fox.

I stood up on my pedals and inhaled deeply of the fields of agriculture. I inhaled the German dead and the allied dead and the drowned body of Kitchener and the shot body of John Roberts. Isn't it true that all wars that have ever been fought record similar events and deployments and death? I took an interest in Agincourt because I read about F. Scott Fitzgerald describing, to his daughter, the British and French tactics in that battle. All these wars are keeping this conversation alive even as we try desperately to separate them and plant them in their own times. These wars are slowly walking over the fields of the earth, and we are pulling shrapnel out of the ground and parading these remnants on our souvenir shelves.

FABIAN WARE

I was becoming obsessed with visiting as many cemeteries as I could squeeze into my little time. As I bicycled down the paved road a spotless white van passed by me, and minutes later I came upon it parked beside a cemetery. Four men piled out. The men were in clean overalls and they opened the rear doors and bent in to slide out lawn mowers and gardening tools. They were wearing earphones. They guided the mowers into the cemetery and yanked effortlessly on their cords. I'd forgotten, that memorials and cemeteries need constant maintenance. When the Newfoundlanders first lay beneath the earth in their new graves they awaited their tombstones. Some had wooden crosses, made by men of the regiment, that were painted to look like marble. The men were proud of their craftsmanship.

At the South African monument in Delville Wood, a man had used a plumb line across the grass abutting a wall to snip a straight line into the turf. These men, I realized, were employed by the Commonwealth War Graves Commission. They were doing an excellent job of tending the memorials. The French civic graveyards I had visited were garish and dark, their gravel walkways imbued with death. You felt you might inhale the ancient vapours of consumption in those civic graveyards. But these walled rooms of war graves were warm, marked with white stone and green grass. You could have a picnic here, as I had done.

These cemeteries for the war dead were moving, not miserable. These fields were beautiful, with a copse on the hillside where the white stone monuments were placed to bury the dead. We have a director of Rio Tinto to thank for that. That director, Fabian Ware, was too old to join the army, so he became a commander of the mobile unit of the British Red Cross. They knew, early in the war, that a tremendous amount of burying would have to be done once the fighting was over. The Imperial War Graves Commission was struck and they decided that crosses would be too difficult to maintain. Crosses could not be placed close enough together and the action of frost and weather on each lone, vulnerable cross could break it. Whereas a stone tablet might hold the Star of David or an Arabic motif—religions other than Christianity could be represented.

Rudyard Kipling agreed to write inscriptions for the graves of the fallen. His son, John, had been dead for two years, but the war was still being fought. They never did find his body. Kipling spoke of the importance of absolute equality and permanence. No remains were to be repatriated. At the start of the war, officers' bodies were shipped home for burial, but as the scale of the war increased, this practice stopped. The graves would be uniform and identical for every man, whether a field marshal or a camp follower. Half a million headstones, Churchill said, would be required for France and Belgium alone. Equality of treatment, Kipling said, confirms and admits equality of sorrow.

The cemeteries, Fabian Ware wrote, "are situated on every conceivable site—on bare hills flayed by years of battle, in orchards and meadows, beside populous towns or little villages, in jungle-glades, at coast ports, in far-away islands, among desert sands, and desolate ravines. It would be as impossible as undesirable to reduce them all to any uniformity of aspect by planting or by architecture."

Each cemetery includes the cross of sacrifice and the stone of remembrance. The plain headstones are thirty inches tall and fifteen inches wide, "upon which the cross or other religious symbol of the dead man's faith could be carved, and his regimental badge fully displayed."

The families were allowed to add an inscription at their own expense to a maximum of sixty-six letters (including spaces); such an inscription cost them roughly four dollars. A decision was made to move each isolated grave to the nearest body of their companions, for "scattered graves look lonely."

The war veteran Edmund Blunden wrote of these graveyards: "I venture to speak of these lovely elegiac closes (which almost cause me to deny my own experiences in the acres they now grace) as after all the eloquent evidence against war. Their very flowerfulness and calm tell the lingerer that the men beneath that green coverlet should be there to enjoy such influence; the tyranny of war stands all the more terribly revealed."

As I bicycled back to Les Galets, pushing on the pedals, I knew I would never come here again. But, I thought, every person should come once. And they should visit Thiepval as well as Beaumont-Hamel. Because these sites are inseparable. They are the smallest unit and the largest upheaval of loyalty, and they exist a few minutes apart. A thousandth of the British army, and the entirety of allied dead.

In bed that night I stared up into the dark and felt as if I was lying in wait, in that Newfoundland cemetery. Waiting for some footsteps to visit me. A student had scribbled a note in the visitors' book: *Remember, you are standing where they did not get.* How can you not teeter back on your heels with this realization? The bees, I thought of the furious bees and Jim Stacey with his gas mask fetching honey. Oxenham's book of thoughtful verse, his bees in amber. How impressed I was of Fabian Ware and Father Nangle, the foresight of men who we now look back upon with hindsight. To bury, to mark the grave.

They were cheered off with a chance to small powder. The idea that, if they were lucky, they might fire off a few rounds. That if they were killed, it would be by a sniper and their head exposed and really it's your own fault. But what they faced was shellfire. They were issued tin hats not to prevent bullet wounds, but shrapnel exploding from shells. It was this debasement of the method of death which was shocking. And at Beaumont-Hamel, the majority of deaths weren't by rifle or shell—but machine gun. The debasement here was that they were trained to be a third wave, a wave not expected to fire a round, but march over territory and occupy deserted land.

The back pages of the *London Gazette* that week were full of acts of heroism and valour and injury. The Newfoundland Regiment performed well in Gallipoli and then were destroyed here in France. All of the tangents of study, machine-gun training, officer training, gas mask donning, bayonet instruction, carrying the Bangalore pipe bomb, lifting ladders and telephone equipment, all of this Scottish training and Turkish experience and Egyptian duration and naval travelling and route-marches and boarding English buses and French trains, all of this was destroyed in thirty minutes.

In thirty minutes, I was asleep.

LOCHNAGAR CRATER

The next day I bicycled to the Lochnagar crater, which is fringed with trees while the rest of the land is cultivated. The British had dug tunnels here, under the German front lines. I had stood at the bottom of Hawthorn Crater, and now I wished to crawl even further down. It turned out that there was a tour I could take, with a guide, of the Glory Hole at La Boisselle.

I walked down into a tunnel carved into the white clay. The heat of the day whipped off me; it was cool down here. The guide and I walked until we were under the German front lines. I thought of the miners stripped to the waist while an officer used a stethoscope to listen for sounds of hostile digging. The guide explained that some tunnels were hard to hide from aerial surveillance because of the colour of the ground. But here the men could put the dirt in sandbags and sprinkle it on the trenches. I told him where I'd been and he said that the Newfoundlanders had planted watercress at Beaumont-Hamel and, after a few days, the effects of tunnelling were hidden.

I climbed out of the tunnel and sat down to eat a *pêche plate*. It was a very flat and juicy fruit. The *plate* made me think of platoons and platitudes. Flat things. I thought again of Kipling, whom George Orwell had said was involved in platitudes, "and since the world we live in is full of platitudes, much of what he said sticks."

After eating, I bicycled on, and up ahead a figure on a bike was heading my way. It was the old man I had met in the rain near Dantzig cemetery. We stopped.

He was seventy-four years old, he told me, on his way to Verdun—more than four hundred miles! He had just been down to the Somme south of Péronne. He wanted to see where King Henry V had forded the river on his way to Agincourt. That was five hundred years ago, I said. He looked puzzled and so I said again the river's name and Agincourt. But I was confusing him. So I returned to the present: How is the Somme? I asked. For I had never seen the main body of it.

He explained its serpentine twists, using his hands, keeping his bike steady with his thighs. The way he moved his hands and the manner in which he carried his mouth told me he thought the Somme was a beautiful river. I know the history of river-making. How a river bends and will lose its shoulders and new twists emerge. I had read the history of the topography of this area, and was surprised to realize that the armies did not line up on either side of the Somme. Instead, the river meandered indifferently through both sides.

Nice weather, he said, and I knocked my knuckles on my head in reply.

As he prepared to carry on he paused and said, I am going to remember you for the rest of my life.

This made me blush and I asked him what he meant.

It's nice to meet someone who's cheerful, he said.

And he climbed upon his pedals and pushed on. I stood there astride my bicycle and felt that perhaps I had just met my older self. Perhaps I too should head for Verdun. But I was at the Somme and I loved the sound of that river. A sleepwalking river.

As I sat back on my saddle I realized I had lost the map out of my back pocket—it had wiggled out somewhere down the road, as though the terrain had its own destination separate from my own. I would have to guess at routes now by the seat of my pants as I headed back, hopefully, to home.

THREE

I climbed the stairs to the top flight of a train to Lille, Flanders, with a connection to Kortrijk. I was on my way now to the end of the war. I left behind the great hinge in the battle that changed everything for Newfoundland and the British empire. "In front of him beneath a dingy sky was Beaumont-Hamel; to his left the tragic hill of Thiepval." That's F. Scott Fitzgerald describing Dick's tour of the Western Front. How he stared at these recovering battlefields through binoculars, "his throat straining with sadness."

We passed over land that the Newfoundlanders fought through for the next two years. The English poet Robert Graves was left for dead out my eastern window at the end of July. He had a wound above the eye—the injury made by a chip of marble from a cemetery headstone in Bazentin.

It took a month for the casualty lists from Beaumont-Hamel to finally reach the newspapers in St John's. There were columns of names. "The land here," Fitzgerald wrote, "cost twenty lives a foot that summer." The colonial secretary stood outside the courthouse and addressed the citizens of St John's on the resolution recording the government's "inflexible determination" to continue the struggle to a victorious end. It was the second anniversary of the start of the war and a full month since the destruction of the men at Beaumont-Hamel. But the truth of that destruction was just now reaching the dominion. John Bennett, abandoning his notes, spoke from his heart and said, "A fortnight ago we sent five hundred men across to fill the ranks; very soon we shall send five hundred more. We shall send five hundred more after that, and shall continue to send them until no more are required." John Bennett's speech was quoted in the next day's *Evening Telegram*.

A colonel in Ayr, Scotland, said of the arrival of that recent draft of men Bennett mentioned: "It is composed of most excellent material."

The Newfoundlanders fought and died and were wounded and taken prisoner and driven insane all along this blurred landscape. The hero of Gallipoli, James Donnelly, was killed at Gueudecourt. Robert Holloway, the photographer who, with his sister, took photographs of the regiment back in St John's and became a sniper, was shot dead at Monchy-le-Preux. A hundred and sixty-five other Newfoundlanders were killed at Monchy—the casualties were the heaviest in the entire division.

CYRIL GARDNER

Cyril Gardner was killed here. Gardner had been the hero at Le Transloy, capturing seventy Germans. When he brought in the prisoners, a British officer of the First Border Regiment raised his rifle. Gardner stepped into the line of fire and said if any German was killed, that officer was next to die. The Germans applauded Gardner and one of them approached and presented him with his Iron Cross. A good story for the morale of Newfoundland. Gardner received the Distinguished Conduct Medal and the British got on it, wrote up the story, and had an artist draw an illustration. The artist wanted to know what the soldier was wearing, what time of day it was, the terrain, the weather, the nature of the country. Cyril Gardner was five foot nine, determined, broad-shouldered, with a quiet unassuming face.

But he was killed here at Monchy. Monchy was part of the Battle of Arras, in April 1917. It snowed here. Siegfried Sassoon wrote that "a snowstorm on April 11 was the sort of thing that one expected in the war and it couldn't be classed as a major misfortune." The Canadians took Vimy and the Newfoundlanders held Monchy, as "the snow melted on the shiny waterproof sheets which kept the men uncomfortably warm." George Culpitt of the Royal Welsh Fusiliers was with Sassoon in this snow. It was the first they'd had all winter. Culpitt was with four others in a hole "unable to move for fear of being seen" and they became gradually enveloped in a mantle of white so that "we were barely distinguishable from the snow-covered ground which was on all sides." The Fusiliers marched for twelve days towards the "life-denying region" of Monchy. Again, Sassoon: "I, a single human being with my little stock of earthly experience in my head, was entering once again the veritable gloom and disaster of the thing called Armageddon."

The Armageddon was Monchy. Edward Moyle Stick was captured here. He was the third of the Stick brothers to sign up for the war. He stood five foot two. He registered as a prisoner of war in July and escaped, with Arthur Hill of the Welsh Regiment, in March 1918. He arrived in England on 19 April and received the Military Medal. Back home he gave a lecture at Broad Cove on behalf of the Patriotic Association of Women of Newfoundland. He told them how Charles Snow had died of heart failure and dropped dead in the street at Marchienne. His death was from exhaustion brought on by neglect. He described Arthur Cummings amd George Attwood dying of tuberculosis brought on by starvation.

Moyle Stick returned to St John's and continued to live in that Devon Row house. He was a teacher but he had pain in his stomach. He moved to Vancouver and claimed a disability due to the Great War. A doctor in Vancouver diagnosed a duodenal ulcer and gave him sippy powders with good results. Stick applied five times over ten years for a disability but was disallowed. He married Edna Rowe in 1946. They had no children. Moyle Stick died in 1986.

The father of these Stick soldiers came from Cornwall, England. Cornish mules, which have been used as beasts of burden, were called moyles.

MONCHY

It was this ground that the Newfoundlanders attacked and defended until there was only ten of them against seven hundred Germans. They were led by the capable James Forbes-Robertson but they were pinned down in a blizzard with forty mile an hour winds, British airplanes almost motionless overhead while around the men were great explosions "the colour of lamp black and wool." The men rationed their ammunition and, after four hours, sent word for help through their runner, Albert Rose of Flowers Cove. Rose not only got a message through about their being pinned down, but returned to the fighting. They were the men who saved Monchy. Beauvoir de Lisle said that if Monchy had been lost to the Germans, it would have required forty thousand soldiers to retake it. Four hundred and sixty Newfoundlanders were killed or wounded at Monchy. Rupert Bartlett was killed while repelling a German counterattack. Rupert was the brother of Bob Bartlett who guided Robert Peary to the North Pole then brought him back. Rupert would not come back. His other brother, William Bartlett, was captaining the *Viking* at the seal hunt that year. It was, in fact, the end of the seal hunt, and the *Viking* had "closed the gates and brought home the key" from the front. Twelve ships had two hundred thousand pelts. The seal fishery was estimated at one million dollars—half for fat and half for skins. It was considered a lucky voyage as it was manned by men not eligible for enlistment.

The casualty list for Monchy was printed in the *Telegram* on the same page as this tally for the seal hunt. Newfoundland, over the course of the war, poured six thousand men into the regiment before no more were required. The fields I was zipping through were sown with dead and now here they were, full of crops. A tractor used a trailer to wrap bales of hay in black plastic. They turn the hay bale the way a spider handles the body of a fly. Raymond Chandler was stationed here, at Lens, with the Canadians. But he was not at Vimy and he was not the sole survivor of his platoon during a German raid. Chandler liked to embellish, but I would embellish too. Raymond Chandler wrote that, when he was in charge of a platoon, his main concern was to space the men. "It's only human," he wrote, "to want to bunch for companionship in the face of heavy fire."

I kept thinking of those sealers, how they thought the only way to survive the blizzard was to bunch together. It had saved some of them.

One of Chandler's companions in the 7th Battalion was a Newfoundlander his own age. Alfred Cullen, of St John's, had signed up, as did Chandler, in British Columbia. But Chandler would elect to try out for the RAF and, in September, Cullen was killed near Arras. The British tried to straighten their lines and the Germans used an elastic defence—as soon as I learn these terms I begin to forget them. The history of war writing is a history that consents with the dimensions and depth of war as a method to communicate. I am not qualified to speak within those rules and assumptions. But is there a new way to talk of war that might break the fruit bowl of the battle narrative? Who owns these fields in Flanders upon which the Germans and the British fought? Whose land had it been? The memorial in Beaumont-Hamel is the only field of battle on the Western Front left as it was when the war ended. Nothing else ever happened here at Beaumont-Hamel except a dormant field occupied by sheep for grazing. How had they felt, these French farmers, selling their land to the women of Newfoundland to make a memorial? And how had that negotiation happened?

It was the work of one man, the Newfoundland chaplain Thomas Nangle.

Of the battles the Newfoundlanders fought over the next two years, Father Nangle said this: At Beaumont-Hamel, "Newfoundlanders taught the world how to die." At Gueudecourt, "they showed the world how they could fight." And at Monchy, "the men of the regiment combined the two."

My train pulled me closer to the end of the war. It was effortless, my travel, and it compressed all of the deaths of the Newfoundland Regiment over the next two years into a few hours. These little towns where the regiment fought, their church spires moving over the rooftops: Le Transloy, Arras, Marcoing, Masnières, Cambrai, Sailly-Saillisel, Gueudecourt, Monchy, Lesboeufs, Scarpe, Ypres, Langemarck, Poelcappelle, Kortrijk.

The spires made me think of Nangle, that Catholic priest, who enlisted after Beaumont-Hamel. He travelled this land and lived with the men in the trenches and marched with the men and buried the men outside of these villages and was wounded with the men and sent letters home about their deaths to their families. Stephen Norris was killed in action on 11 October 1916, and Nangle sent a cablegram to his father:

> Steve killed by big shell, whole trench fell in, body not found, am on the ground myself doing everything possible to locate body, heartfelt sympathy to self, mother, Nell and family.

THE RICKETTS BROTHERS

Tommy Ricketts enlisted at the same time as Thomas Nangle. Ricketts lied about his age and joined up at fifteen, soon after the tragedy of Beaumont-Hamel. He was only fifteen but he told the board he was eighteen. His signature, like that of his brother George, was an x for HIS MARK. He had rowed out from the jaws of the land, away from the family wharf at Middle Arm towards the Reid coastal steamer, the *Clyde*, that was anchored off Seal Cove. Tommy's father was in prison and his mother had left to remarry in Canada. His brother George was in the war and his sister, Rachel, was about to marry a man named Edward Gavin. Edward's brother, Tom Gavin, and a friend named Tom Banks were in the boat with Tommy Ricketts.

The boys rowed out to the steamer and were helped aboard. The steamer dropped off canvas sacks of mail and took on fresh mail and filled several dories with canned goods and flour. Then they raised anchor and took the boys north around the head of Notre Dame Bay and, with a freshening wind behind them, they steamed east on their way to Lewisporte and St John's.

In St John's Tommy Ricketts found a place to board on Colonial Street, which is the first street I lived on when I moved to St John's. He received military training in Pleasantville and attended meetings at the Church Lads' Brigade before being shipped off to England. He was paid a dollar a day, and sixty cents of this dollar he sent home to his sister, Rachel. Just as his brother George had done.

There exists, in the Gavin house in Seal Cove, a photograph of the two brothers in uniform. But it does not mean they ever met each other overseas. It could just be a photographic collage. His brother George had embarked on the *Southampton*, a light cruiser, on 25 June 1916. He was part of the seventh draft of men to join the British Expeditionary Force in France. The *Southampton* had been repaired at Rosyth dockyard after being severely damaged at the Battle of Jutland. A tug collected the cruiser's waste paper, bottles and fat—the *Southampton* had headed the fat list for the current quarter. She was of dark-blue enamel, the stanchions of her awning were covered in pipe-clay canvas, and the decks were snowy white, having been planed by hand by ten carpenters to remove all stains of the Jutland battle.

George Ricketts would have heard about the success of the Newfoundlanders at Beaumont-Hamel, as the newspapers were full of the advance the men had made. But then he would have noticed the injured filling up the hospitals and he would have been on duty to help bury the dead and to retrieve the dead from no man's land. This was the first time in history that a soldier was informed of a battle in print and then came upon some differing truths on the land, having to recalibrate what the news told him with what his eyes saw.

The July drive. A drive in Newfoundland refers to a run of logs from the woods camps, down a river to the lumber mill. A drive sounds positive—full of inertia that one merely has to steer to its natural course. George Ricketts stayed alive for five months then was wounded severely in the face, in December of 1916. He was in a hospital in Rouen. His sister, Rachel, back in Seal Cove, sent a telegraph to the Colonial Secretary in St John's asking about her brother's condition. The secretary replied that George Ricketts was convalescing in Wandsworth.

But then he went missing from the regiment near Masnieres. And six months later, on the second anniversary of Beaumont-Hamel, George Ricketts was presumed dead.

In August of 1919, John Ricketts received a cheque for the balance of his eldest son's pay: $205.89.

LEO MURPHY

The regiment was near Ypres. Leo Murphy described the city as made up of "buildings without doors or windows or roofs." There was a dramatic quality at night, the illumination from the moon, and now and then the sheen of red from gunfire or starshell. They were in a bombed-out building very near the White Chateau. Empty sandbags had been sewn together to create partitions. They decided to host a dinner for the officers from the other companies. They found red and white paper foraged from the ruins of a store in Ypres and cut out red triangles—the badge of their division—to crown the entrances and covered the walls with pictures. There were soldiers busy with scissors and crepe paper. Plates and cups were borrowed, large green leaves were taken from a field to lay the lobster, the divisional chateau supplied alcohol. The officers arrived. Their menu began with Potage à la Quidi Vidi and Lobster without Field Dressing.

Quidi Vidi was the pond near St John's, that "communicates with the sea by a cove of the same name." It was once the seat of military operations for the taking and retaking of St John's. It is where the regiment first trained.

They ate and talked and sang "The Star of Logy Bay," which must have been pretty moving as it's about a girl who is sent away because a man is interested. She could be in France or Spain, the song goes. And here are the men, singing of Logy Bay, while they are in Belgium. Sam Ebsary brought out his accordion and sat on an ammunition box. He played "The Banks of Newfoundland," which is the old rowing song played at the St John's regatta, written in 1820 by Francis Forbes. It was the regimental band's signature tune, and it was played the next summer during Newfoundland Week in Hyde Park to a crowd of ten thousand people. The march was described as a mixture of Irish and Red Indian strains, "as stirring as it is weird."

This was before Gueudecourt, Monchy and Cambrai. When many of the men were still alive.

CAMBRAI

I think of the Newfoundland Regiment's commander, Arthur Hadow, in the snow, a year before the end of the war. This was Cambrai and the snow had fallen during the night. Hadow was thinking of his men, who were on the move. He removed the officers' kit from the General Service wagon and replaced it with the men's blankets. The kits were left to be picked up by the division truck. That night, the truck was stuck with snow, but the men had their blankets for Cambrai.

Leonard Stick was first to join the regiment. His brother, Robins Stick, was also a Blue Puttee. Robins Stick was twenty-six when he signed up. Black hair, five feet seven and a half inches. And during the Battle of Cambrai he was blown up by a shell and rendered unconscious for a half hour and managed to get himself to a field hospital.

There is some dispute about this. Arthur Hadow certified that Robins Stick was "not subjected in the course of his duty to exceptional exposure." Stick disappeared early in the attack but Hadow can find no one in his company who saw him fall out. There was exceptionally little shelling at the time, Hadow wrote. Hadow suggested that further enquiries should be made into the conduct of this officer.

Robins Stick. His brother Leonard's dress uniform is in that glass case in Bay Roberts. And Colonel Hadow's uniform can be seen online—it is owned by a World War One memorabilia collector. I have an odd feeling when I see these uniforms in postures without the bodies, a bit like a scalp is being presented. Or I think of the absurdity that cloth should outlive us.

Where was Robins Stick during the attack? Did a runner see him? Did he know of the action? When was he missing? The Brigadier General, Bernard Freyberg, instigated an inquiry with this terse confidential query: I recommend that the medical authorities be called upon to state definitely whether there are any signs of shell shock. If there are no signs I consider disciplinary action should be taken.

Bernard Freyberg was the youngest general in the British army, and one of its most highly decorated. He had two brothers who were killed, one in Gallipoli and the other in France. On the last morning of the war Freyberg led a successful cavalry charge and was awarded a distinguished conduct medal—one minute before the armistice was signed.

There were no physical signs of shell shock apart from slight tremors in Stick's outstretched hands. Reflexes normal. Dry tongue.

Robins Stick said a shell exploded beneath his feet and all he saw was white flame. Then he came to and a stretcher bearer, with two German prisoners carrying a stretcher, helped him in with an arm around his neck.

Fred Bursey wrote this: I was a runner to Captain Stick. I was with him when we got out of the forming-up trench and stayed close beside him until we reached the second objective on the crest of the hill near three burning tanks. We stopped in that trench for about two minutes and then we left the trench together. I was about ten yards in front of Captain Stick and ran towards a sunken road which was about thirty yards away. There was shelling going on at the time as well as machine-gun fire from the enemy. I thought that Captain Stick was behind me all the way. When I got to the sunken road I saw some dug-outs and commenced to bomb them. I was there for about five minutes. I looked around for Captain Stick but did not see him anywhere.

Beauvoir de Lisle weighed in and said he knew of Captain Stick to be a gallant officer and a fine leader. "I fully accept his statement and have so informed him."

Bernard Freyberg wrote that this officer's past record has been good and that with what he saw of him in the line he is certain an injustice has been done in doubting his statement.

Soon after the war, Robins Stick attended a boat race in Paris. It is not until 1921 that a note says that his excellency has presented Stick with the Military Cross and so "that difficult matter is swept away."

I stared at Cambrai drifting away to the east of my train, and marvelled at the intense British analysis of the actions of one captain. How they shot John Roberts but gave a medal to Robins Stick. It must have been very important to ambush and destroy the independent feelings of a single soldier if those feelings ran counter to the commands of his leader. And if they could not be destroyed, his actions revisited and commended.

While Fred Bursey was writing out this testimony defending his Captain, a telegram reached him to say that he should visit his brother in hospital. But then another telegram arrived saying Goliath Bursey had died. Goliath suffered a gunshot wound to the chest in the same attack as Robins Stick was accused of leaving his command.

Regarding the death of Goliath Bursey, their father Ruben Bursey wrote the paymaster Hugh Anderson:

> Dear Sirs,
>
> In reference to my son who died of wounds in the 9th General Hospital I'm informed that they don't get their full amount of wages when they goes to the trenches. If he got any money then I would like to get it. It's his wish as he leaved me an old broken hearted father to die for King and Country and the Freedom of the world. He was my only help.

Ruben Bursey wrote again about Goliath in April 1918:

> I had correspondence from the General Hospital telling me that his content would be looked after and sent to me later on. I would like to get something belong to him. I haven't received anything yet. I think what belong to him should be sent me. If our King would grant any war instrument belong to him I would like to get something in remembrance of him. To look at when I am alive. He was my youngest and only trust I had on earth.

Ruben Bursey was fifty-nine years old. He worked as a fire warden and still had his son Fred and another son Joseph so no pension was given after the war as there was no dependence shown.

In May 1918 Ruben signed for a package of personal effects of his son Goliath. There was no war instrument, as soldiers and returning convoys were forbidden to bring rifles back to England.

D. H. LAWRENCE

I was travelling now to a field in Belgium where a boy performed an act of courage and became the youngest soldier ever to win the Victoria Cross.

It was a bright sunny morning, with high, wispy clouds. The houses my train passed were brick with white shuttered blinds on their windows. Sometimes an entire row of houses backed onto the train tracks and the sun shone off their white blank necks.

I caught a sign that said: Muskroen Moeskroen and understood that the stations had names with two spellings now, for we had entered Belgium. In Lille there were some buildings with a modern design—buildings that look like they should topple over. But also, sheltered under a massive concrete overpass, were two well-travelled caravans and a tent.

An elderly couple was staring at me; the woman was dressed in white, with a white wimple. Her fierce pale blue eyes. The couple were Arab, and their faces were serious. The man spoke to the woman and together they moved to a table with two pairs of seats facing one another. A family of three kids and their mother sat at another. Out the window now I could see lots of bungalows, stucco and brick, with clay tile roofs. Some block stores. And then a mile of two-storey terraces.

The boys next to me with the mother were dressed the way my son dresses: in sports shirts and shorts and sneakers. Within this geography where, a hundred years ago, all was destruction, now the children are in their pleasant shorts. Spinoza tells us to understand and not be indignant, but another philosopher, Henri Bergson, begs to differ. I will write a little book on the war, I thought, because what happened to the Newfoundland Regiment happened to the entire British army and its people. The loss to Newfoundland is the same as the loss in all of the colonies—except that we in Newfoundland had no poet for the war. No Sassoon to mention our loss, no Wilfred Owen. But one hundred years later, we do have writers and I want to step in to say something—not just to reiterate Ivor Gurney's "red wet thing" but to say something of what an old war means to us now. Does it speak, and do we listen?

D. H. Lawrence, several days before the July Drive, was exempted from military service. He wrote to a friend about it, in the aftermath of the first day of the Battle of the Somme. He was thirty, living in Cornwall with his German wife. "It is the annulling of all one stands for, this militarism," he wrote, "the nipping of the very germ of one's being." He liked the men that he spent the night with in barracks in the south-west of England. "They all seemed so *decent*. And yet they all seemed as if they had *chosen wrong*. It was the underlying sense of disaster that overwhelmed me. They are all so brave, to suffer, but none of them brave enough, to reject suffering. They are all so noble, to accept sorrow and hurt, but they can none of them demand happiness. Their manliness all lies in accepting calmly this death, this loss of their integrity. They must stand by their fellow man: that is the motto."

He also said in the letter that he'd finished his novel—that would be *Women in Love*. He just had to type it and write the last chapter "when one's heart is not so contracted."

I almost don't want to add that Lawrence had a German wife. That he had been accused of being a British spy while in Germany, and a German spy while in Cornwall.

This reproach from both sides reminded me that the Germans at Beaumont-Hamel did not have it easy. The destruction went both ways. A soldier in the German infantry regiment directly facing the Newfoundlanders had this to say about the days leading up to the Big Push:

There was an unbroken stream of calls for assistance from the front line to engage these terrible means of destruction with counter fire. The artillery declared that it was unable to respond to the wishes of the infantry if it was to preserve its guns and so remain ready to fire defensively once the general attack came.

I had to shuck off this attachment to Beaumont-Hamel. I had to, like the regiment, move on to other battles. Twenty-seven killed at Steenbeek, sixty-seven killed at Langemarck. Hundreds wounded. The men buried in thirty graveyards throughout Belgium.

The train arrived in Kortrijk. I was in the land now possessed after the King had bestowed the prefix "Royal" to the Newfoundland Regiment. I took a bus for three euros into the town of Kuurne. It was a quiet town with modern outskirts, which the bus drove through. It looked like a tidier South Shields, which is where my mother is from in England. We passed white shutters and blinds pulled down outside windows. On the second floor of one house was a plastic duck on a veranda. A woman in a doorway held her new baby to see the bus.

Once in the centre of town, I walked down the old main street, aiming for the church steeple. A hearse was parked outside the church and, in beyond the old doors, a glass partition kept the wind out. I walked where Rilke had walked. He writes of wearing his old military uniform while walking in rural places—it earned him more respect, even though he had hated being in a military academy. He wrote a poem of walking and seeing a hill, and the sunlight on that hill, but the hill and sunlight are before him and all he feels is the wind.

Rilke, I had read, wanted to write a military novel.

Kuurne was quiet. To think the Newfoundland army arrived here and heard of peace. Well, it is a peaceful place. A reprieve. The regiment had been pulled from the front line after the first day of the Battle of the Somme. It spent several months retooling—that is the type of word used in the history books. As though the machine of a regiment can be removed from its work station, shipped to a repair shop, honed and sharpened and strengthened. This smothering of the truth: individuals were destroyed, never to be repaired. Then they fought eight battles in eight months.

The governor, Walter Davidson, visited the men and searched for them in French hospitals. He was arranging furlough for the Blue Puttees. But the British knew that if they gave leave to the Newfoundlanders, then the New Zealanders and Australians and South Africans would demand it next. And they did not want these men to leave the front before the Americans arrived—Americans like F. Scott Fitzgerald, who was a commissioned officer in Montgomery, Alabama. The father of the country singer

Hank Williams made it to France and fought near here and was never the same afterwards. But the war ended before Fitzgerald was ever sent overseas, and instead he met Zelda Sayre at a country club. Fitzgerald had to walk over this ground in the same manner as I have, as part of the Thomas Cook industry of cemetery tourism, in order to write his thousand words on the subject. "This was a love battle," Fitzgerald wrote. "There was a century of middle-class love spent here." And yet he gave this line to another character: "You want to hand over this battle to D. H. Lawrence."

The ridiculousness of an alternative, pacifist plan— but perhaps the only solution is to hand over conflict to people like D. H. Lawrence and Charlie Chaplin. Chaplin had entertained the Newfoundlanders in Scotland; one of his favourite holiday retreats was Nairn, five miles from where the regiment stayed in Ardersier. And the men watched his films while on leave in England. There's a short called *Shoulder Arms* where Chaplin has to dress like a tree in order to sneak past German lines and capture the Kaiser. The tree looks shattered and dead, much like the Danger Tree on the field of Beaumont-Hamel.

Kuurne struck me as ordinary, seemingly not marked or halted by events. Which is what I wanted to see: the invisible hand pushing civilization onward. This is where the Newfoundland Regiment was stationed when war was declared over.

I took a taxi out to Ledegem.

In the taxi, suddenly, I felt very moved and wiped away tears. I was beyond the trauma of Beaumont-Hamel now, but the realization was dawning on me that more Newfoundland soldiers had been killed in battle *after* the first of July than before. I had travelled too far towards peace, and had skipped the hard fighting that had accelerated over the last two years of war. I knew I had to find some place of individual conduct; and it was here, in Ledegem, where the tiny blue flower of defending your fellow man had bloomed and was honoured in the Newfoundland Regiment.

The taxi driver dropped me off in the town and I booked him to return in two hours. I asked at a nearby bar if anyone knew where to find the particular cemetery I wanted to see. The people in the bar thought I meant Ypres, but I did not. I realized I must have been one of the few travellers in the world now without a phone or electronic help. I didn't even have a map.

But eventually I found the little cemetery and walked among the graves there. The men in this place all died on the day that Tommy Ricketts won the Victoria Cross. Here were the Royal Dublin Fusiliers, a Lancashire Fusilier, a Worcestershire Regiment, a Hampshire Regiment, a Middlesex Regiment, several Royal Engineers, and down here a couple of Machine Gun Corps (Infantry).

All bright company of Heaven Hold Him in their comradeship.
The Royal Scots, 1 October 1918. J. Duncan, age 19.

At the going down of the sun and in the morning we will remember him.

And below these words: a grass mound, hens and chicks, sedum, red roses.

Something moved. Across from the cemetery was a modern bungalow. A woman ironing clothes in her garage, her young children nearby on bicycles—so very alive. They were pedalling towards a playground, wearing the gaudy colours of youth.

The end of war was here.

I picked seeds from a bush growing twenty inches tall, and plucked a white lavender flower. Tiny petals in a tower, clumps of small oval leaves on a nubbly stem.

And then I took the road, just following my nose, until I came upon an empty field behind the kirk. It was a barren stretch that had collected chunks of wind-blown garbage. I walked into it. I was looking for a field that might be the one Tommy Ricketts had run across to replenish a machine gun with ammunition. He ran a hundred yards for the ammunition and then returned to his Lewis gun, which was manned by a fellow soldier, Matthew Brazil. Any hundred yards around here would do.

Then I watched Tommy Ricketts get killed in action. For there were two soldiers named Tommy Ricketts fighting on this day in Ledegem. What must Elizabeth Pittman of Sop's Island have felt when she heard of Tommy Ricketts hailed as a hero to the country and given the Victoria Cross? And then learned, a month later, that it was not her Tommy Ricketts. In fact her Tommy Ricketts had been killed on the very same day as the other Tommy Ricketts won the Victoria Cross. In 1921 she wrote the government to ask for money enough to help raise Ricketts's sister until she was old enough to take care of herself.

A guard dog nearby started barking, then a tall young man sauntered out, stared at me seriously and waited for me to leave. His posture told me I should not be standing in this neglected field. But I disobeyed him and continued to watch Tommy Ricketts run and retrieve ammunition while twenty-three of his regiment were killed, six from his own company.

My taxi driver found me and drove me into town and I had a late breakfast—excellent lox and coffee in Center Hotel—before taking a train back to Lille.

HENRY SNOW AND THOMAS NANGLE

The work of unburying and reburying. Henry Snow signed up and was used as a stretcher bearer. His wife complained that he hasn't written in four months. After the war Snow agreed to accompany Father Nangle as part of the War Graves Commission to locate and photograph the graves of twelve hundred Newfoundland soldiers. They found, roughly, four hundred corpses. The Nangle name means to dwell in the nook, or a corner of land between two other places. And Father Nangle was in charge of this shift of souls from living to dead. The Nangle motto is: Not in voice but a wish. And it was Father Nangle's wish to create a memorial at Beaumont-Hamel for the Newfoundland dead. And he had a man named Snow with him.

Henry Snow was twenty-eight when he enlisted. On 6 June 1918 his wife was notified that he would win the Military Medal. He was decorated by the minister of militia, Adolph Bernard attended. For conspicuous bravery under heavy machine-gun and rifle fire as stretcher bearer tending to the wounded.

After the war Thomas Nangle was appointed to the War Graves Commission as Newfoundland's representative. In July 1919 there is paperwork preparing him for his new role in identifying the remains of the Newfoundland dead and for authorizing, through the French authorities, a memorial at Beaumont-Hamel. He was being paid, through the Bank of Montreal on Water Street, six dollars a day, half of which was considered a field allocation.

Nangle took the *Sachem* to Liverpool and headed to London.

He asked for ten dollars a day and for Henry Snow to be paid two dollars a day. Snow can live well and cheap, Nangle wrote, at a soldier's hostel.

Nangle, I realized, was in first class while Snow travelled third.

On 14 December 1919, his work done, Henry Snow returned to St John's. Two days later he took up work as a truckman. He was with his wife again at 30 Duckworth Street. That house is gone now, replaced with infill housing.

After the men had been properly buried and the caribou monuments were built and the Beaumont-Hamel park created, Father Nangle left the church and emigrated to Rhodesia. He married and had four children. He ran for office and was elected, in 1933, for one year. He ran again three more times, never gaining a seat. He was a farmer in Rhodesia. People called him Tim.

A REDONE FACADE

I found the bus stop in Lille that would take me to the P&O ferry terminal in Calais. There was a Frenchman at the stop and we waited together for the bus. The Frenchman was impressed with my bicycle tour.

The main avenue in Lille was lined with houses with redone facades, although their chimneys and roofs were still old. A house across from the bus stop had its year of construction outlined in brick at the roofline: 1908. I have a house in Newfoundland, I said to the Frenchman, built that same year. He understood me and nodded, but I remembered that the little life one lives is rarely interesting to a stranger.

Except when those strangers affect you.

I thought of how a soldier in this war had affected a land deal surrounding the house in Newfoundland. I had seen his name at the Beaumont-Hamel memorial: Richard Sellars, for he has no known grave.

When my wife and I bought the house in Western Bay, it came with very little land. There was a field adjacent, and I found out who might own it. Four siblings inherited it from their father. I did a check on the census reports, as there were no deeds to this land and there have been many instances along the shore of people swapping parcels of land or selling land they do not own. The siblings' grandmother, Dorcas Dalton, had been married prior to meeting their grandfather. She had been born Dorcas Crummey and, at twenty, had given birth to a child. Eighteen months later, two days before Christmas in 1897, she married Jonathan Sellars.

Jonathan Sellars died in 1906, leaving Dorcas with a ten-year-old boy named Richard to look after. Six years later, she married Jeremiah Dalton. She was thirty-seven and Jeremiah was forty. Two years after that, war broke out.

Dorcas's son by her first marriage, Richard Sellars, was nineteen now and decided to sign on. He camped at Pleasantville then was shipped to Scotland and trained through the winter of 1915. He joined the British Expeditionary Force during the first days of the Battle of the Somme. He would have witnessed, crossing the channel I was about to cross myself, the wounded returning from the July first onslaught. He was part of that draft, along with George Ricketts, that refurbished the regiment. The sight must have stunned him, as the reports initially were of success.

Sellars went missing at Gueudecourt on 16 October 1916, at the age of twenty. It wasn't until March of 1917 that Richard's mother, Dorcas Dalton, in Western Bay, was notified of his death. But then, news in May reversed that assumption. There was no body and no witness, and much confusion as to whether Richard Sellars was missing or killed. A cablegram sent in early May from Newfoundland begged for a definitive answer: Is there any hope that Sellars is alive? The reply came on 21 May: There is no evidence on hand to show that Private Sellars has been killed in action.

One thing about this dead son: six days after Richard Sellars went missing at Gueudecourt, his mother, now aged forty-one, gave birth to William Fraser Dalton. Dorcas had been pregnant while her only son was overseas. She gave birth to this second son, and then discovered that her firstborn had been killed.

This son, Fraser Dalton, grew up and had a family and raised four kids, and it was these children who were now selling their family land to me and my wife. Here was a family who owned this land because of the simultaneous birth of their father and death of their half-uncle. If not for this war, could we ever have bought that land? If Richard Sellars had lived and had a family, he would have had a stake in this land. Today, my family lives our summers on land meant for a man who fought in the First World War. For him, there was no family. There was not even a body or a grave. Just a marker beneath a bronze caribou.

We are his family.

The bus for Calais arrived and took me and the Frenchman to the P&O ferry terminal. I bought my son a little wooden pirate ship in Calais, then boarded the *Canterbury*. It was drizzly—and I thought about how the sea contains all the seasons at once.

Soon enough, I walked off the ferry and left France and Belgium behind me. I went through customs—and bam, I was back in England. The war was over. I had to make my way to London.

WANDSWORTH

I took a train to London and then the tube and stood outside an apartment complex in southwest London. This was Wandsworth, the military hospital where many Newfoundlanders went. They would tick off boxes on printed forms: am injured; have had operation; am not hurt; am on leave. Many Newfoundlanders at that time could not read or write. This fact alone was one reason why Newfoundland did not follow the lead of Iceland and New Zealand and sustain its independence after the war. It was home to the uneducated and the unlettered, and eventually, after the economic blizzard of the 1930s, it was the only dominion to voluntarily give up its independence and join another country.

I tried to imagine that history while staring at the present, and this building, which housed the Newfoundland wounded during and after the war, seemed a good place to start. Wandsworth went into disrepair after the war, and was about to be torn down in the 1950s, but then received a heritage designation and was sold for one pound. Now, here it was again before me, with fresh apartments and artistic studios, a drama school, and workshops for designers and artists and craftsmen.

During the war, Londoners were asked to be quiet around hospitals such as Wandsworth, and traffic was redirected to help keep the noise down. There were, by the end of the war, over two hundred hospitals in London that held the wounded. War, in one sense, was not over. And Wandsworth had not begun with this war, either: it had been built on subscription as an orphanage for the daughters of soldiers and marines who had fought in the Crimean War. But during the First World War it soon filled up with soldiers and extensions were built: huts made of corrugated iron and painted with asbestos. Then further extensions were added, and satellite hospitals sprang up several miles away. The system of hospitals became as confusing as the knitting together of trenches at the front. The huts at Wandsworth became known as "bungalow town." The main hospital building could normally hold only two hundred patients, but now that number was extended to five hundred. By the end of the war, two thousand wounded soldiers were sheltered at Wandsworth.

Francis Derwent Wood, a sculptor, did voluntary work here. He established the Masks for Facial Disfigurement Department—informally known as the "tin noses shop." This was for faces too badly destroyed for a rubber prosthetic. A cast was made of the face, and a lightweight mask of silvered copper was sculpted to resemble a portrait of the patient before his injury. The mask was painted to match the patient's colouring. My work begins, Wood said, where the work of the surgeon is completed. Twenty thousand soldiers were treated in this way. The masks were uncomfortable, but they did help the soldiers adapt to life back in civilization. They helped the families, too, adapt to the veterans.

Derwent Wood also sculpted "Canada's Golgotha," a three-foot-tall crucified Canadian solider at Ypres. The Germans protested this image, and some say it affected how the allies treated Germany at Versailles.

A Newfoundland soldier named Alexander Parsons was one of the soldiers treated here at Wandsworth. His father was Edward Parsons, an MHA from Harbour Grace. Alexander was a chauffeur and, after enlisting, he had been shipped over to England on the *Florizel*. He trained in Salisbury and landed in Gallipoli in September 1915. There he contracted scabies and pleurisy. And it was because of his pleurisy that he was removed in April 1916 and brought back to England.

His brother, who was a captain in the Royal Army Medical Corps, wrote to the authorities to ask if Alexander Parsons could receive a commission as an officer—he had received a stripe in the field and might get better treatment that way. A tart note came back from the hospital staff stating they made no distinction in their treatment between officers and other ranks. A sea trip, however, would be considered beneficial, wrote the medical officer. The brother replied that he was willing, at his own expense, to accompany Alexander and, gratuitously, three other Newfoundlanders suffering from "tubercule of the lung," on their passage back to Newfoundland. (There was no indication from the hospital that Parsons had tuberculosis. His ailment, pleurisy with effusion, was from exposure.)

And so Alexander Parsons returned to Quebec upon the troopship *Grampian* on 26 June 1916. Five days before the start of the Battle of the Somme.

Once discharged, in 1917, Alexander re-enlisted with the RAF, where he used his skills as a motor mechanic for the remainder of the war. Then he moved to Toronto to live along the east bank of the Don River in a Tudor Revival house—a house I've stood outside—before returning to Newfoundland where, in 1921, he was reimbursed for the customs duties on some woodworking machinery. In those years, and years since, Alexander Parsons and his family ran a cabinetmaking enterprise as well as a caretaking business. There is mention of a photography shop.

That combination of "photography shop" and the surname Parsons made me pause and think. There was a Newfoundland photographer, Simeon Parsons, who had been, like Alexander, from Harbour Grace. I looked at the records and found that when Simeon Parsons moved to St John's he gave his carpentry business to his brother, Edward. And Alexander was Edward's son. Simeon Parsons is the man who took the photograph of the caribou standing on the cliff edge—the image that became the emblem of the Newfoundland Regiment in which his nephew served.

I stared at Wandsworth, where Alexander Parsons was rescued by his brother and returned to Newfoundland. The building has a redone facade now, just like the men with their reconstructed faces. There is a stage inside, with actors who stride across it in masks.

KING'S LYNN

From Wandsworth, I took a train north for two hours, past Norfolk, and stayed at the Duke's Head Hotel in King's Lynn. The exterior of the hotel was a pale blue that reminded me of the Thompson submachine gun my father had made for me out of wood when I was ten. I realize that's a strange connection to make, but I was succumbing to these sorts of associations now that I was focused on war and weaponry. The gun my father built had a drum magazine, also wood, and was called a trench broom. It was meant for trench warfare but ended up not being used much during the First World War. Gangsters in prohibition-era movies swept these guns along the sides of black sedans. My father painted my tommy gun blue so civilians would know it was not real.

Even Sassoon remembered his childhood gun. At nine, he had a gun that "made a noise but discharged nothing." He bought percussion caps at the sweet shop.

On the train up, a young man had been listening to songs through earphones. He was, I noted, the age of Tommy Ricketts—another comparison because I was following in the footsteps of Tommy Ricketts. I felt compelled to see the site where the King invested Tommy Ricketts with a Victoria Cross. Ricketts ran across open ground to fetch ammunition and for this he won the VC. The ammunition was for a Lewis gun, not a Tommy gun. A Lewis gun is set on a tripod. My father recalls an old Lewis gun in a field by his school when he was a boy during the Second World War. There's an awkward nostalgia you have when something old is resurrected in an attempt to help you defend the present—even kids feel it. The Lewis gun was laughed at.

At the hotel I had a shower and a buffet dinner then walked down to the water. I never give up a chance to look at water. I passed a little building with an open door, and a sign that read:

FERRY STREET GYM
BOXING

Inside the open front door, I could see that the space had depth like the interior of a tent. There was a loft with a string of well-lit heavy bags. I took three stairs and entered a small airless gym with red carpeting. In the ring, there were three men and seven boys. One boy was leading with pushups and stretches while instrumental music played from a portable stereo. The youth looked hard. The roof rose taut like an opened umbrella, thick whitewashed beams not far above their heads.

I would have found this set-up attractive when I was a kid. In fact, I did much the same thing as these boys, and in a similar room. I was part of a boxing gym, and we trained and sparred, and then one day our trainer told us about a provincial meet in St John's. We went there on the provincial bus and we bought real boxing shoes in Howie Meeker's sporting goods store on Freshwater Road. I ate a fast-food hamburger for the first time. Then we fought the boys from St John's in the Church Lads' Brigade Armoury, the same building that had kitted out the Newfoundland Regiment in their blue puttees. I fought a boy named Mike Summers. Our bout was billed the "Battle of the Seasons" and it was three rounds long. Twenty-five years later, my mother sent me a newspaper clipping of a Newfoundland referee who was joining the Olympic boxing team. His name was Mike Summers. And in the story, he relates how he first got into boxing and his fight with a boy named Winter. When asked who won the fight, Summers said, In Newfoundland, winter always wins.

The building we had fought in, the armoury, burned down during a winter in the 1990s—I lived in St John's then and watched it burn and heard the flankers from the fire land on the roof of the office where I was working late. The entire downtown of St John's was evacuated. A grocery store next to the armoury caught on fire and the frozen chickens were cooked in their freezers. A string of fish and chips restaurants all had propane tanks in behind their buildings and one after another they exploded and shot high into the sky. But the fire was contained and, afterwards, the Church Lads' Brigade was rebuilt in stone and a fire station rose out of the ruins of the grocery store's cooked chickens.

I left the gym and continued walking down to the water, where I came to a signpost: *The opening of the Estuary Cut to The Wash caused this riverbank to form farther west. The common staithe made of coping stones, now inland, used to be the edge of the quay in 1855.* A staithe, I knew, is a landing area for shipping. I was standing on a wharf that had been pushed inland like the layers forming on a pearl. It reminded me of Ephesus, where the sea was now a mile away from where it once was.

At the corner I found a pub, the Crown and Mitre, and stopped in for a pint of Boathouse Bitter from Cambridge. I took my pint up the stairs into the Vine Room. The pub is laid out like a ship, with nautical tack hanging on the walls. Two men were talking about work. The cigarette is an American powerboat, one said. It does seventy knots.

The Olympic torch is coming through tomorrow, the other said, and I suddenly realized I was dead tired. I had been up since five and I could not listen to Englishmen speak of Americans and the Olympics, of power and competition. I had done my duty to the day.

I headed back to the hotel and washed my clothes in the sink. I had kept my black shirt with the epaulets in reserve to head down to the pub for dinner. Then I looked for the shirt and realized I had left it hanging in the closet in Les Galets. So I wrung out and pulled on my thinnest blue shirt and grimaced with the damp, recalling the many letters from soldiers asking for kit in Scotland to be forwarded to them while they were injured in France and England. And the men in POW camps in Germany, requesting shirts and socks and, if they were in an officers' camp, a full clean uniform.

The still-damp shirt was giving me a chill, so I ordered an iron and board. I was planning to visit the Queen's residence in the morning, and didn't want to go there with a cold.

OLYMPIC TORCH

The morning was warm and muggy so I decided to walk to Sandringham. But after a half-mile on John Kennedy Road I became worried and asked a woman for directions.

Oh yes, she said, this is the direction, but you have to pass through two by-ways.

Is it far? I asked. And she covered her mouth. About twelve miles, she said.

So I returned to where I had started, caught the bus and climbed the stairs to the top deck. The roads we travelled were decked in Union Jacks, and it was wet outside now. I would not have made it on foot. Major routes mixed with little lanes; the top of the bus smashed into low branches. It was a half-hour motor trip.

I jumped off at Sandringham and met two girls selling flags and the *Sun* newspaper for forty pence. I gave them fifty pence and asked where to eat breakfast.

There's nothing up here, they said. You're best off down on the High Street.

But I found nothing on High Street, and decided to head straight for the estate. Tommy Ricketts ate a breakfast at Sandringham, I told myself, and so will I. He had been a little nervous and hadn't eaten much, but it's rare for me to be off my feed. When I'm nervous I tend to eat more, not less. I found a bacon roll and coffee for five pounds. I guessed Tommy might have eaten something like that—or he may have had tea. Temporary coach signs, blue, were being malleted into the grass. And then I remembered that the Olympic torch was on its way. This is "the Norfolk retreat of Her Majesty the Queen" but she was in Scotland on this day, on Jubilee business. Wimbledon was on television, and Andy Murray was playing in the final eight.

At Sandringham I took the nature walk. Lovely gardens and big tall trees. A scent in the air that I could not name. I bought nasturtium seeds from the nursery, apparently from the garden of Queen Alexandra. She liked Norfolk as it reminded her of her native Denmark. I doffed my Danish hat to her gardens.

Fifty people, kids mainly, kicked their feet against the wheelchair ramp, waiting for eleven o'clock. There was a bit of rain and a bit of sun. I watched teenagers ignore their teacher who reminded them of their bags: When you turn round, keep an eye on your bag. Remember, don't touch anything.

An old man told us all: No cell phone rings, please, and no photography.

What low prospects each generation has, to rise up and fix all the damage we've done. But that feeling passed and my composure returned, and eleven o'clock chimed out and I merged into the congested entrance and praised myself for not running away. So often I am mere steps or minutes from a great museum—the Prado, for example—when some small thing puts me off. Having to wait to buy a ticket. Or realizing that part of a gallery is off-limits. The effort it takes to finish a job is not easy for me. And so forgive me, reader, for patting myself on the back for waiting to get into this building.

First, the bathroom study: this is where Prince Charles presents service medals to soldiers from Afghanistan. The Prince is colonel-in-chief of the Royal Dragoon Guards. Sometimes he stands outside on a long red box. Then he dismounts the box and inspects the troops and pins medals on their left breasts. I thought of Sassoon's important breast. The Prince is very adept at this. He will sometimes come to Toronto and visit our old fort from the War of 1812 and inspect our troops there.

We came to a deep dining room with a piano, a drawing room that holds the Christmas tree, a ladies' room and ballroom, and a secret hallway door.

On a table in the dining room was a photo of Sir Dighton Probyn, in this very room at dinner in 1910—and I felt that queer sensation of when a photo from the past is positioned in the same location today. I knew a little about the man in the photo. Sir Probyn had dealt with rumours about Prince Albert Victor, eldest son of the Prince of Wales, and his part in the Cleveland Street scandal, which involved homosexual acts at a male brothel at 19 Cleveland Street, London, in the 1880s. I knew this because after Tommy Ricketts received his Victoria Cross, he was introduced, by the King, to Dighton Probyn. And so I had to look Probyn up.

The table in the dining room could support nine extensions. The room had a pale green wall with white moulded ceilings, and a parquet floor.

A painting of birds was being parsed by our guide. Partridge, the guide said, are smaller, so their eggs are hidden, while pheasants lay larger eggs and the squirrels get them. This is why you don't see eggs in a painting of partridge.

A portable radiator painted pale green stood in the dining room where the Christmas tree would be in December. For some reason, the idea that members of the royal family were kept warm by this portable radiator cheered me up. It was only missing a nest of eggs underneath it.

Finally I struck up my courage to ask what I had come to ask. I found a guard I liked. Her name was Helen Fraser, and as she listened to me I could see her calculate and categorize and finally understand the person I was and the question I had in my mouth. The guards must have memorized all of the questions that are in the mouths of the commonwealth. They were used to providing the unconventional service; you just had to ask for it.

She took me to see Bob. He knows of the room you're describing, Helen said.

A congenial man of fifty pulled his glasses down to his chin, let them sit there and listened to Helen. His hand unclicked the plush red rope barrier and beckoned me to follow him. We walked down a hall, away from the paying citizens, to a staircase, and through a door to a small room with one high window. I felt as if someone had allowed me to walk through Stonehenge.

This, Bob said, is the King's Study.

The room had natural light from a tall window. There was a desk and several portraits of dogs, a kettle and a hot plate. The dogs in the paintings were Borzois. There were bagged lunches on the desk—the clenched rolled top on the paper bag lunches struck me as so new and ephemeral here among the king's dog portraits—dogs that looked like they hadn't been stared at in a hundred years. You can feel that, when a painting has been starved for eyes. This is where we have our tea, Bob said.

The room was mostly gutted of original furnishing. There was a clothes rack so the guards could store their coats here. In a glass cabinet were samples of ship's rigging. On a wall beside the door were brass knobs that might have been used to signal someone in a far-off room of the castle. The paintings and the window and the paraphernalia stored by the guards made me realize that this is what happens with history: someone is always throwing a coat or a bagged lunch over the old stuff, confusing the archaeologists.

I stood by the window and looked out. There was a six-foot-tall gauge in the garden meant for reading the temperature. The King would have stood here where I stand and noted the weather. And so, I thought, I am the King.

The King in question, George V, was born in 1865—a neat hundred years before me. He was the grandson of Queen Victoria and the younger brother of Prince Albert. His brother, who would be king, was engaged to Princess Victoria Mary of Teck. But Prince Albert died of pneumonia during the great influenza pandemic of 1892. He died here at Sandringham. George, the younger brother, and Mary grew close during the mourning and he proposed to her in 1893, a year after his brother's death. In 1901 Queen Victoria died and George's father became King Edward VII. That same year George and Mary toured the British empire, including a visit to Newfoundland. This tour was to reward the dominions for their participation in the Boer War. This was the year Thomas Ricketts was born. George's father died in 1910 and George V reigned until his death in 1936.

When Thomas Ricketts met the King, both men had lost their older brother.

The thermometer, made by Negretti and Zambra, is in Fahrenheit and centigrade. The King stood here and looked at the temperature while Tommy Ricketts ate his breakfast. A cold day in January. It was snowing in parts of England.

It would have been a comfortable breakfast. The study is off the main room, now called the saloon, and the people I had left were just there, behind a wall with a fireplace.

That, said Bob, pointing at the wall I was looking at, was the original ballroom. When more people came to live here, they built a new ballroom. And this door was camou-flaged so you wouldn't know the King had a study here.

I stood beside the table where Tommy Ricketts had eaten his little breakfast before being invested with the Victoria Cross by King George V.

I thanked Bob for the tour and returned to the saloon to see the hidden door from that side. And there it was: a fine outlined perimeter of a door concealed in the wallpa-per and the mouldings.

Outside, vendors were selling postcards and I found one with the hidden door. For my son. *In behind that door*, I wrote, *is where Tommy Ricketts ate his breakfast with the King.* As Tommy Ricketts toured the gardens, Queen Mary picked a white rose and gave it to him.

I walked past kids parked on the grass and people lining the road, all waiting for the Olympic torch. The kids had paper torches with orange paper funnelling out of the top. These had come as free inserts with the *Sun* newspaper. I wondered if any of the children would keep their torches for souvenirs, tuck them in the back slip of a photo album, and their grandchildren a hundred years from now would find them and think, think what? What would they think?

1916 had been an Olympics year. The games were sup-posed to be held in Berlin. It wasn't until April that people realized the war was not going to end and the games were called off. In a strange way, you can see the preparations for the Battle of the Somme as a substitution for those summer games. Near the end of the war Pierre de Courbitin met with his Olympics committee to set up a games for 1920. Antwerp was chosen. Hungary, Bulgaria, Austria, Turkey and Germany were not invited.

I thought of Eric Robertson, a Blue Puttee, who asked permission to run for Newfoundland in the Olympic marathon. There's a photo of him at Stob's Camp, in Scotland, kitted out in athletic gear. Fair hair and blue eyes. It's as if he spent the war thinking about the 1916 Olympic Games, and when they were cancelled he gunned for 1920. He played the drum in the regimental band. He needed thirty pounds for the Olympic entry fee, he wrote, and had been training for three months. But there were paperwork problems, since Newfoundland was not recognized as an independent country, so in the end Robertson ran for England.

Arthur Wakefield had sporting conquests too. After the war he joined the 1922 Everest expedition as a medical doctor. He was forty-six. He witnessed, through binoculars, the avalanche that killed the seven men with George Mallory. "The whole wall was white, and there was no string of ascending climbers." At the 1924 Games the expedition members all received an Olympic medal in alpinism. Wakefield lost his religion after the war, and kept the windows wide open in all weather and "never hugged his children".

Eric Robertson, in Antwerp, finished the marathon in three hours and fifty-five minutes, or thirty-fifth out of a field of forty-nine—last among those who finished. His war wounds were bothering him but he refused to get into the ambulance. Robertson had been shot in the leg with three exit wounds. After his Olympic run, he was commended "for playing the greatest game of them all"—fighting in the war. War was still being judged as the final, grandest form of sport.

I believe that type of statement should carry with it a jail term. Robertson fought at Gallipoli, where he suffered dysentery and a perforating gunshot wound to his right leg. He fought at Beaumont-Hamel. He was laid up in Wandsworth and was diagnosed with syphilis after a Wassermann reaction turned up positive. He was discharged in August 1917 and returned to St John's, but remained employed by the regiment as a masseur.

It was a cool wet day in August in Antwerp—a good day for a marathon, much like today at Sandringham. Though there was no torch relay back then. The theft of fire, I thought, for the benefit of civilization. Prometheus means forethought. I waited in a line along the road and then the line wavered and you knew there was a commotion not far off. People were bending their hips and necks into the road. Finally, bobbing over the tops of heads, the torch arrived. The real torch, compared to the paper torches, was fully alive, and its bearer, wearing a pennant and number, ran past with some urgency, as though the animated quality of the torch might be doused in the light rain. She turned and headed into the estate. It must have been something to have that torch of fire inside.

BOY IN THE GLADE

I walked along and peered into a small outdoor museum—a warehouse full of cars. The beauty of wooden panels on shiny dark green enamel. When cars were still pretending to be horse carriages, the way the Egyptians built furniture ending in an animal's feet. This was the Daimler belonging to Queen Mary, a car she used for shopping. The museum offered up the history of the royal family through vehicles. Well, I thought, I am walking and I shall search out my own history through nature. I followed my nose into a flower garden and crossed a little stream. It was the same width, I judged, as the Ancre. On the other side was the Glade: a brook in which stood a four-foot stone boy, all green, grey and charcoal. He was carrying over his head a large pail and water poured perpetually from the pail. You are supposed to walk in a flow past this stone boy, but I paused here. There was something about this boy that had echoes of things I'd already witnessed on this trip. A classroom of kids saw me staring, and stopped to look at the brook as though it must be important.

Kid: What's in there?

Another kid: Water.

On my way out, I came across a monument to the war dead—a twenty-foot cross surrounded by chain that looked like elegant barbed wire. It appeared to be a First World War memorial, so I had to walk completely around to see. Yes, it was dedicated to the Sandringham Company—a company that was wiped out at Gallipoli. They had entered a woods and not a soul had returned. Not even the company flag was brought back.

Sandringham was part of the Norfolk Regiment. Bernard Ayre was with that regiment and killed on July first.

I asked a gardener to direct me to the church that held Prince John's grave. It was up a slope through a gap in the wall and into another garden. As I stepped through the gap, I admired the brickwork in the wall: loose, small, brown flat stones in mortar; stones like large Weetabix; and then framed in proper brick, the top, bottom and sides with rounded cement caps. The British exported this type of wall around the world. There are corned-beef facilities in Uruguay surrounded by these walls. Beef that fed the British army—a million tins a day.

Inside the church I spotted a revolving carousel with postcards, indicating that I must be in the right place. I asked a minister where I might find the gravestone of Prince John. I was thinking of a song by Al Tuck, the line: "in the days when the people were small and few." It's a song that tackles history, but really it's about the singer's girlfriend walking amongst the graves, and his perplexity at her interest in the past.

There are two princes buried here, the minister said, both named John and both died very young. This is why no prince in England is given the name John. They are on the east side of the church. And he showed me around the corner. There was little John, who lived for one day in April 1871. He was directly under the stained glass window. His pink granite looked so new I thought it must be refurbished. The minister understood my suspicion. That stone wears well, he said. It could be original.

Like he was buried yesterday, I said. One day old, that's what keeps your headstone new.

I thought of the little teddy bears many of the soldiers carried in a tunic breast pocket, the head of the little bear staring up. I had visited a museum in Toronto that was full of these bears. They were given by loved ones and when the soldier peered down, he had a loving, loyal face staring right up at him. In an adjoining gallery, after the bears, was the shock of a colourful, praying Hitler. He is kneeling and gazing up at Christ.

That is what happens in a graveyard, too. We look to heaven, waiting for a visitor to peer down on us. It is a terrible punishment to be buried staring at the earth, not facing the sky.

Against the church wall there grew tall purple-and-white foxglove. And next to the one-day-old John was the John I was looking for:

JOHN CHARLES FRANCIS
FIFTH SON OF
KING GEORGE V AND QUEEN MARY
BORN JULY 12, 1905
DIED JANUARY 18, 1919

The gravestone had a Celtic design. *And in thy kingdom he shall have rest.*

This Prince John, this boy of fourteen, had died the night before the investiture of Tommy Ricketts. Prince John took things literally. He was told, after the death of his grandfather Edward VII, that dead people "went on the wind." Days later little John was seen collecting leaves.

What are you doing? someone asked.

Collecting grandpa's pieces.

He had a fit early in the morning and died late that night. The family mourned and then the next day the King bestowed upon Tommy Ricketts the Victoria Cross. It must have been awkward for the King, to see this young man who had signed up at fifteen. To see this beautiful young soldier awarded the highest honour of valour, while in a room not far off his own son lay dead.

There was a story that Cluny Macpherson, the Newfoundland Regiment's doctor, told of Prince John. In 1911, Macpherson oversaw the laying of the first stone of the King George V Seamen's Institute in St John's. The laying of this stone was to be done on the day of the King's coronation in London. The governor of Newfoundland, Ralph Williams, was to read aloud a proclamation from the King. Cluny Macpherson thought about this and wondered if the King himself could lay the stone. The King, on his way to his coronation, could press a button in Buckingham Palace and send an electric signal through the Anglo-American underwater sea cable, a signal that would jolt a mechanism that laid this first stone. The button could be anywhere, reasoned Cluny—even hidden in a wall as the King walked to his coronation.

The Palace, to the amazement of Ralph Williams, agreed to this plan.

The night before the coronation, it rained heavily in St John's. In a trial run the next morning, the mechanism for laying the stone malfunctioned. Macpherson raced to a corner store and bought a ten-pound tub of butter and liberally applied the butter to all the mechanisms except for the electrical ones. He got the contraption working again just as the coronation began. A gong had been set up to go off when the stone was laid. As the governor said a few words, the gong sounded—and to everyone's relief, the stone was laid.

A few years later, Ralph Williams was in England to meet the King and young Prince John came in. You were the Governor of Newfoundland? he asked.

Ralph Williams said he was.

I saw the button, Prince John said, and wondered—what if I had pressed it beforehand? Would it have worked?

Ralph Williams said he didn't know; only Cluny Macpherson knew the answer to that question.

Now I was standing before the grave of this young Prince, the boy who probably did push the button at his father's coronation—the boy who had died the day before Tommy Ricketts was invested with the Victoria Cross.

After visiting the church, I tried to leave Sandringham, but there was now a crush of people lining the roads. Buses are leaving at half three, a driver told me. You could try walking to Derbyshire and finding a bus there. So I started for Derbyshire, but then thought: What am I fighting against?

I returned to Sandringham for leek soup and fried haddock. I took it easy. I observed people waving Union Jacks with "I saw the flame" printed in black on the red horizontal bar. And I thought of Thomas Ricketts having his breakfast in the King's study. The red upholstery.

The King had been staying at York. The Queen was notified of Prince John's death and the King was sent for.

They had a cry. The Queen wrote of her sadness at her son's death. Then the next morning Thomas Ricketts entered the ballroom and was invested with the Victoria Cross in what is now the saloon. He shook hands with Sir Dighton Probyn on his way out. The King remarked, One of the oldest surviving winners of the Victoria Cross has just met the very youngest.

LONDON

Back in London, at the Swiss Cottage youth hostel, I did a load of washing. My jacket and jeans were stiff with sweat. I thought about how the men in the regiment had boiled their clothes to kill the nits, and sometimes wore their shirts inside out until the lice crawled around to the other side.

I emailed home. My father had good news: I had received an either-sex caribou licence, in the area that I like. So I'd be hunting in the fall.

I walked from the South Kensington tube stop to the Ritz, looking for a spot to eat, but I couldn't settle on any of the shiny flanks of modern buildings. It would be like eating in a bank. At Sainsbury's I picked out a sandwich, a pop and bag of chips for three pounds. Just to tide me over, I thought, but soon it seemed this was what I would have for dinner. I ate en plein air. *Esprit de corps!* I thought, to cheer myself up.

In the morning I ate the hostel breakfast and purchased from a teller an eight-pound travel card. It felt strange to be whizzing about on trains again, after days of biking. A lot of the men at the front did this: went on leave and returned to London, bought new clothes and visited relatives in parts of England. A bicycle moves the farmland around.

I took the packed tube to Kew Gardens. The tennis player Andy Murray was in the semi-finals at Wimbledon now—I discovered this when I took the Wimbledon train for a bit, surrounded by patrons of tennis with a day of professional sport ahead of them. Next to me, standing, was a couple. She was blond, about thirty-five, well dressed. He was mixed race, handsome, younger, with a good shirt cuff and watch. He was helping her. She may have been drunk. But she was in love with him. It looked like they were still dressed in clothes from the night before and hadn't yet gone to bed. She wanted to have sex with him. She swung into his chest and pressed him against the plastic wall of the train. She wasn't looking at him, or looking at his shoes. Her eyes were closed. Then she bent her head and he whispered into her blond hair. He was urging her to behave, or perhaps to misbehave. Her head under his chin, she had both hands now at his new belt, as if to unbuckle the belt. The train was crammed and I was next to them but they had made a little island for themselves. It was as if they were the British Isles and we were the rest of the world, politely ignoring their antics. Except I had been away from love for too long and so took a vicarious interest. There were many young men in suits—striped blue shirts and dark shoes and trousers with a tapered front or a little curve. The trouser leg here was still shorter than in North America. Three of these men held printed sheets and were going over talking points, with one ear straining to hear what the man and woman were whispering to each other. We had all been recruited into their illicit behaviour.

At my stop I had to ask the woman to shift over so I could remove my bag from under her feet. The man casually lifted one of her feet with the side of his shoe.

Watching this couple, seeing their desire for each other's company, made me incredibly lonely.

I walked towards signs that indicated the National Archives and found myself in the company of nine women and two men. We were forming a little platoon, all marching to arrive at the archives at the stroke of nine. I signed up for my reader's card and did a fifteen-minute tutorial online. The original Newfoundland regimental diaries were here and I ordered them. Meanwhile I found a series of wounded/captured testimonials. Photocopies were twenty pence each. I read bureaucratic statistics of the numbers of men who had enlisted from Newfoundland

and how that compared to the rest of Britain's former colonies. The purpose of these notes was to counter the notion that Newfoundland was not "rowing its weight in the boat" in terms of numbers of men signing up. Close to two thousand Newfoundlanders served in the Naval Reserve and there were a hundred and eighty fatalities. Many of these men's names were listed on the memorial at Beaumont-Hamel "for they had no grave but the sea."

Rowing its weight. I remembered how oarlocks back then were thole pins—a pair of pegs in the gunwale that kept the oar steady. Thole means young fir. But to the Scots it's a word that means to endure, and both definitions apply to the young Newfoundlanders.

I pored over numbers and names and statistics and troop sizes and divisions. When war broke out the Newfoundland male population was 123,239. Category A—men who were fit to serve—totalled 30,816. The number serving was 4500.

These general overviews formed a blizzard of paper that travelled over the ocean and across the land to generals and colonels, and then back to the colonies in the mouths of returning soldiers who toured the outports to drum up enlistment. These files full of papers also formed a collective experience that allows historians now to say things such as "they were the generation that supplied men for the wars" and "those who survived returned home to work in the factories."

But sometimes a fact will pop out of this neutral display of numbers, this tide of human affairs, and it's like in books on chess when a grandmaster has made a surprise move, and the dry notation, which looks like columns of letters and numbers, is accompanied by an exclamation mark. The exuberance transfers from the page to the researcher. The exclamation mark occurs in your mind. And in this vast acreage of a room, hundreds of people were working with the past, their heads lit with wonder. I was struck by the fact that we were all working at the same flat elevation. Historians might say of us: We were the generation that supplied labour for the dissemination of historical records.

A woman with a very good camera took stills of her computer screen, I guess to save her the expense of the twenty pence. She was attractive, partly because she was working. I've always found industry and concentration alluring. I thought of Elsie Holloway back in Newfoundland, taking pictures of the regiment and even of her own brother. And how she must have reacted to receiving the telegram one day that her brother was killed.

While I waited for the regimental diaries, I found in a census for 1911 my own grandfather, the one who served in the Second World War. He was aged two in the census. Walter Hardy. He was a toddler being held in someone's arms as he was counted and the street address noted, the town and county. A person had come to my great-grandparents' door with a sheet of census paper, and written down the boy's full name and his age, this boy who would grow up through the Great War and marry and have a daughter who was evacuated during the Second World War and marry and have me, who grew up through the Cold War. And this old man, my grandfather, who was two on this piece of paper, would mail me comic books full of the wars that he had grown up on and fought in. Exclamation mark.

The regimental diaries, I could tell from the photocopies I was making, were wrapped in fragile paper with a handwritten title on the cover. Inside, the pages had a printed header:

WAR DIARY

OR

INTELLIGENCE SUMMARY

and on every page INTELLIGENCE SUMMARY is crossed out. These pages were part of a punch-hole binding, filled with the careful print of the commanding officer.

I spent the day at the archives and photocopied enough material to cover the entire floor white. But the original diaries I never got to handle. Someone had taken them out before me. Somewhere, across these several well-lit acres of industrial study of the past, a set of eyes was reading about the Newfoundland Regiment. It was the only fact I could not research. Who. Reading was the only activity in the room not ordered or catalogued.

I took the tube back to my hostel and asked a stranger where I might buy toys. She pointed down the street. To Hamleys. Three storeys of toys. This is the oldest toy store in the world. Hamleys was here during the First World War, and had a hard time of it as foreign toys were not allowed and Germany was the largest producer of toys. So they sold domestically made dolls wearing khaki clothes and tanks and wind-up submarines. I remember my mother telling me that, during the second world war, she had a doll made of pottery and one side of the doll's head was smashed. She used to cover that part of the head with a blanket.

I bought a bag of army men, a volcano that uses baking soda, a flashlight with twenty-four NASA pictures, a dart board with magnetic darts, a mini tabletop football set, and a pair of walkie-talkies with two nine-volt batteries. The toys of violence and geologic change and competition and distant territory.

I walked through Trafalgar Square then and petted the enormous lions at the base of Nelson's column. The lions were sculpted by Edwin Landseer. Their tongues were hanging out because he had never seen a lion, so he copied the posture of his dog. This was his first sculpture.

The last commander of the Newfoundland Regiment, Adolph Bernard, was married in this Square. Bernard was not a Newfoundlander, but the first officer from the regiment to command. By then the war was over. Bernard's medical condition was poor: bad teeth, loose bowels, no energy. And on the first of June 1921 he married Maud Harris of St John's. He was supposed to marry her in St John's, but he could not get away from his post here in England. So there was a reception in St John's and an eight-year-old Gordon Winter, future lieutenant governor of Newfoundland, "looked very smart as a page." Then Maud Harris sailed to England and was married at the Church of Saint Martin in the Fields, just over there. Adolph Bernard was in his forties. He lived another sixteen years. They had a daughter.

I walked west to eat in South Kensington. I was starved and tired and carrying a bag of toys. My bottom lip felt sore from windburn and sun. I heard, up the street, someone yell. From a large Hummer limousine, a young woman was stretched out the window. She blew a kiss to a man standing and riding hard on the pedals of a rickshaw. A number of people were impressed with this and clapped. It was dusk.

I ate at a packed oriental canteen—the whole square in behind South Kensington was very nice, and it was much better to eat here than near the Ritz, which was polished and buffed like the wood in Queen Mary's car. There was an open courtyard, with tables on the paving stones. It was modern, but it harkened back.

Two men with rented Barclays bicycles tried to cross a busy divided road. They nudged the front wheels of their bicycles into the street while traffic swerved around them. They were looking for hesitation. Finally, they forced a black cab to brake and they sauntered over to the divider to join the traffic heading that way.

I finished my dinner and took a little walk into Hyde Park. I thought of Tommy Ricketts being feted in London after his investiture. The news of his being the youngest man ever to win the Victoria Cross was printed in the *Daily Mail* and the *Daily Mirror*, and he became a much sought-after man in London. He attended Drury Lane Theatre as one of Sir Edgar Bowring's party for the Prisoners of War and Men in Hospital fund. His name was brought into the pantomime as a gag—a penalty of fame. Drury Lane, built a century before, housed three thousand people. Bowring's party saw a production of "Babes in the Wood," which was taking over from the waning "Shanghai." It starred Stanley Lupino, Lily Long and Will Evans. There were goblins and cross-dressing and fairies and slapstick comedy. There were moments when the audience was expected to join in the chorus. What did Tommy Ricketts think of all this?

I stopped in front of the Peter Pan statue. George Frampton created it just before the war: Peter flies out of the nursery and alights beside the Long Water. The author of *Peter Pan*, J. M. Barrie, was disappointed with the sculpture. It doesn't show the devil in Peter, he said.

Barrie had modelled Peter on a boy he knew named George Davies. And then George Davies grew up and joined the army and was shot to death in March 1915. To die will be an awfully big adventure, Peter Pan says in the book.

I found a suede top for the woman I live with. There was something aboriginal about it, but London too. Wild and urban at the same time—that's the type of woman I'm with.

It was dark now and I walked down towards the Thames. London is not one big city, I thought; it's fifty little Londons all living on top of one another.

IMPERIAL WAR MUSEUM

The next day I walked to the Imperial War Museum, which is on the south side of the Thames. The wide waterway was full of trade. I passed a full-scale replica of Francis Drake's ship: the *Golden Hinde II* is one of those floating museums covered in kids and period costumes. It lures tourists through its proximity to Shakespeare's Globe Theatre. I thought hind "deer" and drake "duck." Drake's motto: Virtue is the safest helmet.

The Imperial War Museum. Here resides all of the machinery of several centuries of war. I looked at planes and cannons and tanks from all eras, and I felt I was experiencing, in three dimensions, the disorienting sense of reading my childhood comic books. Every war the British had fought was sitting here one top of the other. I read labels and posters and escaped to the Somme battlefields which was an interactive display with examples of trenches and models of men in battle stance.

What do museums do? Marx said that the tradition of all past generations weighs like an alp upon the brain of the living. Decades from now we will attend theme parks and don the attire of the infantry and experience shrapnel and whiz-bangs and trenchfoot. We will understand, in a safe environment, what it's like to walk over no man's land. The Imperial War Museum was pursuing that type of interaction with the infantry. The word "infantry": does it refer to the Spanish princess, the infanta, who led an army to victory? or is it derived from the Italian infante, meaning youth? The infantry began warfare before firearms were invented. They used shields and long spears. You joined the infantry because you did not know how to ride a horse. You were a foot soldier.

The museum was screening a film that was shot over the first few days of the Big Push, a film that was first released in England in August 1916. *The Battle of the Somme* begins with horses. The horses are led, with affection, to tall troughs of water. The horses's eyes are covered in fringes to protect them from dust and flies. Excited dogs approach the marching prisoners and the Germans are given cigarettes and water and several of them double back when they realize there is a movie camera. A British medic does the same, pulling out his long curved pipe from his pocket and, while moving around, keeps his face square to the camera to make sure he is in the frame. The pipe may not be his but something captured from the Germans. It is hard to believe he would march to the front with sixty-five pounds of materials and this large ornamental pipe. This medic stays in the picture and, unlike today if you take video of someone (most people think you are taking their photograph) these soldiers know the mechanics of moving film and they mirror the cinematographer, winding a hand at their ear as John McDowell handcranks his camera while panning across the men. The camera, which we never see, is in a narrow wooden box on a tripod. McDowell is interested in men and their machines, the various sizes of the bombs, the dugouts, and how the men form a team to move large wheeled cannon and use pulley ropes over the wheels to double their momentum. He is interested in bombs exploding in the vast empty land between the British and the German lines. The French houses that have been shelled and gutted of their glass windows and tile roofs. Everything torn to reveal structure.

This is a scene out of Walter Benjamin. His description of rural men fighting at the front: "A generation that had gone to school on a horse-drawn streetcar now stood under the open sky in a countryside in which nothing remained unchanged but the clouds, and beneath these clouds, in a field of force of destructive torrents and explosions, was the tiny, fragile human body."

There are several action scenes of men entering battle and yes these scenes are probably edited in from training camps and the most famous scenes of men going over the top of the trench are re-enactments, but what could be a genuine document of an event like this? There are millions of pages of first-hand descriptions and memoirs and histories by historians who repeat the same numbers and facts as though they themselves came up with these conclusions and nothing is as accurate or real as these clear unadorned images of dead British soldiers in ruptured soil with fractured tree trunks sheared off like wood that has been savagely harvested in winter.

The film includes footage of an advance of British troops over open land, moving right to left in the frame as they descend an incline. From where the Hawthorn mine exploded this advance could be the Newfoundland Regiment. You see the soldiers fall after they hit the barbed wire. They are funneled to gaps in the wire and the Germans are training their machine guns on these gaps.

Half of Britain watched this film that was shot over ten days in early July 1916, they watched it a month later. It is one of those most viewed films in history, and no one seems to make these films now. Have we seen ninety minutes of footage of Afghanistan taken in the same way as this? There are various regiments here and the monograms on some caps suggest Newfoundland is one of them. The monogram is so distinctive, the profile of a stag caribou with his full antlers. A caribou prepared for rut. There are good scenes of General Beauvoir de Lisle on a magnificent horse instructing the men before the July first advance.

Owen Steele discussed this great advance the British were to make and how proud he was to be a part of what, he thinks, is the beginning of the end of war. He is caught up in the historical future, of being a segment of something large—a Waterloo for their generation. They have fished and started careers and married and had children and built houses and woken up in ports in various parts of the world, but a war is something else and a man like Owen Steele senses this is part of becoming a man and a nation with its place in history and he is honoured to have a part in that placement. They are proud and they are loyal and duty-bound and Owen Steele takes his command seriously—the Newfoundlanders are the only colonial troops present for this Big Push. Owen Steele is not selected for battle but kept in reserve and lives for several days after July 1 before being killed far from the front by shrapnel from a random shell. In his remaining days, healthy, he writes not a single word about what happened on that first day of battle, he merely jots down the numbers of the dead and wounded.

DINNER WITH CHURCHILL

I thought I should see my English agent.

My plan had been to walk to her like a foot soldier, but I was late so I took a cab. We got stuck in traffic and I thought, Why on earth am I meeting a literary agent when I haven't a book or the sense of a book? But I remembered that this did not stop the filmmakers who shot *The Battle of the Somme*. The driver remarked that he didn't get Newfoundlanders often. That's because we take the bus, I said. The bus, he said, is in your DNA. But sometimes, I added, we hang the expense.

I tipped the cabbie well and removed my jacket and changed shirts right there in the warm street. What do I care, I thought. I don't know anybody. I shoved an arm into the sleeve of my newly washed blue jacket that a Frenchman in the Somme had thought made me look so typically English. I would see this meeting through. I found the agency in a little back alley. It looked like a one-storey garage. Perhaps I had written the address down wrong? I had thought the address so posh. A mews. Then I realized: this is what a mews is. I was in London, where every square inch of the city has been turned into usable space.

How many times had the Newfoundland officers visited London, and the regimental headquarters at 58 Victoria Street? This was where Hugh Anderson had worked and shipped out letters and packages and managed a considerable volume of overseas correspondence. This was the home of the Blue Cross, too, which helped rescue horses in wartime. The London Society for Women's Suffrage—advocating for a woman's right not only to vote but also to work—shared this street address. The Newfoundland trade commissioner had operated out of the building, and it soon became the centre for correspondence and pay for the Newfoundland Regiment. Sometimes the men, like Leonard Stick, requested to join the Indian Army, or asked for furlough, like George Tuff. Many members of the first contingent, the Blue Puttees, had not returned home after three years of war. Some others were denied leave by Hugh Anderson, "through their own fault." Which meant because of venereal disease.

Home for those men was twenty-five hundred miles away. Incredible to think that a man could leave the front and get back to London, then take a train to Southampton and sleep six days on a ship for Canada, find a train back to Newfoundland and spend ten days shooting birds around Kelligrews, then return to England on board a troopship and be part of a draft that took him back to

France before the war was over. And then be shot and killed. But this happened to some of the Blue Puttees.

When I entered the mews, my agent, Zoë, asked me what I was reading. I pulled out of my knapsack the letters of Frances Cluett and the memoirs of Jim Stacey. I described the only time Jim Stacey wore his gas mask—to collect honey from a bee hive. Diaries, I said, are so much more in touch with contemporary life than potted histories.

They remind you of the truth, Zoë said. Of what must be tried.

And she asked me what I was writing. I explained this little book on the war. How my narrative wends its way in and out along the shoreline of history and modern life the way the tines of a caribou's antlers branch out and then return again towards their source. When I finished and saw her hesitation, I said, The way it comes together in the end all depends on a few things. For instance, there was a man reading a book at the Imperial War Museum called *Dinner with Churchill*. A title like that can sell a book.

But not *Walking the Fields of the Newfoundland Dead*, Zoë said.

How about *Breakfast with King George*? For I had told her the story of Tommy Ricketts and how, near the end of the war, when he heard his name was being put forward for an award for action in the field, he received a letter from Seal Cove—from his father, complaining that now that he was out of incarceration he had no money. His eldest son, George, was dead and Thomas was somewhere in France. Why was Thomas not sending his allotment to his father instead of to his sister, Rachel, who was married now?

Tommy Ricketts could not read or write, so he heard his father's letter read aloud, a letter that had been dictated in the first place, for his father had told his troubles to the local minister. Tommy Ricketts signed his mark and the allotment was transferred over to his father. A month later Ricketts received word that he was to be on his way to England to have breakfast with the King.

Yes, how to sandwich moments of war with moments that happen during peace? I thought of that scene when Helen Mirren, playing Queen Elizabeth II, is surprised by a stag in the movie *The Queen*: the queen of civilization meeting the king of the wilderness. Or the poet Sassoon, and how his work is so powerful because he has moments where his high class of living—a batman! champagne!— happen alongside the slaughter all around him. What would be this book's moment?

I thought of other ways people had lived through the war. Like Sir Edgar Bowring who, in his fifties, had used his position as a businessman to help the Newfoundland Regiment. He had put his name forward for committees and associations that raised funds for hospital beds and biplanes and Christmas chocolate. But I don't make the mistake of thinking the rich got off easy. Edgar Bowring himself suffered loss. His grandchild Betty Munn drowned on the *Florizel*, the very troopship that had carried the original Blue Puttees and many other drafts of men. The *Florizel* had returned to being a passenger ferry and made a mistake in navigating the southern coast of Newfoundland. It foundered on the rocks outside Ferryland during the winter of 1918. The survivors were rescued from the wheelhouse. There was not much room there to survive, a witness said, but plenty of room to die. What did Bowring do? Beyond grieving the loss of his grandchild, he commissioned a cast of the Peter Pan sculpture I'd seen in Kensington Gardens and installed it in Bowring Park, St John's.

The papers on the desk behind Zoë made me think of the cabinet notes I'd seen in the Imperial Museum describing what the British army might expect in manpower from the dependencies. Draining the Commonwealth to pour brute force upon the Germans. Before the war, such calculations had been made about raw material exports. And now Zoë mentioned that the British had traditionally had a right to the book market in the Commonwealth. But eventually the terms had changed to a thirty-day window in which the British could publish a book in the former colonies or forfeit the right. She was talking about books, but the principle was the same—a shadow of a former structure that had ruled the world.

My visit with Zoë was pleasant and I was glad that, at some future date, she might remember the man from Newfoundland in the little blue coat that a Frenchman thought was so British.

I set out to return to my youth hostel, on the way stopping into the British Museum. When I was twenty-two and coming home from Egypt with a foot infection, I'd had an overnight layover in London and managed to limp my way through the British Museum. Now I went to see the caryatids again and relive my youth and folly. On the way out I was struck by a room full of paintings of dogs. They were big black and white Newfoundland dogs. One was called *A Distinguished Member of the Humane Society*: a Newfoundland sitting on a seawall with his front paws hanging daintily over the edge. He had saved twenty-eight people from drowning. I had forgotten the name of this type of dog and then I saw the painter: Edwin Landseer. And remembered that these Newfoundland dogs were called Landseers because of the painter. And now I could see that this magnificent dog here on the seawall had the same posture and structure as Landseer's lions in Trafalgar Square. Still another painting showed a large galloping Newfoundland called *Lion*. I looked closer: the background was the same Scottish mist and mountain crags that appeared in Landseer's painting of the stag in *Monarch of the Glen*.

SASSOON AND THE MERSEY

I had an extra day before my flight home, so I took a train to Liverpool to see Knowsley Park, where Lord Derby had trained the first Pals battalion for the new army. Liverpool was where Eric Ellis returned after shooting birds in Kelligrews. And while these fields and ports were interesting, I remembered Edward Carter Preston. Preston designed the death penny given to families of dead soldiers. He had, I was told, some sculptures in the Anglican cathedral here.

In the entrance, I was welcomed by an odd, cheery bronze Christ by the artist Elisabeth Frink. Inside the cathedral was an incongruous Tracey Emin pink neon sign:

I FELT YOU AND I KNEW YOU LOVED ME

And then I saw what I was looking for: the sculptures by Preston. He'd spent thirty years on these figures. This was after he had designed the death penny. Five inches in diameter, these bronze plaques were presented to families well into the 1930s as soldiers died of injuries suffered during the war. It is difficult to say who is the last soldier to have died in the Great War. Even the most decorated soldier in the British army, Bernard Freyberg—the man who began the scrutiny into Robins Stick's activities at

Cambrai—ended up dying, in old age, of a wound from the war that had never properly healed.

Preston called his design for the penny "Pyramus." The name comes from a story in Ovid's *Metamorphoses*. There is a crack in the wall between houses where the lovers Pyramus and Thisbe live. This story is also the origin of Shakespeare's *Romeo and Juliet*. Pyramus and Thisbe whisper their love to each other through this crack and promise to meet at the tomb of Ninus under a mulberry tree. Thisbe arrives first but is scared off by a lion that has freshly killed something beforehand, and she leaves behind a piece of clothing stained with blood. When Pyramus arrives he sees the blood. Thisbe is dead, he thinks, and so kills himself. Thisbe discovers her lover's dead body and decides to end her life. Because of this, the gods changed the colour of the mulberry fruit to the stain of blood.

And the sculptures here did not move me. Except to make me think of the dead as sculptures. The sealing disaster prompted the idea of the frozen body. And the memorial figures I was passing by had the same deathly quality. Nothing matched the life I had seen in that caribou.

Now, I thought, I could return home. I walked over the Mersey and peered down at this wide expansive river, and remembered that Sassoon was garrisoned here at Litherland. He wrote a letter condemning the war, then tore off his Military Cross ribbon and threw it in the Mersey. He was disappointed with how light the ribbon was, how his action created very little effect.

HOMECOMING

London. I took the Gloucester underground to Victoria and the slow Gatwick train to the airport. My flight home was three hours late taking off. I waited and watched as a little girl lifted her foot out of her shoe. A man stroked the adjustment knob on his rucksack strap. Another yanked out the retractable handle on his wheeled carry-on suitcase—the sound, I thought, like the bolt action of a Lee-Enfield.

Finally we got on the plane and, once we had achieved altitude, a steward dispensed, from a blue tray, a hot wet napkin. He used tongs. He reassured a Middle Eastern woman that her special meal was vegetarian. I was sitting next to a woman of Caribbean descent who was reading a bible study much like the material my mother reads.

Two Muslim girls in front of me had their hair covered and both wore jean jackets and fancy sneakers. One was twelve, the other about eight. The eight-year-old just sat on her mother's lap. The twelve-year-old had a blue headscarf of thick material, with silver studs in a diamond pattern on the forehead. Then a yellow fabric of looser, thinner material over the blue turquoise one.

We flew back home, racing the sun, and I read my little memoirs of the First World War. We hit turbulence where the Gulf of Mexico mixes with the cold Labrador current. We were over a sea full of bright icebergs.

We continued through the day and gained hours as we pushed the nose of the plane westward ho. Then, with the sun still behind us, we descended into Lester B. Pearson airport in Toronto. It was Pearson who had won the Nobel Peace Prize for resolving the Suez Canal crisis, and who is considered the father of peacekeeping.

I found my way to the city bus that took me back to Kipling Station, and so at last I returned home to my wife and son and our little apartment. The leap he made into my arms. He had his postcards that I'd sent him lined up on his windowsill. Did you see the secret door? I asked and yes he found it. We unpacked his little toy soldiers, figures that were perhaps from the second world war, and we lined them up and I described how the Battle of Agincourt was won.

TORONTO

Over the next year, my wife and I threw all our resources at a mortgage, declared total war on our finances, and bought a house in Toronto and renovated it. I was trying to commit to life here, and my son had started going to a French school. I walked and bicycled around the neighbourhood, studying the place, to get a sense of where I might grow old and where my son would become a man.

There's a man in British Columbia who designs camouflage patterns for the Canadian army. He's also provided hyperbaric chambers for professional hockey teams. If you do a deep search for him on the internet you see that he's staked claims to helium-3 mineral rights on the side of the moon that faces earth and challenged Stephen Hawking by suggesting that you can change the direction of time's arrow. Guy Cramer is now working on an invisible cloak for the military. The cloak obscures the target from thermal imaging by turning the human shape into background noise. He's made an orange disappear.

I thought of him as I watched, with others, some modern Canadian soldiers on parade in our neighbourhood. A woman carrying a bag made out of a rice sack was taking a photograph of these soldiers as they marched past the Elderly Vietnamese Society building that was gutted and now being rebuilt. There used to be tangerines and geraniums in the Vietnamese window and stacks of magazines and new immigrant information and a poster of an eastern god that had slowly turned blue from the sun. The woman pulled an apple from the rice bag and started to eat it while taking photos, as though the camera were propelled by fuel from her combustion of the apple. The building was dressed in scaffolding and the woman stood still with her weight on one leg. When I asked her if she knew these soldiers she said one of them was her sister and she pointed— the soldiers are stationed at CFB Petawawa.

They were all wearing the Guy Cramer pattern of computer-generated pixels, the type called temperate woodland. Cramer is working on material that will break up the pattern of a soldier's joint movements, the knee and elbow while walking, so as to make the target harder to detect. I was hunting with my father once, and we shot a moose. We gutted and quartered the animal. Then we each hoisted a quarter onto our shoulders. While carrying the animal to the truck on the woods road, my father stopped and turned and asked me not to follow him so closely. From a distance, my father said, we look like a moose.

It shocked me, this realization of the two of us carrying the sides of a moose, close together, mimicking the very moose that had lived and breathed on this marsh. Cramer has fabric that is light sensitive so that it changes colour as you step from sunshine to shadow. He's also written about the Americans possibly bouncing rays off the moon that could strike underground targets in Russia without using nuclear explosives.

That is where our soldiers and army are these days, I thought, as I took the subway to the Toronto Research Library to read General Haig's private diaries and Beauvoir de Lisle's reminiscences of sport and war. De Lisle wrote, in 1939, that Neville Chamberlain will be remembered for pushing onward civilization. There used to be a call for a duel and two men would have to undertake it or be ostracized. Now that notion is ridiculous. So, too, de Lisle thought, Chamberlain's quest for appeasement will one day be looked upon as a brave and civilizing concept for governments. What a gutsy, sobering thought to consider in 1939.

The library is at the corner of Yonge and Asquith. George Yonge was responsible for administering the British Army a few hundred years ago. Herbert Asquith was the Prime Minister of England during the First World War. Yonge Street is a thousand miles long. Asquith Avenue is less than a thousand feet.

When I wasn't in the library I was destroying the house—gutting it, they call it. Just so we could fix the wiring and plumbing and remove asbestos and knock down a foundering chimney and insulate the attic and move a few walls around and hammer on a new roof. The house was built just before the war, and I would think of the people who lived here then. Sometimes I took a break in the backyard. My son was tossing sandbags into various-sized containers, I had told him the number of points for each and he was getting the range. The neighbour, a woman in her eighties, was planting a garden. I could see little slats of her between the wide broken fence palings. She was bending over, coaxing the vines of some vegetable plant up a trellis. But it was hard to see her. I had to stitch together strips of her from through the fence. The fence was ours, built by someone even older than my neighbour. The husband and wife who owned our house were from another culture and country—and we have been erasing them from the electoral lists carried by door-to-door canvassers. They probably moved here to avoid a war, or to recover from the effects of a war. Political refugees and displaced persons. I have not heard the neighbour speak a word of English. And somehow this fractured portrait of her through the fence is accurate to the modern predicament. It is the spatial equivalent to the broken shards of the past that we receive in touring the land where events occurred and the museums where evidence of those events are now compacted.

THE PEOPLE WHO WERE MURDERED FOR FUN

And yet we still had the place in Newfoundland.

In the summer we returned. And the drive from St John's to Western Bay is a hundred minutes, which is exactly how long it took me to travel, by train, from Amiens to the end of the war in Kuurne. We passed the little towns of Topsail and Bell Island and all the little places along Conception Bay that provided men for the war. The last surviving soldier of the regiment, Wallace Pike, died in Bay Roberts—the birth-place of the first man to be recruited, Leonard Stick. Pike was born in 1899 and died in 1999. He was a boy in Millertown which is in the very heart of the island. Millertown is on Red Indian Lake, which is the last home of the Beothuk. The Beothuk had been driven from the sea coast and beaten from the rivers and hunted deep into the interior until they finally died here in the heart of the island sixty years before the birth of Wallace Pike. There's a magazine article about their extinction called "The People Who Were Murdered for Fun." Pike worked in a lumber camp and joined up in 1917 because he had friends in the army. He was sent to Scotland and then saw action at Cambrai. They were outnumbered and, out of a hundred men, only nineteen survived. Wallace Pike had four friends. Now he had none. He made a vow that if he survived the war he'd devote his life to God. In the last month of the war he was wounded in the hand by a shell. The doctor wasn't sure he could save the hand. Pike said he didn't care as long as he didn't have to go back to the war. When he woke up he was surprised to see that only part of his hand was gone. After the armistice he returned to Clarke's Beach and went to church and the minister spoke about reneging on vows. Pike remembered his vow. And so he joined a new army, the Salvation Army, and spread the word throughout the country of Newfoundland. He was awarded the Legion of Honour, from France, in 1998.

COLEY'S POINT SURRENDERS

We drove past Spaniard's Bay and a little graveyard to the left; it's a new graveyard and they have eleven graves all placed in the southwest corner. At Harbour Grace we saw a little boat on its way out to the *Kyle*. We had heard on the radio that Kelly Russell was going out there to read his father's poem, "The Smokeroom on the *Kyle*." And there he was. I slowed the car down to a lookout spot and shut the engine and rolled down a window. Then we all got out and I sat our son between us on the hood of the car for him to experience a little bit of Newfoundland culture. My son was born here but neither of his parents were. The little boat circled around the great shell of the steamer and a rope was secured and figures climbed aboard.

The *Kyle* is an old passenger boat that was used to truck fishermen down the Labrador coast to prosecute the Labrador fishery. She ran aground here in 1967 and was a rusty hulk for years. But recently they've painted her up, though the interior is in hard shape. She was built in 1913 in Newcastle upon Tyne. During the war the *Kyle* was used as a troopship ferrying Newfoundland soldiers on leave, from New York back to Newfoundland—Jim Stacey had used the *Kyle* to get home from the war.

The first Newfoundland casualty of the war happened on that vessel. Sampson Hamel of Muddy Bay, Labrador, fell ill on board and saw a doctor in Bay Roberts. He visited some friends in Coley's Point, went unconscious that night and died the next day. As the historian David Parsons points out, once Hamel boarded the *Kyle* for military service he was considered on active duty.

There was a clearing of an amplified throat. Then a loudspeaker. And the whole harbour was filled with Kelly Russell's voice:

Then tales were told of gun barrels bent
    to shoot around the cliff,
Of men thawed out and brought to life
    that had been frozen stiff.

Kelly's father, Ted Russell, was born in 1904. So he was too young for the war. He would have been fifteen when the war ended. But he must have thought to himself, while the war was still on and conscription had been brought in, that he could be sent over. He grew up in Coley's Point. And there are a number of connections to the war from that small town.

If you look at Coley's Point on a topographic map it is like the torso of a man surrendering, his two arms above his head. Those arms are peninsulas of land that stretch out past Bareneed and Beachy Cove, all around Bay Roberts. Dozens of men here volunteered for the war. Strange, I thought, that Sampson's family name, Hamel, is the same as the place of Newfoundland's worst military tragedy.

The *Kyle* was named, as ships were named then in Newfoundland, for a Scottish town. When war broke out, the *Kyle* was immediately used to ship men from along the shore to St John's for military training. My grandparents were alive in Newcastle when the *Kyle* was built, they were children. My father told me of my grandfather, who worked in the shipyard during the Second World War, being proud of the *Mountbatten* and seeing her sail down the Tyne. And then hearing her bombed and sunk and having to go and remove the dead soldiers from the burning hull. How it affected him. How it affects me to hear it.

A FENCE IS NOT ALIVE

We piled back in the car and headed for Western Bay. The house is along a dead-end road towards an abandoned community and an automated lighthouse. As you drive there, parts of the modern world melt away and I feel, in my heart, that I'm living closer to whatever one might call a traditional life. I'm suspicious, of course, of what is traditional. Instead of buying my son a toy pistol, I cut him out a wooden one with the help of a coping saw. We planted the seeds I'd found at Sandringham—the nasturtiums—and some other seeds from cemeteries. We dug trenches and laid down seed potatoes. Later in the summer you hill them up, and when we did that I felt like we were artificially burying the past. But the past grows up through.

There are fences here that require tending, and I caught myself feeling disappointed that a fence can't take care of itself like a tree. The fences here are made of stakes and rails that are the trees themselves, with their branches limbed off with an axe. The trees have not been processed further, and look very much like themselves. And yet their ability to heal themselves and grow has been extinguished. The Christmas tree and the maypole are extreme examples of a fence that pretends to be alive.

The trees at Beaumont-Hamel take care of themselves. No one paints the leaves or varnishes the bark or replaces a rotten root. All this effort poured into cemeteries. A reminder that nature and our inventions are distinct classes of matter. The army makes every effort to break this sense of renewal. And yet, when the mind cracks they send you out at dawn and shoot you. Or leave you in the wire overnight screaming your head off. They have no interest in the blue flower of the mind, the forget-me-not of the self.

Our little cemetery at the end of the road, everyone in it died before the war. The last date I can find is 1899.

A fence can be said to keep animals out, to delineate property, but there is a poacher's quality to a fence too—it tempts one to scale it. A fence encourages an invasion or an escape to an activity that, prior to the fence, was merely meandering. The Newfoundlanders at Beaumont-Hamel were shot carrying lengths of bridge to ford trenches and breach barbed wire and those lengths of bridge were like sections of fence. There was an old letter we found in the Newfoundland house, the man worked as a cook on a delivery boat. He said he should be home, for the fences need mending. It was the time of year to fix fences.

Newfoundlanders are used to seasonal activity. Even now they work sixty hour weeks in Alberta or three weeks straight on the offshore and then return home to play hard with their snow machines and heavy-duty trucks and all-terrain vehicles. The origins of this modern behaviour are in the seasonal work necessary to survive here: during the fall they piled aboard coastal steamers to fish the Labrador. They entered woods camps in winter and they hunted seals in the spring. They had homes during the summer fishery out along the headlands and then, before winter blizzards hit, they returned to homes sheltered in the bottom of the bay. They hunted game and snared rabbits and kept gardens and built cellars to store root vegetables through the cold months. Sheep grazed, everyone had a cow, a horse was given a boat ride to the tall grass on an island. There are roadsigns in Newfoundland for places like St Jones Without and St Jones Within—traditionally, the same community, just a people involved in seasonal transhumance. The winter houses were built differently, with porches that were meant to be filled with firewood. The summer houses did not have these porches, but bigger kitchens on the back so the heat of the cooking stoves could escape the house.

So the temporary nature of a war, of digging a trench or living from rations and sleeping in tents, this was all understandable, tedious and short-lived work. War sounded like a seasonal activity mixed with a sense of loyalty and a promise of steady money, an adventure with a duration no longer than Christmas. You return home with medals and valour and French luxuries for under the tree. There had been older wars that were more like the wars we've had very recently, limited wars.

No one knew yet of total war. First they had to melt off all the novelty and exhaust the latest strategies and the generals and the politicians searched their pockets for facts and the only truth that came up after the colossal failure of the first day of the Somme was this: we have the numbers. There are more British and French and Russians than there are Germans. But then the Russians became Soviets and withdrew and the Americans were hesitating. The English called it a war of attrition and the Germans called it a war of material.

A SOLDIER VISITS WATERLOO

I spent a few weeks in the museum in St John's called The Rooms. The museum stands upon the archaeological remains of a star-shaped citadel built in the 1770s to protect England's fishing interests. I looked at photographs and read letters. I found an original package of blue puttees in their wrappers—the wrapper has two little orange foxes. I thought of Hitler's dog. The attestation papers of the soldiers are full of height and weight, hair and eye colour, and identifying marks—scars or tattoos. The only reason to note these things is to identify a body or locate a person who has run away.

One day the archivist handed me a box with four boy-scout notebooks in it. Stacked together, they were smaller than a deck of cards. A tiny pencil was slipped down through the back binding of one of the books. The inside covers had symbols for distress signals and tools to remember before venturing into the woods. Quick notes on how to read a map and how to allow for magnetic variance in a compass. These were notes that instill adventure, for a campaign that should result in thistle scratches and a nosebleed and wet clothes.

In these notebooks a soldier named Eric Ellis wrote about his experiences during the war.

He spent those years in Scotland. He took musketry lessons and other studies involving gas attacks and the firing of mortar shells and the throwing of bombs. There were tactical procedures involving a red side and a blue side, and exams to write. He was kept back from the front to train other soldiers. He visited museums and the Robert Burns monument. He noted officers wearing crepe after Kitchener's death by drowning. In a former skating rink he watched movies with a Miss Dunn. He made identity tags for the boys before they were shipped over to France and he bought a pair of boots from a soldier accompanying a draft. He took part in trench digging. He read newspapers from home and learned of the *Florizel* being shipwrecked off Ferryland. He ate breakfast with women working in a munitions factory and played Klondike whist at parties. You can throw a stone clear across some sections of the Clyde, he noted; and he described how Nellie from home had given herself an awful cut on her foot from a hayfork. In a parcel he received a piece of wedding cake.

Ellis managed to stay out of the war entirely until the very last month, when it was obvious the Germans were surrendering. That's when he crossed over to Boulogne, stayed in the Hôtel du Louvre and took in the sights. He boarded a slow train to Calais and met up with some of "ours" and went to the cinema. It was 7 November 1918 and civilians were celebrating at night, singing and flying flags. The armistice terms had been completed but not yet signed. He met a nurse from Bishops Falls, stationed at the

10th Canadian General Hospital, while the Germans met with General Foch. He caught up with Captain Sydney Frost and heard about Frost's Military Cross and the loss of five hundred Newfoundlanders, mostly wounded, during the last twenty-eight days in the line. The regiment had advanced eighteen miles. They had gone over the top six times and had taken Ledegem station.

On November tenth, Ellis reached Ledegem. Beautiful scenery, he noted. He passed through the recent fighting zone and saw villages and towns shelled to pieces.

On the morning of November eleventh, the weather was fine and cold. The news broke widely that the armistice had been signed. The day was declared a full holiday, but Ellis noted that there was very little excitement. He stayed at a coffee shop near headquarters and was billeted in a place where a German was buried in the garden.

A week later, he finally joined the Newfoundland Regiment. He marched in their parades and he was brought before the commanding officer for not stamping his letters at six o'clock, as required. He received a lecture from his commanding officer, Arthur Bernard. "He is anything but a gentleman," Ellis writes in his diary. "Spoke about me sitting at the depot for two years doing nothing, and getting well so suddenly."

On the twenty-third of November the regiment advanced towards Germany, and they took a sidetrip to see the battlefield of Waterloo. They got a lift in a truck and it cost one franc to visit the museum. There was a painted mural, Ellis writes, of the entire battle of 1815. You climb stairs and from a landing you experience the battlefield in the round, with the foreground littered with the bodies of horses and the dead. It was most beautiful. This Waterloo panorama had been painted in 1912 by Louis Dumoulin. This long-ago battle with Napoleon impressed Ellis greatly—he was thrilled to be on the very ground where an ancient battle had taken place. He understood, suddenly, what war must have been like. This was his first experience of war.

And there I was, in this museum, reading of the Newfoundlanders visiting a museum a hundred years ago, a museum dedicated to a battle a hundred years before that!

THIS WAY TO THE MUSEYROOM

Thomas Hardy did much the same with his long dramatic narrative, *The Dynasts*, which depicts the last years of Napoleon. At the Battle of Waterloo Hardy describes the English arising from their bivouacs in the morning, the "red dye washed off their coats from the rain." Both Wellington and Napoleon are forty-six and they can see each other through field glasses. It was an era when the spyglass was not yet outstripped by rifled bullets.

Wellington disapproved of soldiers cheering as it was "too nearly an expression of opinion." He called his soldiers the scum of the earth for breaking ranks at the Battle of Vitoria.

What's amazing about Hardy's account is his inclusion of the women near the rear guard of the action. There are a group of women who seek their husbands, and once these men are dead, they continue to help the wounded and dying by shredding lint to use as dressings. There's a surgeon's horse "laden with bone saws, knives, probes, tweezers" and a woman who has just given birth. A man rides in with his face falling off in red. Hardy describes the light flashing off fixed bayonets and the armour of cuirassiers, the flash of priming-pans and muzzles, and the "furious oaths heard behind the cloud," the "steam from the hot viscera of grape-torn horses and men." Hardy's "stage directions" are fantastic. When an aide asks Wellington for relief he replies that every Englishman afield must fall "upon the spot we occupy, our wounds in front."

Thomas Hardy visited the camps of soldiers during World War One. He saw the Australians but also the German POWs. He went to Salisbury and must have witnessed the Newfoundlanders training there. He wrote *The Dynasts* when he discovered that Wellington's top colonel was from Dorset. The Newfoundlanders have an immigrant connection with Dorset. Hardy would have heard men with the accent of his grandparents. Frank George, the relative who was to inherit Hardy's estate, was killed in Gallipoli just before the Newfoundlanders arrived. It was, in fact, because of failures in Gallipoli that the Newfoundlanders were sent there to assist the 29th Division. George's death brought the Newfoundlanders into Turkey.

In the Great War, instead of wives seeking their husbands all along the front, there were brothels. This was one bonus for the stalemate of trench warfare, the establishment of brothels. And while the men were buried with no distinction made between officers and other ranks, they did not share the same brothels. Other ranks went to "knocking shops" that had a red lamp hung outside. Officers received a blue light package, which contained condoms.

Impressions. Hardy wrote of impressions, that "poetry rested on seemings, not convictions." Often, history is convictions that have been fleshed out with details that might give, in retrospect, the appearance of seemings. That's the kind of book this is. There will be no battle narrative here. The kind of book I am after is one Siegfried Sassoon might enjoy reading.

For aren't we all solitary creatures, in the end? After community and nation and family, in the small dark hour of the night, aren't we but lonely individuals which the army obliterates to form some machine that can service the guns and tanks and weaponry of war? Forgive me, but I aim to break down the patriotism, the false honour, the received sentiment, that vast fatalism that total war pours upon the soul. I want to highlight the trouble in the brain, the reason why so many men cannot speak of what happens in the theatre of war. The absurdity of this campaign, and the tragedy of dramatized recreations that aim to honour the sacrifice of men to some greater ideal. The words we are asked to chant are "never forget" and remembrance. And the politicians would have you believe that it is the dead we should not forget. I will say one last outrageous thing. It is not the dead we should remember. It is the atrocities that occur when men in charge throw individuals in to war and kill them for some idea. It is this we should never forget.

Sassoon, just before the Battle of the Somme, carried a volume of Hardy to the front. He read from it there. Sassoon, while the Newfoundlanders were destroyed, "came back to the dug-out and had a shave." At ten o'clock in the morning he ate his last orange.

Eric Ellis's first taste of battle—Waterloo—was over in a day. The bodies lay where they died. An artificial mound was built from the ploughed remains of the war to commemorate a twenty-three-year-old prince who had been shot in the shoulder. Steps led up to a statue of a lion looking towards England. From there, Ellis wrote, one could see the original battlefield for many miles. Hundreds of officers of every rank took in the sight.

When the Duke of Wellington returned to Waterloo just two years after the war, he said disapprovingly, "They have altered my field of battle."

Eric Ellis arrived back at his billet around noon. He watched an old man of about seventy take a wash in the river.

COLOGNE BRIDGE, 1918

Over the next few days, as the regiment marched towards the German border, they met some prisoners of war who said they had been badly treated. They'd had to work behind the lines. In the villages, people had hanged dummy Germans from their houses. At one stop, the Newfoundlanders went to a skating rink and ate dinner in the road. The regiment crossed the Rhine on a pontoon bridge. On the other side, the shop windows were filled with toys for Christmas. They were led by two mounted soldiers, Adolph Bernard and Arthur Raley.

Bernard and Raley were English school masters at Bishop Field in St John's. They had been on vacation in England when Britain declared war. They took the next sailing back to St John's. Scotland, Gallipoli, France. It was Arthur Raley who was on the telephone and received the order for the men to advance at Beaumont-Hamel. He thought it was a very bad order. The grass was long that time of year, and he lay in it and watched the Regiment get mowed down. It was Raley who described the soldiers bracing themselves with an advanced shoulder, as they did in a snow squall back home.

They crossed the Rhine into Germany and a photograph was taken of them with Raley and Bernard on horseback. It is one of many photographs of various regiments crossing the Rhine in preparation for occupying Germany. They were used as Christmas postcards home.

They arrived at Hilden and the lady of the house where they were billeted put away, bit by bit, everything of value she owned.

I lay down Ellis's little notebook and stared out the large windows that overlooked St John's harbour. A harbour is much like a salient, I thought. A safe salient. This very piece of sea in which the regiment had floated at anchor overnight while waiting for the Canadian convoy back in 1914.

VICTORIA CROSS

I picked up Eric Ellis's diary and kept reading. Two days before Christmas, the Newfoundlanders learned that Tommy Ricketts had won the Victoria Cross—the only man in the regiment to do so. There was much cheering. On Christmas Day, the men were up early and took church parade. Some received holy communion. The officers appeared to have no use for the men. The King was not toasted. Mick Nugent was the only one to give a proper speech. On the whole, Eric Ellis wrote, the worst Christmas I ever spent.

Mick Nugent was forty-two when he signed up. Black hair and brown eyes, he was married and had a family of twelve to support. He fell ill after Gallipoli and missed the Beaumont-Hamel catastrophe. In June of 1918, he was part of the sports day for the Newfoundland Regiment, overseeing a sideshow stall. He asked Hugh Anderson for advice on buying one hundred coconuts at Covent Garden for a coconut shying event. He survived the entire war.

Matthew Brazil was another Newfoundlander who joined up early and lived. He was a miner, almost six feet tall, and weighed 165 pounds. From reading the records in the museum, I got the sense that Matthew Brazil enjoyed himself while he could, but also looked after the men that were in his company. One of those men was seventeen-year-old Tommy Ricketts. Brazil was wounded in the face and leg, had a scalded hand, and was gassed at the very end of the war. He was afflicted with recurring bouts of gonorrhea and was hospitalized because of it for eight solid months. Brazil, I imagined, took to heart Lead Belly's bread-wagon song: "when the boys go over the top, he won't be dodging shotgun shells but doing the eagle rock."

Captain Sydney Frost was the officer who wrote up the citation selecting Tommy Ricketts for the Victoria Cross. But he also put forward Brazil's name, and it may have been decided by others in the British army that Matthew Brazil was not the man to represent the Newfoundland army and shake the King's hand.

EDWARD JOY

I left the archives to walk around the city. I was looking at houses where a soldier had returned unharmed and, adjacent, the mourning family of a soldier who had perished. I thought about the way military operations get written about by civilians. The way historical events are treated with the bias of hindsight. The revisionism of one's modern place and the translation of the past into an experience relevant to contemporary life. Even a forty-year-old describing the thrill and fear of a twenty-year-old. Who am I to judge and weigh and pooh-pooh?

They loved it. The food was better. The hours at the front were not long. They saw the world. They brought home other perspectives. They broke the class system. Promotion was earned and not bestowed.

A lot of the city has changed. There is a whole section in the center that was demolished in the 1960s and the great concrete bunker of City Hall was built. My first job after university was working with city planning. On the first of July the mayor had invited all municipal workers to join him in singing "O Canada." But it was raining. The rain kept everyone indoors. Everyone except me. I felt patriotic and hang the weather, so I sang, in the rain, on the City Hall steps. I sang "O Canada" and then sang, for it was July first, the bits I remembered of the "Ode to Newfoundland." The mayor and his aide finally did come down the stairs but they noticed I was alone. They turned around and walked away.

I phoned the mayor about this, about being gutless and not singing, in the rain, with an employee. Who is this? he shouted into the phone, and I hung up. But the call was traced, and the next week I was handed my pink slip.

I stood in front of City Hall and remembered that first job, and how I had realized then that the development of a city is methodical and planned. Scale models are built to attempt to predict traffic congestion and housing needs if certain economic factors occur. Buoyed with research, I thought too of Sergeant Edward Joy, who was one of the last of the Blue Puttees to go over to England with the *Florizel*. He was born and grew up on this hill, which was the central slum of St John's, on a street that no longer exists. City Hall, Mile One Stadium and the two hotels stand on the hill that was Joy's neighbourhood. His attestation papers describe his colouring as "fresh." During his training in Scotland in early 1915, his conduct sheet is peppered with reprimands for being absent from tattoo, absent from church parade, fighting in barracks, absent from coal parade, drunk and disorderly, creating a disturbance in camp, using obscene language and violently resisting arrest. When I read these judgments I was filled with pride for the individual who could not be broken. Joy then fought for four years and saw action in Gallipoli and Beaumont-Hamel and Gueudecourt. He was decorated for bravery at Monchy and Marcoing (a bar to his Military Medal). My God, he survived everything. In a letter to his father, the chief staff officer wrote that "During an attack when his own officer was killed, Joy took charge of his platoon and showed the greatest courage and leadership in encouraging and leading his platoon. His personal example was the greatest asset to the whole company."

In May of 1918 Joy found himself returning to Newfoundland for four months on Blue Puttee leave. He was home, he was alive! He caught a cold while in St John's and got more ill on the trip back to England in the reinforcement draft of late September. He disembarked in Devonport on 12 October 1918, wrapped in blankets. The blankets were returned to the ship. He died of pneumonia two days later, and is buried in the Plymouth cemetery.

In January of 1919, Joy's parents received their son's medals and a letter which expressed regret that their son "will not be able to have the honour of wearing them."

SPANISH FLU

Influenza is what killed Edward Joy, and it had spread through St John's during the last year of the war. It went from neighbourhood to neighbourhood, much like I was walking now, and Edward Joy had returned home to catch it. The virus crept through the world killing more people than had died in four years of fighting. For twenty-four weeks during that summer and fall of 1918, the virus travelled through armies and civilians alike. It may have been the cause of the final collapse of the German army. It certainly prolonged the peace talks, as many of the officials detailing the negotiations became ill or were still recovering. The elderly, usually the first to be killed by the flu, were generally spared: they had survived the Russian flu of 1892, and so carried some resistance.

This flu had a strange process: a cytokine storm caused those with a strong immune system to react more violently than those with a weak system. The bodies of fit young soldiers were struck at a greater rate than any other group. This was a puzzle. During peacetime, when someone is very sick they remain home and do not have much interaction with the general population. Those with milder symptoms continue on with their day. In this way, the milder strains of the flu get disseminated through the population while the more severe strains are treated in isolation, and those patients die at home.

In the war, when a soldier was struck ill he was transported from the front to a hospital in the rear. Along this route he came into contact with many people before landing in quarantine. A soldier with mild symptoms remained where he was. Therefore the aggressive strain of the flu was passed around far more widely than the milder strains.

The virus caused a violent reaction—and the stronger the immune system, the worse the reaction. So it killed the young. War governments censored the press, but in neutral Spain news about the outbreak was allowed to be published. The flu was called Spanish because the world heard of it mostly from Spain.

I walked down to the harbour and saw a restored schooner from the White Fleet docked where the *Florizel* had docked a hundred years before. The Portuguese used to fish the Grand Banks and then tie up at the harbour right up into the 1980s. Tall wooden ships receiving provisions and the fishermen took rest in this lively port. There used to be a sign posted in Bannerman Park that said:

PROIBIDO JOGAR FUTEBOL

The Portuguese sided with the Allies in March of 1916, and a year later sent fifty-thousand men to the Western Front. Seven thousand were killed in the war. The hull of this vessel was now decked out in steel. I climbed aboard and stared at the city. It is always nice when you live by the sea to be on the water and look back on the place where you live. It makes you, for a moment, a stranger.

I had a clear view of the courthouse on Water Street. The building looks exactly as it had when it was built in 1904. But I knew that every stone in the exterior of that building had been removed and sandblasted and repaired or replaced. This was where John Bennett had addressed the citizens of St John's on the resolution recording its "inflexible determination." A year later, from the Colonial Building near Bannerman Park, the fallen heroes of Beaumont-Hamel were honoured. There was a giant naval and military parade. In front of the Colonial Building, between the pillars on the top stone steps, were the German machine guns captured by the regiment at Gueudecourt. A parade assembled at the Church Lads' Brigade and marched to the Colonial Building. "It was the largest gathering of citizens ever seen to assemble at the Colonial Building. And while honouring the dead there was much to be proud of." The premier, Edward Morris, said that this celebration, he hoped, would inaugurate an anniversary to be cherished by future generations.

Governor Davidson sent a message declaring his wish that July first become a national holiday for Newfoundland. This will be the day, Morris said, we celebrate, when our heroes fell facing their foe. He compared Beaumont-Hamel to the passing of Thermopylae for the Greeks and the holding of the Bridge by Horatius for the Romans.

Davidson, educated in England, resorted to the history lessons of his school years, when the British Empire searched for classical examples of expansion that would excuse colonial behaviour. But he preached these values on the steps of a modern world devastated by these attitudes, to a population no longer convinced by this method of conduct.

William Lloyd of the Opposition drummed up the proud reputation of being "better than the best." He spoke of the war as a struggle of endurance, and brought up the submarine menace, and the tonnage problem.

The band rendered "The Banks of Newfoundland" and the parade made a tour through the city, returning to the Church Lads' Brigade Armoury where it was dispersed.

Morris had written a letter to Prime Minister Borden praising the Canadians on their Jubilee—their fiftieth. Morris wrote that the Canadian people are their greatest resource.

The very next year, 1 July 1918, was another mammoth parade but "very little bunting." People came not to cheer but to remember their fallen sons. "They did not attend the parade to have a gay time." The new governor, Charles Harris, insisted that it should be "primarily a commemoration of the fallen and not an occasion of rejoicing." James Moore had suffered a gunshot wound to his head at Gallipoli and a gunshot wound to his thigh at Beaumont-Hamel.

Both of his legs were sheered off below the knee by a shell at Gueudecourt. He spent a year at Wandsworth and then two artificial limbs were fixed for him and he was sent home. He was there, in his house at 31 Duckworth Street, all dressed and waiting for someone to come help him with his crutches, but he was forgotten for the parade.

That was two years after Beaumont-Hamel. Beaumont-Hamel was to become Newfoundland's defining moment as a nation. The historian Robert Harding writes about this attempt at celebrating the July Drive. Like Vimy for Canada, Beaumont-Hamel was our statement to the world that Newfoundland had arrived as an independent nation. The political powers were determined to make July first a day of nation-building.

Until Confederation with Canada. And with confederation came a revisiting of the tragedy of Beaumont-Hamel. To what it is seen today—a symbol of how we lost a generation of young men who could have risen to power and made Newfoundland strong and viable. Instead, the destruction of the regiment was the beginning of the loss of our status as a self-governing nation. We sat on our bed, crutches at our side, waiting for someone to take us to the parade on the very day the rest of the nation celebrates Canada. And there we mourned our stripped independence.

James Moore's house was a five-minute walk from the Colonial Building.

The war ended. On the next anniversary there was a terrific attendance at a shrine in Bannerman Park. The event was close to the signing of the Peace Treaty "in which," the governor said, "we hope to find the inauguration of a finer and better age." Newfoundland was not represented at that peace conference, but this celebration "has been the spontaneous act of the officers of the Regiment itself."

Charles Harris brought up Thucydides, who records a speech in which Pericles pronounced a eulogy over those who had fallen in one of the wars of the Athenian republic. "That was not an isolated event," Harris said. "It was the regular practice of the Athenians, the most striking historic instance of a powerful democracy, to appoint a regular day in which they could commemorate the virtues of those who had given their lives for the State."

RICHARD SELLARS

We often travel on the first of July to spend our summers in Newfoundland. We have a guidebook and I've tried naming all the wildflowers. Every year I learn the local names of all the things that bloom here, and then, through the winter, I forget them. Truth be told, I've even forgotten the family tree of the people who have owned this house, and I would have to consult this book to recall how Richard Sellars is related to the land I am now standing on.

We bring on the plane to Newfoundland the potted Christmas tree we had in Toronto—kept alive through the winter—and plant it in the barren acre of grass behind our house. This way, our son will have a memory of his Toronto Christmases when he visits Newfoundland. "There," he will one day say to his children at the height of summer, pointing to a grove of spruce and fir. "Those are my winters in Toronto."

Our house in Newfoundland dates to 1908. It was built so that the family of George Loveys could move out of his parents' house. George and his brother Ormsby, who is listed in the census of 1912 as a carpenter, worked on it.

When we bought the house it had no running water. We went to visit Nellie Loveys, ninety-seven years old, who had been born in the house. We told her we had a son whose first nights on earth, after being born in the hospital in St John's, had been in the house she'd been born in. I asked her where the well was. Oh, she said, we always meant to dig a well.

So what did you do for water? I asked, and she mentioned taking a bucket to the brook. I went to the brook at the back of the property and almost didn't make it back. My feet found, hidden in the brambles, an old dry bed of stone where a brook had run many years before.

The house is on a small parcel of land with community pasture in behind. To the west is land that used to have a house on it—you can see the foundation still and, in amongst the rocks, a ceramic door handle, a rusty hand-forged nail.

We needed the land if we were to put in a well and a septic field. And so I set about hunting down who owned it.

If you talk to the old people of a place, they will tell you very specific stories about who owns what and how fields were swapped—someone might need hay for a horse, while another family would like a vegetable garden. A bit of this kind of thing happened with this land. It is how I found the story of the Daltons and their uncle, Richard Sellars. I walked over the field of Richard Sellars where we had dug a well and rocked over the well and added good soil and planted the seeds I had collected from cemeteries all over the Western Front. I walked over this land and understood how the story of Richard Sellars had affected me, and I felt I should get to the origins of Newfoundland's larger personal story. Which meant retracing the steps of Tommy Ricketts and where he lived and worked and loved and died.

THE HOLLOWAY PHOTO

In England, January 1919 was a dull and wet month. The mean temperature was below normal—the least number of days of sunshine since 1901. The first major snowfall of 1919 occurred in the first week. Heavy snow occurred in the Midlands and northern England, causing damage to telegraph wires in the north and a foot of snow to fall at Buxton, Derbyshire. The fog on 13 January made it impossible, at Dover, to see ten yards ahead of you. It rained non-stop on January twentieth and there was hail every day at the end of the month. It was the most flooding in Southport since 1882. Near the end of the month there was another heavy snowfall.

On 30 January, Tommy Ricketts and a large contingent of the Newfoundland Regiment left England aboard the *Corsican*. A week later, the ship's captain asked if they should continue on to New Brunswick or Nova Scotia—the ship was delayed because of impenetrable ice. The minister of militia replied that the ship was to come into St John's "as it was out of the question to take the soldiers so far out of their way and no arrangements had been made for transportation other than that for debarkation at this port."

The ship would have to steam south to get around the ice floe, and therefore would not arrive until late in the night. Because of this, the city holiday was postponed.

The *Corsican* came into St John's harbour the night of 7 February, a Friday. The next day the men were let off.

Brigid Browne, in St John's, wrote to her son studying in Toronto that they will have a great time when the boys come home. Ricketts, she wrote, is among them—our Victoria Cross. They are making up money to educate him. He belongs to a little place where there are no schools. He went back for the ammunition twice in the face of the German gunfire.

Thomas Ricketts climbed out of a rowboat on the harbour apron a hero. The men carried him on their shoulders and placed him in a horse-drawn carriage. The horses were unhooked and men took the yoke and pulled him through the city. He stopped in at one house—the home of a doctor whose son Ricketts had seen die in the war—then continued on. He was asked to stay at the Crosbie Hotel but he insisted he return to his boarding house on Colonial Street. This was where he roomed before sailing off to war. He had been gone for a thousand days. He was nineteen years old and promoted to a sergeant.

When he entered a cinema, everyone stood and applauded him.

A reception was organized on Bell Island, where Matthew Brazil and Bertram Butler and Walter Greene were from. The ice came while he was on the island and he ended up walking over the ice back to Portugal Cove.

He got his photograph taken at Holloway Studio. Robert Holloway had been killed in the war and Tommy Ricketts had been there when he was shot. Elsie took his photograph. Did he say anything to her about her brother or about the war? It must have been strange to them both to know the predicament they were in, this celebration of a heroic deed when her brother was dead. Ricketts was wearing his new sergeant stripes. His gaze is dispassionate, handsome, interior. He looks towards the camera but his eyes are staring inward. He is not stiff. Elsie Holloway must have said something to put him at his ease.

CAPTURED

He lived with the Storeys. A fund of ten thousand dollars was struck for his education and he was taught how to read. Edgar House tells of him fishing and catching an eel. He skinned it carefully and cooked it and they pretended to enjoy it. Edgar saved the skin and they dried it and cut it into strips and made bootlaces out of it.

He studied at Bishop Feild College and then enrolled in Memorial University College. He was encouraged to use a gift fishing rod to fish trout in Virginia River. I know that river, having fished the length of it and caught many good trout there. There's a falls and a deep pool and the mouth of the river flows into Quidi Vidi at Pleasantville at the grounds where the regiment first gathered to train. But it was Tommy Ricketts who was captured. His son has said this. His son lives in Scarborough near us in Toronto. He was captured by the people of St John's. Unlike Bert Butler and Matthew Brazil, Tommy Ricketts couldn't return to his life.

EDNA EDWARDS

He would have returned to White Bay and been a fishermen. Instead, Tommy Ricketts lived in town at various boarding houses. His grades weren't strong enough to become a doctor. And so he tried pharmacy. I suspect even that was too onerous for him. He may have become a druggist, which is a step below pharmacy—he always hired a pharmacist at his place of business.

For more than a dozen years he stayed a bachelor. The hero of a nation could not take conventional steps through courtship and marriage. Indeed, many soldiers were halted in their natural development. The women, too—Elsie Holloway never married and neither did Francis Cluett.

At the age of thirty-two Tommy Ricketts started seeing the daughter of the owners of a boarding house at 131 Pennywell Road. He was living there too. Edna Edwards.

She was nineteen. There was some discrepancy between when they were married and the birth of their first child, Dolda. Did they marry because Edna was pregnant? Did they keep Dolda's presence absent from the census because they didn't want it to be known?

Dolda means "hidden" in Swedish.

They certainly wouldn't be the first to marry with child.

The house where they met was torn down, but the houses it was attached to are still there. I got to know one of the neighbours and she was astonished at what I told her. She said they have a poster of Tommy Ricketts in their stairwell. The stairs that would have been joined to the Edwards boarding house.

There is evidence of that house still—a cement footing for a bay window and the concrete front step. This, I thought, is where Tommy Ricketts met Edna Edwards. She played records and was a flapper and was very young and they were in bedrooms close to one another up there on the second floor. A foundation block to carry a chimney against one of the houses. You can still enter the front door that hangs in the air, which I do, and sit in the first-floor rooms where they met.

Tommy Ricketts had waited fourteen years to get married. What pressure there must have been on him to learn a profession, to settle down.

If you stand in the gap between the houses there is a

rough path that pedestrians use as a shortcut to Prince of Wales Street below Pennywell Road. It is a rogue path, made by feet, not by hand. And I realized I had lived in the basement of a house directly across from this gap, after coming home from travelling in Turkey and Egypt and England. I had lived across from the house where Tommy Ricketts met Edna Edwards.

When I mentioned this to a friend, he said: I know Edna. I talked to Edna every day for years.

My friend had worked in a home where Edna visited her mother. She was a true lady, he said. She drove a green Chevy Nova. I don't dye my hair, she said. It's tinted. She'd go in and do her mother's make-up.

RICKETTS DRUG STORE

He was set up in business on the corner of Job Street and Water Street. He brought in Edna's younger brother, Bert Edwards. And Bert worked for Tommy Ricketts for ten years, before setting up his own pharmacy further west, at the Crossroads. In the newspapers of the 1950s there is a major renovation of the Edwards Pharmacy. And in the paper are large ads for automobiles and furniture with companies named after prominent men, T&M Winter and Ayres and other men that Tommy Ricketts had fought with and who did not win a Victoria Cross but now they had half-page ads in the paper. And in a column down one page a postage-stamp-sized ad saying bingo tickets were available at the following outlets. In the list is Ricketts Drug Store.

His son says his father was not a businessman. He didn't have the aptitude. A man who worked for him in the 1960s says Ricketts paid him twice the going rate and he kept terrible accounts. But he served his customers and the west end of St John's well. He was a quiet man.

You can walk along Water Street and recognize the old stores that have been standing for over a century. There are terrific photos of the buildings that have been knocked down: Ayre & Sons, for instance, is replaced with Atlantic Place. Ayre can mean wind or the air itself or a narrow bank of sand created by the sea. Ayr was the place in Scotland where the men had trained. Because of the geography of the harbour and the hills it is easy enough to pick your way back to the past of St John's when the roads were cobbled and horse-drawn streetcars were here and there were cinemas and hotels and department stores. But as you draw towards the far end of Water Street, into the west end, things turn a corner and the past begins to be constricted by the new arterial routes that have thrown the wide shadows of overpasses onto the street and the street itself splits into a divided highway and your sense of a pedestrian becomes threatened by auto routes. Still, there are small buildings that exist here, like O'Mara's Pharmacy that is an apothecary museum that never opens and the shades are drawn tight. Brennan's Barber Shop, a narrow building squeezed into a row of buildings, and inside there is a Nestle hair machine that looks like it could electrocute you, photos of a man selling braces of rabbits and fish being sold on the harbour apron and a book open to 1964 and the customer's rates jotted in pencil. Pencil was used a lot for journals. I decided to wait at Brennan's and get a haircut. Tommy Ricketts could have easily had his hair cut in this very chair—for his drug store was nearby. The Newman's vault is here where they stored casks of wine. The Coastal Railway station is across the road and they used to display the Ricketts Victoria Cross before it was transferred by the family to the national war museum in Ottawa. Inside they have little floor tiles of train tracks for kids to follow as they look at costumes and scale models of trains and boats that shipped mail and goods and people around the island. I've taken my son there. I enjoy looking at the fabric of clothing, the thick wool weave, the stitching, how well-made and abundant fabrics were in the past. There was an article in the daily paper about house fires and how the roof trusses in new homes are built to withstand snow loads but, in a fire, they are consumed four times more rapidly and can cause roof collapse. That sort of thing. And yet, here was a newlywed couple, sleeping in separate berths because the sexes were still separated back then, and the train derailed and the oil lamps in the women's train caught the fabrics alight and the bridegroom rushed in to try to save his new wife and they were both consumed by smoke. No, I do not want to live with open flames around me. I do not want to live in the past.

Across from what was the railway museum is a memorial plaque commemorating Tommy Ricketts and his pharmacy. He sold comic books and candy to kids. Ricketts travelled to London once, in 1929, to attend a dinner given by the British Legion at the House of Lords. He met General Hart, the oldest living Victoria Cross winner. Ricketts was still the youngest.

There is a story that, when King George VI visited St John's in 1939, Tommy Ricketts declined an invitation to join him at an event. So the King had his car stop in front of the pharmacy until Ricketts ventured out to shake hands with him.

The last photo I've found of Tommy Ricketts in his pharmacy shows him holding a magazine from off the rack, opened to a story called "How to Fool Smart Ducks." This is *True—The Man's Magazine*, and the ducks story was written by Ted Trueblood. It's the October 1954 issue. Ricketts was fifty-three.

True's masthead reads "'Tis strange, but true; for truth is always strange—stranger than fiction."—Byron.

Ted Trueblood had been the editor of *Field & Stream*. He was a conservation leader and led the fight to preserve salmon rivers from hydro dams. He popularized catch and release methods. He fished, in the 1950s, for salmon in Newfoundland. He was similar to Lee Wulff, whom I saw perform when I was a boy at the Arts and Culture Centre in Corner Brook. Lee Wulff and his wife, Joan, practised spey casting and I watched, with my father, as Lee Wulff cast his line with a red bow on the end, cast it across the stage and then changed direction and flipped that line out into the audience. The red bow landed daintily on the top of a bald man's head. We all stood and applauded. It was my first time in a theatre, and for a long time I associated theatre with the practice of fly-fishing.

Lee Wulff, on catch and release: Game fish are too valuable to be caught only once.

Tommy Ricketts, who was captured by the Newfoundland people, died in February of 1967. He collapsed on the floor of his shop, right here, on this spot, in this store that no longer exists, but the space exists, the land where last he stood and where I now stand. He was buried with full military honours, a state funeral in the graveyard near Quidi Vidi. A red cushion held his medals. The coffin placed on a gun carriage. There was snow on the ground as there was when he came home from the war, when he was carried on men's shoulders.

MORGAN MACDONALD

If you keep walking west from Ricketts's old pharmacy, up along Waterford Bridge Road, you'll come to Bowring Park. Here is Basil Gotto's *The Fighting Newfoundlander* and the replica of the Beaumont-Hamel caribou. The caribou was a gift of Major William Howe Green. Green served as a musketry instructor during the First World War and was a cousin to Edgar Bowring. It's a strange thing to see this same statue in a different place. The sculpture of Peter Pan is here too, the one Bowring had made when the *Florizel* broke to pieces.

The caribou, over the years, had been damaged. The kids swing on the antlers, a deputy city manager said. Morgan MacDonald removed the caribou and took it to his foundry. He cut the caribou open and installed a structure inside to reinforce the antlers. Morgan MacDonald is in the memorial business. He has created several recent war memorials for Newfoundland outports. There is the sculpture of two modern Newfoundland soldiers in Conception Bay South, a man and a woman, modelled on soldiers fighting in Afghanistan. He dreamt up the idea of making half-size models of the caribou for local monuments. He built one for my hometown—and his—in Corner Brook. That's how I got to know of him, walking past the old Co-op grocery store, where the new City Hall is, and seeing his caribou in the same posture as the Beaumont-Hamel caribou. The caribou, while half the size of the original sculpture, is about the same size as a real, living animal—something monumental brought back to normal dimensions.

CALYPSO

That fall I drove west to hunt with my father. I had a caribou license. I passed the turn-off to many bays and coves where the men of the Newfoundland Regiment had been born. Halfway across the island I darted into Lewisporte, for I wanted see the wreck of a ship that had trained the Newfoundland sailors for the British Navy. The *Calypso* was built in 1883, and was one of Britain's last sailing ships. There are engravings of her in full sail, and she looks like something that fought during Napoleon's time. She had steam engines, but could be propelled entirely by sail, which allowed her to serve where coaling stations were rare. She had been used by the British in fleet exercises and war games, where the fleet was divided and one side protected England while the other attempted to invade. This was back in the late 1800s.

And there she is, you come around a corner and look for her bow and she's there, near the shore in Embree. A calm sea, her masts cut down, but there is the bow of the *Calypso* jutting out of the lowtide water. I got out of my car and mar-velled at this quiet deck of wood and iron. It would be noth-ing if you did not know her story. But when you are informed, it is easy to slip into the danger that Nietzsche outlined: over-attention to the past turns men into dilettante spectators.

The ship was named after the nymph Calypso, who kept Odysseus hostage for five years. Calypso, daughter of Atlas, lived on the island of Ogygia. Plutarch wrote that Ogygia is five days' sail west of Britain. Which, when you think about it, suggests Newfoundland. The Newfoundland sailors who trained on *Calypso* were kept from home for the duration of the war, from their island home, for five years. The word "calypso" means to conceal knowledge.

See, Nietzsche said, the great thing is already here!

I got back in my car and headed for my father.

HUNTING CARIBOU

It's a long drive—eight hours—but soon I was motoring along the Humber River, past the hometown of Hugh McWhirter, to the area of Newfoundland I hunt in and know well. There is a woods road and a marsh that cuts across the road near Big Falls. You can hear the water rushing although the falls is too far to see. It is like some big battle rumbling in the distance. I hunted with a rifle my father found for me. It is a Lee-Enfield, from 1943, but pretty much the same rifle they used in the First World War. My father knew I wanted a bolt action: the gun that built the modern British army. James Paris Lee, who invented the Lee-Enfield, moved from Hawick to Canada at the age of five. The family lived in Galt, Ontario, which is near Waterloo. I had a reading in Waterloo a few years ago, and drove into Galt just to stop and take in Lee's childhood home. There is a plaque there much like the plaque at the site of Tommy Ricketts's pharmacy.

We hunted near territory that the Beothuk roamed over. I have canoed, with friends, down the Exploits and slept in a tent on land where you knew the Beothuk had once built a mamateek. Natural points of land that provided good views of game and places to fish and shelter from the prevailing wind. They dug a round shallow pit for their mamateek and we set up our tents in one of these cavities. I carried a shotgun and crept up on some ducks. I shot six but there was one duck I'd only wounded and I had to track him down the river. He hid himself beneath the dead roots of a tree overhanging the riverbed. I bent down to get him and he turned one terrible, innocent eye to me. I pulled him out from this overhang of earth and felt I was involved with events of the grave. I wrung his neck. We dug a hole and built a fire and plucked the ducks. When the fire was rendered to coals we put a pot with the ducks in the hole and buried the pot. Again, cooked in their graves. Then we unearthed the pot and ate the ducks. They tasted gamey: fish-eaters. We slept in our tents on the Beothuk site and I thought of the sculpture of a Beothuk that stands someplace in the woods near here, a memorial to a people now extinct.

We were on the river for three days, deep within the heart of the island, and it felt like we had returned to an earlier, pre-industrial time. There was a sharp turn in the river that almost switched back onto itself, and there in the distance was a glint through the trees of something metallic and fast. Then you heard it, above the noise of the river: the Trans-Canada Highway.

The Beothuk used to build fences to corral the caribou to openings where they lay in wait with bow and arrow. The Germans did much the same with the Newfoundlanders at Beaumont-Hamel that morning of the Big Push. They waited for the men to climb out of their trenches and allowed them to be funnelled down to the gaps in the barbed wire and permitted them to walk through these gateways before opening fire with their machine guns. Mown down in heaps is the way Arthur Hadow described it in the regiment's diary. The Newfoundlanders had met their Red Men. And, when their bodies lay open to each other, through gunshot and shrapnel, Ivor Gurney's red wet thing was made evident to them. They had become, to each other, their own red men.

I did not fire a shot that hunting season with my father. We saw nothing alive in those woods and across that yellow marsh, a field very much the size of the field at Beaumont-Hamel. And as I emptied the magazine from my Lee-Enfield I remembered that not one member of the regiment fired a shot that day.

We spent the night in the log cabin my father had built when I was a child. I had noticed, in the trunk of my father's car, a portable tent. I asked him about that. He said in winter he doesn't trust the roads. If there is a blizzard, he said, and I can't get through, I want to be able to abandon the car and hike into the woods. You won't find me trapped in a car, he said, under six feet of snow. He'll be in the shelter of trees in his tent with a fire, his snares set; he'll be ready to go ice fishing on a nearby pond.

I told him about the shelter of trees I had found the Newfoundlanders buried under at Beaumont-Hamel, trees taller and bigger than they would be here because these Newfoundland trees had grown up in the climate of France. My father knew that I was writing this book about war, so he told me then that he'd had the chance, when he was eighteen, to go for national service. He'd deferred until he'd finished his apprenticeship at the shipyard. National service was for two years and everybody had to do it if they passed the medical exam. My father was a borderline case because of his eyes. The doctor asked him if he wanted to go and he said yes. He served from February 1956 to February 1958.

I thought of those years, and clicked through the wars the British had been involved in. The historian Will Durant calculated that "only twenty-nine years of human history have not been marked by war." I asked my father if he had been worried about the British in Kenya or the war in Korea. He said that none of his entry got posted abroad, which was a big surprise. Every entry before his—about a hundred and twenty men—had been posted to Cyprus where there were terrorist bombings. But just about all of the men in his entry were given home postings. He went to the Royal Air Force in Driffield, the Yorkshire Wolds country. It was a great camp. The first words my father heard when he arrived were, "Food's good here." And it was. Food was lousy in every other camp he was at. He was an engine mechanic working on all-weather night-fighters— jets. They would refuel, fit starter cartridges, do preflight and after-flight inspections. Check oil. He also got to run up the engine after a bigger servicing. He got to sit in the cockpit, start up the engine and run it up gradually until it was screaming. He also guided pilots to their parking stations using batons, like you see people doing at airports today. But most of the time he and the others were just playing darts, waiting for the planes to come back. It was pretty boring. Being near home, he got a lot of forty-eight-hour passes at weekends, so he was able to see my mother quite often. They were engaged before he went away.

After his service, my father went back to his old job in the shipyard.

GEORGE TUFF

I drove back to Western Bay without a caribou. But before leaving Corner Brook I took a turn up Elizabeth Street towards what I used to think of as the Old Age Home. I wanted to see a house where Arral Tuff had lived. Arral Tuff was the widow of George Tuff. George Tuff lived in Old Perlican, near our place in Western Bay. He was the second man to sign up for the Newfoundland Regiment. He was a commercial traveller. He had sandy hair and grey eyes and for a while I confused him with a sealer who had survived the *Newfoundland* disaster of 1914. But that George Tuff was from Bonavista Bay. My Tuff had been left a parlour organ in his father's will. I wondered if that had spurred him to become a commercial traveller. Sassoon once wrote that there was something attractive in the "idea of being a commercial traveler, creeping about the country and doing business in drowsy market towns and snug cathedral cities."

I had gone to Old Perlican to find where George Tuff had lived but no one remembered him. Maybe you mean

New Perlican, an elderly man told me, which is along the Trinity side down near Winterton. Sometimes people get tangled up, he said. It was, in fact, the anniversary of the sealing disaster and I'd already been tangled up with that other Tuff.

I'd been tangled up a few times. At The Rooms I had discovered that it wasn't at Sandringham at all that Tommy Ricketts had met the King, but at York Cottage which was on the Sandringham estate. I was close, but the entire scenario I had conjured up was wrong and I had to pull up stakes and reset the event in another building. What odds, I thought. How accurate can we be about the past? I had stood in the footprints of Gavrilo Princip, the Bosnian Serb who shot Francis Ferdinand and his wife, in Sarajevo. The footprints are artificial impressions in a cement sidewalk and a plaque on the wall explains them. But are they genuine? Did Princip stand exactly here? Even the meticulously kept trenches at Beaumont-Hamel, so often declared the only stretch of the Western Front preserved intact, have filled up with soil and grass. The archaeologists have to dig down several feet to find vials of morphine and belts of cartridges.

So I gave up on George Tuff, even though I knew his father had been a magistrate at Old Perlican and had married twice. Then it struck me: marriage. That's the way to find a person. Had George Tuff been married? He had fought at Gallipoli and Beaumont-Hamel and Cambrai and survived everything the war could throw at him and returned and—yes—he married a woman thirty years younger than himself. Arral Tuff was from Stephenville Crossing—the other side of Newfoundland. George Tuff had cleared out of the east coast of Newfoundland and lived his days on the coast where I grew up. He wasn't the only soldier who did so: Bertram Butler, the hero of many campaigns, did the same, working for years with the Bowater pulp and paper company.

In 1988, Arral Tuff wrote a letter asking for a widow's compensation for her husband's veteran status. She wrote this letter from 26 Churchill Crescent in Corner Brook. I was sitting in my car outside that door, looking into the front window where that letter was written. Arral Tuff had been a senior citizen living in an old folks' home that I passed every day as I walked to school as a kid. To think of the woman who'd married a man who'd survived the entire First World War—and I had probably walked very close to her several times without knowing it. She was one of those women counting out coins from her clutch purse at the Co-op grocery store, the store I loved because it had the city's only escalator. I now knew, from her correspondence, that Arral Tuff hadn't received a widow's compensation.

REMEMBRANCE DAY

A friend of mine went to a recent Remembrance Day ceremony at the war memorial in St John's. I went there, she said, for you. There was icy rain, driven at a slant. Very cold, she said. Water was running in the streets. An old lady was up to her ankles in lace-up leather shoes. There was a young girl, either a soldier or a cadet, standing with a rifle by the statues, on one end. The girl wasn't moving, her eyes downcast, bun at the back, incredibly beautiful and young and rain dripping steadily off her chin. She was trembling from the cold, but otherwise completely still. They had to cut the ceremony a bit short—too many elderly people in the freezing rain. The cannons really boomed. They seemed to tear up the sky and my friend thought she could smell the smoke. She missed the "Ode to Newfoundland."

Later in the evening, she was in a restaurant across from the memorial and there were three photographers, in the dark, after the rain, taking pictures of all the wreaths. A reporter on the radio said that it was a lazy wind: soon as cut through you than go around you. One woman: The weather was nothing compared to what was going on overseas back then.

The smell of cannon smoke. The Victoria Cross is made from the bronze of a Russian cannon captured by the British during the Crimean War—at least that's what they thought until they analyzed the metal and have decided now the iron is from a Chinese-made cannon captured by the Russians. So the Victoria Cross is an early example of a Chinese export.

The Crimean War was the first major war covered by journalists. It was suggested that a medal should be struck that honoured the bravery of the individual soldier. Up until then the only medals handed out for courage were to officers. The Victoria Cross is awarded "for most conspicuous bravery or some daring or pre-eminent act of valour or self-sacrifice or extreme devotion to duty in the presence of the enemy." There was some opinion against the award: a medal for bravery might encourage individual behaviour that could weaken the strength of a fighting force.

There had been a customs house here at King's Beach where the war memorial was built. It had been destroyed in the Great Fire of 1892. After the war the cliff face was blasted away to make room for the memorial. Governor Allardyce lit the fuse. Two ex-servicemen were given the contract to lay the first concrete. One of the men, Ernest Churchill, had been on the regiment's hockey team and then been gassed at Passchendaele. The memorial was paid for, through Thomas Nangle, with five pounds for every missing Newfoundland soldier and merchant marine, and Royal Navy reserve seaman.

During the fundraising for the caribou memorials in France and Belgium, Nangle had grown exasperated: If one hundred pounds is all that can be spared per monument, I recommend that we erect nothing at all, he said. Let us forget we ever had a Regiment.

The word "monument" means to remind, to advise and to warn. And they are often the last things to survive a civilization.

MIDDLE ARM

I had one last place to visit. One last tour of duty. I drove across the island again, this time in December, trying to beat a snowstorm. Past Botwood, where I learned that Rachel Ricketts—Tommy Ricketts's sister—had remarried after her first husband died. She married Edward Purchase of Fogo in the school chapel and they lived in Botwood. Edward had a brother Arthur, who was a Blue Puttee. Arthur Purchase, after his year was up, did not sign on for the duration of the war. Very few soldiers did this. He returned home, and Rachel Ricketts married this man's brother. Rachel was two years older than her brother Tommy. Tommy Ricketts, the youngest of three children, just like me.

The weather turned poor as I drove to Seal Cove. A snowplough was churning a tall wave of snow and salt and sand and the wave hit the car with a whump as the plough passed by at full speed. I promised myself to turn around before two in the afternoon, to allow enough time to retreat before the final big freeze of the year and a snowstorm which would mean abandoning my car with only all-season tires until April, much like soldiers abandoned equipment when they were forced to withdraw quickly.

The hills here were steep and the road followed these hills up and down. On the final down you're in Seal Cove. A beautiful, quiet place with a public wharf and men who still fish out of here. I used the post office and sent my family a postcard. I let them know I was okay and near the end of my journey. That I might be back before they got this note. While I licked my stamp I recalled the earliest report I could find for a John Ricketts—the father of George and Rachel and Tommy. Herman Pearce was in his post office in 1903 when he noted in his diary that John Ricketts of Seal Cove was on his way to visit his brother. It was a dirty cloudy day in December, Pearce wrote, then the wind blew from the northwest and it became fine and clear.

The same weather was happening again. I asked the post office clerk if she knew how one could get to Middle Arm. There are no roads to Middle Arm and the closest community is this one. Seal Cove is where the fishermen of Middle Arm dealt with their product and accepted supplies and received word from the outside world.

The clerk confused my query about Middle Arm with another Middle Arm in the adjoining bay, Notre Dame Bay.

I mean the one where Tommy Ricketts was born, I said.

She understood then. It was just around the corner, she said. But Middle Arm is a place no one goes to anymore. Then she brightened. Alonso Osbourne might help you, she said. And she pointed out Alonso's yellow bungalow.

Bungalow, I thought, is an Indian word, as is Bangalore. Puttee, too: a puttee is a bandage. Alonso was the name of the father of Hank Williams.

I knocked on the door to the yellow bungalow and Alonso Osbourne's daughter went to fetch him. Come in, she said. A small man in his seventies, Alonso Osbourne was born in Middle Arm in 1936. He weighed a pound and a half and his parents decided to let him live with the midwife here in Seal Cove. The midwife was his grandmother. She put me in a shoebox, he said, with cotton and placed me behind the water warmer of the woodstove. That was my incubator, he said.

He knew Tommy Ricketts. Tommy would have ended up in Seal Cove if he hadn't won the Victoria Cross. A school was built out of concrete in his honour but it was abandoned in the 1940s and torn down ten years later. An ordinary Tommy Ricketts would have fished out of Seal Cove.

I thought: It's a pretty spot here, the houses ringing the bay.

Alonso Osbourne drove me around to a man who might take me to Middle Arm in his boat. But the man wasn't home. He may be out turre hunting, Alonso said. You can walk there, but be careful on the ice in the tickle.

I said I wasn't about to walk on strange ice. I did that once when I lived in Trepassey, and the neighbours were waiting for the day when they'd have to come fish me out.

There is a woods road, Alonso said. Look for Nobles, on your way to Western Arm.

So I drove out to Western Arm. And on the way I stopped at a river that flows from Flatwater Pond into Middle Arm. I felt an urge to walk down to it because it was a river that Tommy Ricketts would have crossed as a boy. It was as wide, I judged, as the Ancre. Ricketts liked to fish at Virginia River in St John's. He was a fly fisherman, like me, and he returned to Middle Arm in the summers to fish with his friend Tom Gavin. How to fool smart ducks.

I drove on and came upon a sign for Nobles Woods Road and turned off onto it and drove along a raised frozen white ground. I passed a pair of those tall galvanized cylinders that woods trucks drive through to align their loads, then crossed a Bailey bridge, which is a type of pre-fab truss bridge used by the British in World War Two. I crept up the snowy hills and was worried about getting stuck in there. I checked the odometer because I didn't like the state of the road or the weather. The road rose alongside the hill until it crested and I saw the ice over Middle Arm. I got out of the car and walked across the snow with the stumps of blackened trees sticking out of the snow. The entire hill and valley had been burned over, and snow was falling on it. I couldn't tell if the place had been logged or burned or both.

I knelt down and formed a snowball with my bare hands, thinking: my son would build a snow fort with this type of snow. When you create a shelter like that you pile the snow and leave it overnight. The snow goes through a binding process called sintering. A lovely word, sinter. Many things go through such a transformation. Art, you hope, does.

The snow fell onto my eyelashes and I hugged myself to stay warm. I was thinking that if I had to, I could build a snow fort here. Who would be the last person to spend a night in Middle Arm? But I'd need a shovel. You heap snow and pat it down and then you take a shovel and slide it into the bottom and carve a hole. You scoop out as much snow as you can and then you enter the hole with an axe. You chop out more snow from the ceiling of the fort. All of this excess snow you throw on top of your fort and you repeat this process until you feel like it could go on in an infinite spiral of progression. One can let one's mind go with this ever-expanding roof built from the snow carved from within—and it is easy to see how many projects are like this, how scenes are carved one upon the other, building layers upon the primary source. Here I am, I have confirmed that the hometown of Tommy Ricketts no longer exists as a habitable space. The regiment he served in is now a reserve battalion for militia. Bishop Feild College where he studied is a primary school for youngsters my son's age. The house where he met his young wife Edna is demolished. The pharmacy where he died is torn down. The only thing left of Tommy Ricketts is a field in Ledegem. A field much like this one before me.

The wharves and houses where the community had existed have been erased from the landscape. Out there someplace in the bottom of the bay is Sop's Island, where the other Tommy Ricketts came from, the one that was killed the day this Tommy Ricketts won the Victoria Cross. Buried at Ledegem. Sometimes people get tangled up.

The sense that anything had ever happened here, that a child could be born, that anything could evolve from this place and animate itself and create a difference in another part of the world—all that seemed unlikely. This land had reverted back to land dominated by the industry of animals and insects.

I turned and looked back at my car. It was the only modern thing in view. I remembered hunting with a friend in the winter and we were in the woods for three solid days and he collapsed in the snow one day—we had been whispering all morning, and he said, in a normal shocking voice, that not only had we not seen a caribou, we hadn't seen another living thing. And it struck us that the entire animate world could have been destroyed and we would not have known it, out there in the field waiting for movement, for purpose.

The only evidence of civilization in Middle Arm was this recent forest fire buried under a cloak of snow. The bereft fields here were startling: the burnt hill and valley covered in snow, just the charred stumps climbing out of the white frozen ground. These were the shattered black trunks of trees harvested by Nobles, probably. I was trying to think what this vista reminded me of, and then I remembered the photos in the archives of battlefields on the Western Front, the destroyed land. That experience of the earth had marched right into the backyard of Tommy Ricketts, had turned this homeland into a black-and-white photograph. I was alone in this photograph like some lonely stag, at a site of birth and death, while the wind freshened and some serious snow began to whip into my face.

UNITED KINGDOM: OCTOBER 1914 – AUGUST 1915

14 Oct 1914 – Devonport (arrival)

20 Oct 1914 – Salisbury (Pond Farm Camp)

7 Dec 1914 – Inverness (Fort George)

19 Feb 1915 – Edinburgh

11 May 1915 – Hawick (Stob's Camp)

2 Aug 1915 – Ayr

19 Aug 1915 – Aldershot

20 Aug 1915 – Devonport (to Gallipoli)

WESTERN FRONT: MARCH 1916 – NOVEMBER 1918

1 July 1916 – Beaumont-Hamel

9 Aug 1916 – Ypres

12 Oct 1916 – Gueudecourt

19 Jan 1917 – Le Transloy

2 Mar 1917 – Sailly-Saillisel

14 Apr 1917 – Monchy-le-Preux

16 Aug 1917 – Langemarck

9 Oct 1917 – Poelcappelle

20 Nov 1917 – Masnieres / Marcoing (Cambrai)

10 Apr 1918 – Bailleul (Passchendaele)

28 Sept 1918 – Ypres

2 Oct 1918 – Ledegem (Kortrijk)

Abbreviations are as follows:

TFN: The Fighting Newfoundlander
MBP: Memoirs of a Blue Puttee
LOWS: Lieutenant Owen William Steele
LML: Letters of Mayo Lind

Many of the attestation papers and family correspondence of the soldiers are available online at: therooms.ca.

p. 4   "Is he a prisoner of war . . ." (attestation papers, The Rooms).

p. 7   "For who could tell what swift blizzard . . ." (definition of "nunch," *Dictionary of Newfoundland English*).

p. 8   "men wore their hair short . . ." *The War the Infantry Knew 1914-1919: A Chronicle of Service in France and Belgium* (Abacus 1988).

p. 9   ". . . there was a photo of him in the newspaper . . ." (*Evening Telegram*).

p. 11   ". . . it is not by men but by devils . . ." (*Twillingate Sun*).

p. 11   "Bernard Harvey," (Commonwealth War Graves Commission).

p. 13   "drinking to the health of everyone else . . ." (*MBP*, p. 35).

p. 14   "the strike of 1902 . . ." (Briton Cooper Busch, "The Newfoundland Sealers Strike of 1902", *Journal of Canadian Labour Studies*, 1984).

p. 15   "I thought you were killed" (*MBP*, p. 157).

p. 17   "the sculpture is of two large toy soldiers . . ." Douglas Coupland.

p. 18   "and left on his way rejoicing . . ." (22 August 1914, *Twillingate Sun*).

p. 18   "had built a wall ..." (Danette Dooley, *Evening Telegram*).

p. 20   "before more nurses had their hands ..." (*Twillingate Sun*).

p. 21   "good luck and a chance ..." (*Twillingate Sun*).

p. 23   "... and a dozen postcards cost ..." (*MBP*, p. 29).

p. 24   "very hardy and accustomed ..." (*TFN*, p. 118).

p. 24   "a mile is a thousand..." (conversation with Jean Dandenault, Toronto).

p. 24   "that forest of ships" (*MBP*, p. 35).

p. 25   "...that care taken for an individual life ..." Frederick George Scott, *The Great War As I Saw It* (F. D. Goodchild & Co.,1922).

p. 32   "Jim Stacey only visited ..." (*MBP*, p. 38).

p. 35   "many's the drop of salt water ..." (*TFN*, p.127).

p. 39   "... a slip from a rose tree ..." (*Your Daughter Fanny*, p. 99).

p. 42   "a tent-load of brother privates" (*TFN*, p.126).

p. 54   "... essential for a writer to travel ..." James Salter, *Paris Review* (No. 133, Winter 1994).

p. 61   "They had milk in their tea ..." p. 39 (*TFN*, p 129).

p. 62   "It is very exciting ..." (*LML*, p. 9).

p. 62   "Christmas dinner: goose and roast beef," (*LML*, p. 5).

p. 62   "You couldn't escape it." (*TFN*, p. 131).

p. 62   "abdominal disease," Jack Chaplin attestation papers, The Rooms.

p. 63   "When you're weaving ..." (Jonathan Cleaver, from an interview with Rebecca Gordon, *STV News*, 12 July 2012).

p. 66   "Troop Train Disaster" (*The Times*, 1915).

p. 68   "... soft end of the plank." (*TFN*, p 138).

p. 68   "... selling coal from a cart," (*MBP*, p.45).

p. 68   "... sheep wandered around the tents." p.43 (*LML*, p 35).

p. 68   "A detention camp ..." (*LML*, p 15).

p. 68   "... one of the men made a movie of their march ..." (*LML*, p.28).

p. 68   "final 'polish'" (*LML*, p. 41).

p. 70   George Ricketts (attestation papers, The Rooms).

p. 70   Patrick Tobin (attestation papers, The Rooms).

p. 71   "Real good . . ." (Eric Ellis diaries, The Rooms).

p. 72   "They were not prepared . . ." (War Brides, "Land & Sea" Episode, CBC TV).

p. 72   "Come, sit with Mary . . ." ("Sons of Martha," Rudyard Kipling).

p. 74–79   "Gas mask . . ." (The material here is culled from "Notes on Cluny Macpherson,1879-1966," Faculty of Medicine Founders' Archive, Memorial University of Newfoundland).

p. 80   "They are sure to be in fine condition," Lieutenant Owen Steele, p. 116.

p. 81   ". . . the coastal steamer *Prince Abbas* . . ." (*MBP*, p. 52).

p. 81   Hugh McWhirter (attestation papers, The Rooms).

p. 83   James Donnelly (attestation papers, The Rooms).

p. 83   "Owen Steele in shorts . . ." (*LOWS*, pp. xvii & 80).

p. 83   "The Turks used dogs . . ." p. 52 (*LML*, p. 74).

p. 83   "Dr. Wakefield led the Presbyterians in prayer . . ." (*LOWS*, p. 25).

p. 87   "It reminded one of the *Greenland* disaster," (*LOWS*, p. 100).

p. 89–90   George McWhirter (attestation papers, The Rooms).

p. 93   "a pillar of the community," (obituary, *Western Star*).

p. 95   "He was a racewalker . . ." (introduction, *LOWS*).

p. 101   "the peach trees were in bloom . . ." (*MBP*, p. 74).

p. 101   ". . . tea and cakes along the way . . ." (*LML*, p.111).

p. 107   ". . . John Roberts." (*Shot at Dawn*, p. 98, Julian Putkowski & Julian Sykes, Pen & Sword 1998).

p. 108,   ". . . inculcate the offensive spirit . . ." (*Goodbye to All That*, Robert Graves, 1929).

NOTES

p. 112   "Arthur Wakefield, who had . . ." (*Into the Silence*, Wade Davis, Knopf Canada, 2011).

p. 112   ". . . caribou through the snow." (*Labrador Memoir of Dr Harry Paddon 1912-1938*, ed. Ronald Rompkey, McGill-Queen's University Press, 2003).

p. 115   Bertram Butler (attestation papers, The Rooms).

p. 119   ". . . a uniped." (*Saga of Erik the Red*).

p. 126   "their bayonets glistening in the sun," (*TFN*, p. 266).

p. 126   "Brandenburg cuffs . . ." (from a thread on the Great War Forum website).

p. 127   "World War One is coming." Conversation with Mark Ferguson.

p. 132   The Norman Collins interview is from audio supplied by Mark Ferguson of the Rooms.

p. 134   "Men who would never . . ." (Hugh Trevor-Roper, *The Invention of Scotland: Myth and History*, 2008).

p. 135   "alive with bees," (*MBP*, p. 88).

p. 150   "The general who would have fought this war differently . . ." (video, *Line of Fire*, Part 3 of 12).

p. 153   ". . . so that forevermore . . ." (*Evening Telegram*).

p. 154   "Much could be written . . ." (*Memoirs of an Infantry Officer*, Siegfried Sasson).

p. 167   "He recommended lying down . . ." (General Sir Henry de Beauvoir de Lisle, *Reminiscences of Sport and War*, 1939).

p. 168   "better than the best. . . savours of extravagance," (*TFN*, p. 493).

p. 168   "The best small-boat seamen . . ." (Richard H. Gimblett, *Citizen Sailors: Chronicles of Canada's Naval Reserve*, 1910-2010).

p. 168   "eight million horses perished . . ." (Jilly Cooper, *Animals in War*).

p. 170   ". . . ribbons on a mule . . ." (*MBP*, p. 75).

p. 171 "... seven times more likely ..." (The British historian Dr Clare Makepeace makes this point and discusses venereal disease and brothels in several published articles).

p. 173 Ernest Chafe (attestation papers, The Rooms).

p. 176 "Goodbye, Jews!" (Louis CK interview, Conan O'Brien, TBS, 2013).

p. 180 "I venture to speak ..." (Edmund Blunden, introduction to Fabian Ware's *The Immortal Heritage*, 1937).

p. 182 "miners stripped to the waist ..." (*Shots from the Front: The British Soldier 1914-1918*, Richard Holmes).

p. 188 "... twenty lives a foot ..." (F. Scott Fitzgerald, *Tender is the Night*, 1934).

p. 189 Cyril Gardner (attestation papers, The Rooms).

p. 190 "... unable to move for fear of being seen." (George Culpitt war diary, http://www.culpitt-war-diary.org.uk).

p. 190 Moyle Stick (attestation papers, The Rooms).

p. 191 "... the colour of lamp black and wool." (James Forbes-Robertson, attestation papers, The Rooms).

p. 192 "... closed the gates ..." (*Evening Telegram*, 19 April 1917).

p. 195 Thomas Nangle (attestation papers, The Rooms).

p. 195 Tommy Ricketts (attestation papers, The Rooms).

p. 196 "two brothers in uniform," *Two Newfoundland VCs*, p. 84, Joy B. Cave (Creative Printers, 1984).

p. 198 "buildings without doors," Leo Murphy, *Veteran* magazine.

p. 198 "communicates with the sea ..." Lewis Amadeus Anspatch, *A History of the Island of Newfoundland* (1819) p. 86.

p. 199 "as stirring as it is weird ..." Glenn Colton, "Imagining Nation: Music and Identity in Pre-Confederation Newfoundland" (Newfoundland and Labrador Studies, Vol. 22, No 1, 2007).

p. 199 "Hadow, in the snow ..." (*MBP*, p. 148).

p. 200   Robins Stick (attestation papers, The Rooms).

p. 201   "I was a runner ..." Fred Bursey (attestation papers, The
             Rooms).

p. 202   "that difficult matter is swept away," (correspondence, The
             Rooms).

p. 203   Ruben Bursey's letter. Goliath Bursey (attestation papers,
             The Rooms).

p. 206   "It is the annulling ..." (D. H. Lawrence, letter to Catherine
             Carswell, 1916).

p. 207   "There was an unbroken ..." (Landwehr Lieutenant M.
             Gerster, Reserve Infantry Regiment 119, speaking of events
             about 29 June near Beaumont-Hamel).

p. 213   Henry Snow (attestation papers, The Rooms).

p. 215   Richard Sellars (attestation papers, The Rooms).

p. 220   Alexander Parsons (attestation papers, The Rooms).

p. 234   Eric Robertson (attestation papers, The Rooms).

p. 234   "The whole wall was white ..." (Arthur Wakefield on Everest
             1922: no 'passenger', Ronald Bayne, *Alpine Journal*, 2004).

p. 238   "... a colourful praying Hitler" is the sculpture "Him" by
             Maurizio Catellan, Ydessa Hendeles Foundation, Toronto.

p. 238–241   Material on Prince John is from "Notes on Cluny
             Macpherson, 1879-1966" (Faculty of Medicine Founders'
             Archive, Memorial University of Newfoundland).

p. 245   "... rowing its weight in the boat." (*Evening Telegram*).

p. 245   "When war broke out ..." Western and General report no.
             92 , Part I, British Empire and Africa, 30 October, 1918.
             Records of the Cabinet Office.

p. 249   "... looked very smart as a page." (*Newfoundland Quarterly*,
             1921).

p. 253   "... a generation that had gone to school ..." (Walter
             Benjamin, *The Storyteller*, 1936).

p. 270   Wallace Pike (attestation papers, The Rooms).

p. 270   *The People Who were Murdered for Fun*, Harold Horwood
              (*Maclean's* magazine, 1959).

p. 271   "Sampson Hamel ..." (David Parsons, CBC interview, 4
              July 2012).

p. 277–280   Eric Ellis diaries (The Rooms).

p. 279   "beautiful scenery, he noted," (notebooks of Eric Ellis,
              The Rooms).

p. 284   "on a pontoon bridge" (*TFN*, p. 504).

p. 284   "he thought it was a very bad order" interview with Arthur
              Raley, Oral Histories of the First World War, Library and
              Archives Canada.

p. 286   "Mick Nugent was forty-two ..." Mick Nugent (attestation
              papers, The Rooms).

p. 286   "Matthew Brazil... was a miner, almost six feet tall," (attes-
              tation papers, The Rooms).

p. 286   "When the boys go over the top"; "I'll be down on the last
              bread wagon," Lead Belly, *Lead Belly's Last Sessions*.

p. 287   Sydney Frost (attestation papers, The Rooms). Tommy
              Ricketts is third on Frost's list of recommendations for a
              Victoria Cross.

p. 287–289   Edward Joy (attestation papers, The Rooms).

p. 291   "The Portuguese sided with the ..." footnote, p. 47, *Grand
              Bank Soldier*, ed. Bert Riggs (Flanker Press, 2007).

p. 293   "Davidson, educated ..." from a conversation with Stephen
              Crocker.

p. 293   "James Moore had suffered ..." (*MBP*, p. 163).

p. 293–294   these anniversary speeches were printed in the *Evening
              Telegram*.

p. 294   "... beginning of the loss of ..." Robert J Harding,
              "Glorious Tragedy: Newfoundland's Cultural Memory of

the Attack at Beaumont Hamel, 1916-1925" (Newfoundland
and Labrador Studies, Vo. 21, No. 1, 2006).

p. 298   "... a dull and wet month." (National Meteorological
Library & Archive, England).

p. 298   "The ship would have to ..." (*Evening Telegram*, 6 February,
1919).

p. 302   "She said they have a poster ..." from a conversation with
Michelle Bowes, St John's.

p. 303   "She was a true lady ..." from a conversation with Tom
Whalen, Bradley's Cove.

p. 308   "the kids swing on them," Paul Mackey, quoted in the
Evening Telegram, Bonnie Belec reporting, 30 July 2013.

p. 314   "only twenty-nine years" (from p. 3 of David Facey-
Crowther's introduction to *LOWS*).

p. 315   "But that George Tuff ..." Thank you to Bert Riggs for
this clarification.

p. 315   "... he was a commercial traveller ..." Sassoon, MOAIO.

p. 318   "a friend of mine ..." I thank Lisa Moore for the
description.

p. 319   "... on the regiment's hockey team ..." *For King & Empire*, p.
110, Norm Christie (CEF Books, 2003).

p. 321   "... on his way to visit his brother." (NL GenWeb, Diary
of Herman Pearce, 17 December, 1903).

p. 322   "She put me in a shoebox ..." from a conversation with
Alonso Osbourne, Seal Cove.

For those interested in a complete battle narrative of the Royal New-foundland Regiment, please consult Gerald Nicholson's official history of the regiment, *The Fighting Newfoundlander* (McGill-Queen's University Press, 1964).

The following three books provided much insight into a Newfoundland soldier's life:

The Letters of Mayo Lind, Newfoundland's Unofficial War Correspondent, 1914-1916, Francis T. Lind (Creative, 2001).

Memoirs of a Blue Puttee, A.J. Stacey & Jean Edwards Stacey (DRC Publishers, 2002).

Lieutenant Owen William Steele of the Newfoundland Regiment, ed. David R. Facey-Crowther (McGill-Queen's University Press, 2002).

FURTHER READING

Trenching at Gallipoli, John Gallishaw (reprint by DRC Publishing, originally published by S. B. Gundy, 1916).

Your Daughter Fanny, The War Letters of Frances Cluett, VAD, ed. Bill Rompkey & Bert Riggs, (Flanker Press, 2006).

Grand Bank Soldier, The War Letters of Lance Corporal Curtis Forsey, ed. Bert Riggs (Flanker Press, 2007).

The Danger Tree, David Macfarlane (Macfarlane Walter & Ross, 1991).

The First Five Hundred, Richard Cramm, (C.F. Williams, 1921).

Two Newfoundland VCs, Joy B. Cave (Creative Printers, 1984).

General Sir Henry de Beauvoir de Lisle, *Reminiscences of Sport and War*, 1939.

W. David Parsons, *Pilgrimage*, (DRC Publishing, 2009).

Ernest Junger, *Kriegstagebuch 1914-1918*, (Klett-Cota, 2013). Thanks to Brigid Garvey for the translation.

Booklet on the History of the War Graves Commission, 1929.
The Private Papers of Douglas Haig 1914-1919, ed. Robert Blake, (Eyre & Spottiswoode, 1952).

MUSEUMS

The Rooms, St John's, Newfoundland
Canadian War Museum, Ottawa, Ontario
The National Archives, Kew, Richmond, Surrey, England
Imperial War Museum, London, England

ONLINE RESOURCES

The Newfoundland Regiment and the Great War:
www.therooms.ca
The Great War Forum:
http://1914-1918.invisionzone.com/forums/index.php
Wallace Pike information from the Canadian Orange Historical website: http://www.canadianorangehistoricalsite.com
The Browne Papers (Letters and Diaries of William Joseph Browne), ed. Madeleine Snow, 2000.
Mike O'Brien, "Out of a Clear Sky: The Mobilization of the Newfoundland Regiment, 1914-1915" (Newfoundland and Labrador Studies, Vol. 22, No. 2, 2007).
Antonia McGrath, "Museum Notes, Early Photography in Newfoundland," 1980.
Notes on Cluny Macpherson (1879-1966): Faculty of Medicine Founders' Archive, Memorial University of Newfoundland.

ACKNOWLEDGEMENTS

I'd like to thank Mark Ferguson, manager of Collections and Exhibitions at The Rooms, St John's for guiding me to various archival sources. Special thanks to Michelle Bowes, who dug up excellent material on Thomas Ricketts and his family. Bert Riggs of Memorial University answered some specific questions. I appreciate the generous help from the staff at MUN's Centre for Newfoundland Studies. Many thanks to Michael Renshaw and Julie Renshaw for their hospitality and conversation while in Auchonvillers. I'd like to thank the staff at the Imperial War Museum in London, the National Archives in Kew, and Helen Fraser at Sandringham Estate, Norfolk.

At Doubleday Canada, my thanks to my editor, Lynn Henry. And thank you to everyone within Random House of Canada who has been part of making this book, especially Brad Martin, Kristin Cochrane, Scott Sellers, Scott Richardson, Peter Phillips, Zoe Maslow, Susan Burns, and publicist Nicola Makoway.

I would also like to thank Christine Pountney for her many insightful comments.

Note that the names of many commissioned officers, commanders, and civic and political leaders have been shortened in my account to a single given name and surname. In the historical records many of the "other ranks" barely have a first and last name. I wanted, in the spirit of Kipling, to level the value in human life, to make no distinction of the kind that middle names, initials, and honorific titles tend to encourage.

The only name I have kept in its entirety is General Sir Henry de Beauvoir de Lisle. It is such a beautifully ludicrous name and I hope the reader understands something about the character of the person who bore it and the nation and family that bestowed it.

A NOTE ABOUT THE TYPE

Into the Blizzard is set in Centaur, designed originally for New York's Metropolitan Museum in 1914, then adapted for general use in 1929. While a so-called modern face, Centaur is modelled on letters cut by the fifteenth-century printer Nicolas Jenson. Its italic, originally named *Arrighi*, was designed in 1925 and is based on the work of Ludovico degli Arrighi, a Renaissance scribe. Centaur is considered among the finest, most elegant faces for book-length work.

The display face, Twentieth Century, was designed by Sol Hess between 1936 and 1947, and is based on the geometric shapes and unadorned aesthetic of the Bauhaus movement of the early 1920s.